MW00846803

The University as a Site of Resistance

The University as a Site of Resistance

Identity and Student Politics

GAURAV J. PATHANIA

Oxford University Press is a department of the University of Oxford.
It furthers the University's objective of excellence in research, scholarship,
and education by publishing worldwide. Oxford is a registered trademark of
Oxford University Press in the UK and in certain other countries.

Published in India by
Oxford University Press
2/11 Ground Floor, Ansari Road, Daryaganj, New Delhi 110 002, India

First Edition published in 2018

ISBN-13 (print edition): 978-0-19-948841-4
ISBN-10 (print edition): 0-19-948841-X

ISBN-13 (eBook): 978-0-19-909369-4
ISBN-10 (eBook): 0-19-909369-5

Typeset in Bembo Std 10.5/13
by Tranistics Data Technologies, Kolkata 700 091
Printed in India by Rakmo Press, New Delhi 110 020

To Michelle

Contents

Tables and Maps

TABLES

MAPS

Preface

While I was on my morning walk, a small crowd gathered around a tree near the library caught my attention. It was the fifth day of my pilot field study at Osmania University in Hyderabad in December 2012 and I enjoyed walking around campus, observing student life. Inquisitively, I approached the crowd. I thought that some students may be protesting or preparing for an agitation that day, which is routine at Osmania's College of Arts and Social Sciences (known as Arts College). Making my way through the crowd, I found that they had taken down the body of a young student who had hanged himself. One student had tears in his eyes as he read the suicide note found on the body. The letter stated the financial crisis his family faced and how his education did not lead to a job. The letter concluded with an appeal to the government to grant separate statehood to the Telangana region in the state of Andhra Pradesh.

Two students made calls to the family of the deceased young man. I heard spectators commenting that this area had become a 'suicide point'. Listening to the discussion, I discovered that the victim was not a student of Arts College but of another college of Osmania, and that this was part of a growing trend, whereby outsiders committed suicide at this 'suicide point'. Later, I returned to Narmada Research Scholars' (NRS) hostel where I was staying.

After about an hour, I noticed a larger crowd of students carrying the corpse, holding banners and shouting the slogan '*Jai Telangana, Jai Jai Telangana*'. I stopped at the nearby tea stall to see if I could understand what the commotion was about. Media and police personnel were sipping tea and discussing the incident as if it was routine for them. As I approached Arts College where students were protesting, I saw that they had blocked the main road and burned an effigy of the chief minister. Approximately 25 student leaders took turns addressing the gathering and each renewed their demand for a separate Telangana state, chanting, '*abhi nahi to kabhi nahi!*' [(Telangana,) now or never!].

After a few hours of protest, police warned the crowd to disperse but the students were determined to stay. In the meantime, a government minister arrived and met student leaders. I noticed that from all the student leaders speaking to the crowd, only one of them could speak fluent English. As a result, he had been nominated to serve as the national spokesperson of Osmania University-Student Joint Action Committee (OU-JAC). He told the media that it was an unfortunate fact that thousands of students had lost their lives in the 50-year long struggle for separate statehood, while the government continues to 'play its dirty politics'. Amidst this rally, I was curious to understand how an 'outsider' could leave his college to commit suicide near the Arts College building. 'This is a sacred place for Telangana activists', one leader told me. While chatting with him, I came to know that he faced more than 100 criminal charges since he led the biggest student agitation in 2009 for the same cause. It shocked me even more when he told me, 'There are 50 other student activists who are facing a similar number of charges and need to appear in court almost every week'. He expressed himself in broken English with the help of his friend. Once he left, I enquired about his age and was told that he was the senior most student leader of Arts College, more than 40 years old, and had gained tremendous respect among students since he took an oath to remain unmarried to serve the people of Telangana. There were other activists who had made the same promise. During the protest rally, I met a much older man, an alumnus of the campus who had written 80 novels and stories, and had publicly vowed to produce a book on Telangana every month until it became a state. Such was their passion that some students even used 'Telangana' as their surname. This piqued my interest in such an intense movement for statehood that I felt the need to explore this university as a site of resistance.

This book is the outcome of nearly a year of fieldwork in Hyderabad and presents an ethnography of activists' everyday life on campus. How did their activism deal with the issues and problems of the Telangana region? How did their demand for Telangana statehood succeed? The volume also provides a theoretical debate on old and new social movements and argues that the Telangana movement should be viewed as new social movement. This book attempts to establish the Telangana movement as a cultural movement, rather than merely a political one, as many scholars argue.

Social movement is a process of consciousness and representation that requires material and cultural resources for its existence. But consciousness of cultural resources has largely been given an industrial answer. Culture[1] cannot be reduced to mere economic or political factors, it cannot be understood, either, without understanding the economic context that surrounds and shapes it. What Telangana student activists gained after joining an institution of higher education is access to cultural capital and consciousness of cultural resources unique to their identity. That is why cultural identities, whether custom or costume, food or festivals, language or life-world, caste or region, are instrumental to the functioning of Indian politics.

Without the help of my activist-friends from Arts College, Osmania University, Hyderabad, and the English Foreign Language University, this research would not possible. I would like to thank Dr Kolluri Chiranjeevi, Dr Sujatha Surepally, Kota Rajesh, Mohan Dharawath, Mothe Sammiaha, P. Mukhesh, Panthukala Srinivas, Shankar Sampangi, Stalin, Sunil Shetty, and Srinivas Gellu for their unwavering support. Similarly, several discussions with the late Professor G. Krishna Reddy of Arts College compelled me to reflect on the importance of the concept of Joint Action Committee (JACs) in the Telangana movement. His sudden demise in 2016 was a huge loss for scholars working on Telangana issues. Several interactions with Professor Keshav Rao Jadhav, one of the key figures of Telangana movement, shaped my understanding of a mass movement.

During my fieldwork at Osmania, I also spent some time in the library of Hyderabad Central University. I also benefitted from the discussions with Dr Nagaraju Gundimeda, Dr Silveru Harinath, and my friends Anthony Raj, Dickens, Kishor Aleti, and Prem.

At my alma mater, Jawaharlal Nehru University (JNU), I am grateful to my supervisor Dr S. Srinivasa Rao for his guidance and insightful comments. I also valued inputs from Professor Debal Singharoy (Indira Gandhi National Open University, New Delhi), Professor N. Sukumar

(University of Delhi), Professor G.G. Wankhede (Tata Institute of Social Science, Mumbai), Dr Shivali Tukdeo (National Institute of Advanced Studies, Bangalore), and Professor Nina Asher's (University of Minnesota-Twin Cities) suggestions on the concepts of identity and movements. JNU Ambedkar Chair Professor Vivek Kumar and Dr G. Srinivas offered not only moral support but also gave me full access to their personal libraries. I thank the staff of Dr B.R. Ambedkar Library and Zakir Husain Centre for Educational Studies Library at JNU, New Delhi, Anveshi Research Centre for Women's Studies, Hyderabad, Ramesh Mohan Library of English Foreign Language University, Hyderabad.

During the process of writing this book, I shifted to the United States of America for my postdoctoral studies and had to leave several books behind, but my JNU friends have helped me by providing missing references from those books. I am indebted to my JNU friends, especially Amit Kushwaha, Anil Yadav, Ankur, Atu Ozukum, Gaurav Vijay Pratap, Imsutoshi Naga, Monika Batham, Narender Yadav, Poonam Shah, Pragyanshu Amaoni, Rakesh, Rashim Pal, Saheed Meo, Shashi Deo, Shahid Reza Khan, Shekhar Tokas, Vaishali Sahoo, and Vinay Bhushan for listening long stories of my field work. Shashi Bhushan and Prabhakar's weekend cooking at our place added the missing flavour to our intellectual fervor.

I'm deeply grateful for the encouragement I received from my professor-friend Bill Tierney from University of Southern California, who sowed the seeds of publication in my mind. I am indebted to Dr Nina Dey-Gupta (University of Delhi) who always made time to edit my writings. I'll never forget the time when she was admitted to the hospital but happily rose from bed to help edit my latest commentary. I am thankful to Professor Werner Menski from the School of Oriental and African Studies (SOAS London)—I published my first research article in his esteemed journal *South Asia Research*. Intellectual companionship of my mentor Dr Sushrut Jadhav was unparalleled. I thank Professor Sangeeta Kamat from University of Massachusetts, Amherst, Balmurli Natrajan from William Patterson University, Amit Thorat from Jawaharlal Nehru University, Narender Thakur from Ambedkar College of the University of Delhi, and Rajbir Parashar from RKSD College, Kaithal, Haryana. Sanjay Kumar (assistant commissioner, Ministry of Labour and Empowerment) has always been kind to make regular phone calls to listen to my questions, discuss in detail and suggest new readings.

People who have helped me with every possible way during the process of writing are Alex and Lenore Bolourchi, Blake Pederson, Kirti Kyab (Brandies University, Boston), Derek Mitchell and Kathy Sreedhar, Yizreel Urquijo, Viviana Alejandra, and Ashok Panikkar from Washington, DC.

Words fail to express my gratitude to the untiring contribution of my mother, who never had any formal education but keeps my thesis in her safe like a sacred book, and the pillar of courage and motivation, my father, who left this world suddenly as I embarked on writing this book. He was the only educated person in my family with whom I could share my thoughts. His unwavering support and our long discussions kept me motivated to achieve my dreams of higher education. My brother, Naveen, and sister, Bharti, took all familial responsibilities while I was busy writing. My niece, Faven Sharleen, has been a source of joy whenever I see her on WhatsApp video calls from my hometown. The unwavering trust of my childhood friends from my village, Paramjeet Pathania and Pravesh Virmani, and my college friend, Sunil Kumar, kept my writing spirit alive.

Many thanks to the OUP team for their professionalism in bringing this book out. Working with them was a valuable learning experience.

Gaurav J. Pathania
May 2018

NOTE

1. Culture is ontologically super-organic only in the sense that it is not transmitted genetically and in the Boasian sense that cultural variation among population is not a function of their biological variation (Schwartz 1992: 327).

Abbreviations

AASU	All Assam Student Union
ABVP	Akhil Bhartiya Vidyarthi Parishad
AGP	Assam Gana Parishad
AIBSF	All India Backward Students Forum
AIMIM	All-India Majlis-e-Ittehaud-ul-Muslimeen
AISF	All India Student Federation
AMS	Andhra Maha Sabha
APCC	Andhra Pradesh Congress Committee
APRSU	Andhra Pradesh Radical Student Union
ASA	Ambedkar Student Association
BAPSA	Birsa Ambedkar Phule Student Association
BASO	Bhagat Singh Ambedkar Student Organisation
BC	Backward Caste
BDO	Block Development Officer
BHU	Banaras Hindu University
BJP	Bharatiya Janata Party
BSF	Bahujan Student Front
BSP	Bahujan Samaj Party
BSU	Black Student Union
CM	Chief Minister
CMS	Chaithanya Mahila Sangam
CPI	Communist Party of India
CPI-M	Communist Party of India-Marxist
CPI-ML	Communist Party of India-Marxist-Leninist
DARAKAME	Dalit Rachayitala Kalakarulu Medavula Aikya Vedika

DFDM	Democratic Forum for Dalits and Minorities (*Dalit Writers, Artists and Intellectual Forum*)
DMS	Dalit Maha Sabha
DSU	Dalit Students Union
DYFI	Democratic Youth Federation of India
EFLU	English and Foreign Language University
FIR	First Investigation Report
GKSF	Golla-Kuruma Student Federation
GVS	Girijana Vidyarthi Sangam
IIT	Indian Institute of Technology
INC	Indian National Congress
JAC	Joint Action Committee
JNM	Jana Natya Mandali
JNU	Jawaharlal Nehru University
JNUSU	Jawaharlal Nehru University Student Union
JNUTA	Jawaharlal Nehru University Teachers Association
KCR	Kalvakuntala Chandrashekhar Rao
KU	Kakatiya University
MCC	Maoist Communist Centre
MCR	Marri Chenna Reddy
MHRD	Ministry of Human Resource and Development
MIM	Majlis-e-Ittehad-ul-Muslimeen
MLA	Member of Legislative Assembly
MP	Member of Parliament
MRPS	Madiga Reservation Porata Samithi
MSF	Madiga Student Federation
MSO	Muslim Student Organization
MSP	Mahajana Socialist Party
NDSF	National Dalit Students Federation
NRS	Narmada Research Scholars
NSUI	National Student Union of India
NTP	Nava Telangana Praja Party
NTR	Nandamuri Taraka Rama Rao
OBC	Other Backward Classes
OU	Osmania University
OU-JAC	Osmania University-Joint Action Committee
OUSU	Osmania University Student Union
PDSU	Progressive Democratic Student Union

PRP	Praja Rajyam Party
PSP	Praja Socialist Party
PWG	People's War Group
RCS	Rytu Coolie Sang-Hams
RDF	Revolutionary Democratic Front
RJD	Rashtriya Janata Dal
RRS	Rayalaseema Rashtra Samiti
RSS	Rashtriya Swayamsevak Sangh
RSU	Radical Student Union
RTI	Right to Information Act
RYL	Radical Youth League
SC	Scheduled Caste
SCR	Srikrishna Commission Report
SEZ	Special Economic Zone
SFI	Student Federation of India
SIMI	Students Islamic Movement of India
SRC	State Reorganisation Commission
ST	Scheduled Tribe
SUCI	Socialist Unity Centre of India (Communist)
TBVV	Telangana Bahujan Vidyarthi Vedika
TCF	Telangana Cultural Forum
TDF	Telangana Development Forum
TDP	Telugu Desam Party
TEJAC	Telangana Employees Joint Action Committee
TeNA	Telangana NRI Association
TGVP	Telangana Girijan Vidyarathi Parishad
TISS	Tata Institute of Social Sciences
TKS	Telangana Kala Samiti
TLSO	Telangana Liberation Student Organisation
TMP	Telangana Madiga Yuvasena
TNM	The New Materialist
TNSF	Telugu Nadu Student Forum
TPF	Telangana Praja Front
TPS	Telangana Praja Samiti
TRC	Telangana Regional Council
TRS	Telangana Rashtra Samithi
TRSV	Telangana Rashtra Samithi Vidyarthi Vibhagam
TS-JAC	Telangana Students-Joint Action Committee

TSA	Telangana Student Association
TSF	Telangana Student Front
TSU	Telangana Student Union
TTF	Telangana Teachers' Federation
TVS	Telangana Vidyarthi Sangam
TVUV	Telangana Vidyarthi Udyama Vedika
TVV	Telangana Vidyarthi Vedika
UAJAC	United Andhra Joint Action Committee
UGC	University Grants Commission
UoH	University of Hyderabad
UNDP	United Nation Development Project
UP	Uttar Pradesh
UPA	United Progressive Alliance
VC	Vice Chancellor
VHP	Vishwa Hindu Parishad
YAF	Young American for Freedom
YFE	Youth for Equality

Introduction

Over the past few years, Indian universities have made headlines that have sparked widespread debate among intellectuals about the university autonomy, academic freedom, and freedom of expression. At the start of 2016, the administration of the University of Hyderabad (UoH) rusticated five members of the Ambedkar Student Association (ASA). Two weeks later, on 17 January 2016, one of those students, a lower-caste PhD student named Rohith Vemula, ended his life by hanging himself in a hostel room. His death led to intense protests at UoH which gradually turned into a massive student movement in India known as the post-Rohith Vemula agitations. Uproar from Rohith's suicide burst out through protests, marches, and hunger strikes. From Hyderabad to New Delhi, the incident spawned numerous media analyses and parliamentary debates. Rohith's suicide note was a searing attack on the casteist and hierarchical society where, in his words, 'the value of a man was reduced to his immediate identity and nearest possibility, to a vote, to a number, to a thing', and where he described his birth as a 'fatal accident'.[1]

Meanwhile, another incident occurred suddenly after Rohith's suicide, and being in the nation's capital at one of the country's most liberal institutions, it attracted rampant media attention. On 9 February 2016, Jawaharlal Nehru University (JNU) gained notoriety for allegations of being an 'anti-national' campus. A group of JNU students were allegedly opposing the death penalty while commemorating the death anniversary of Muhammad Afzal Guru (a Kashmiri who was executed in 2013 for involvement in a terrorist attack on Parliament). Some students in the group were filmed sloganeering for a free Kashmir and criticizing the Indian state. The media was called in and filmed the event which became national news overnight. After right-wing student body, Akhil Bhartiya Vidyarthi Parishad (ABVP), complained to the police, the JNU Student Union (JNUSU) president, Mr Kanhaiya Kumar, and two others were arrested on 12 February on charges of sedition and criminal conspiracy for organizing a programme wherein anti-India slogans were raised. The media seized upon the nationalist *vs.* anti-nationalist binary, and soon, public actions and behaviours were interpreted in these inverse categories. Kanhaiya's time in jail triggered a wave of student activism in India.

Across universities, thousands of students and teachers participated in protests. They argued against the government, voicing that dissent is a vital right, not a crime.[2] For weeks, media vans camped outside the campus gates. After 20 days of imprisonment, Kanhaiya was released on 2 March on interim bail. The entire movement became known as the *Azadi Campaign* or Campaign for Freedom. Kanhaiya Kumar then spoke to a huge crowd gathered in front of JNU's administrative building and raised the slogans: 'We want freedom not from India, but within India. We want freedom from hunger, freedom from poverty, and freedom from caste system'.

Numerous video messages were posted on social media by army personnel, discrediting the university and advising for its closure. JNU[3] was tagged as 'anti-national', 'a den of drugs, terrorism, and Naxalism'; its students were labelled as 'traitors' and 'sex-workers' by the mass media. These narratives by army and media created an image of JNU students as social misfits in a 'moral' society, and overshadowed past contributions JNU[4] has made to the county through its scientific research and democracy building by questioning the university's very existence. In its defence, the JNU community decided to engage civil society and educate the country about nationalism, which they felt was grossly misrepresented by corporate media and the ruling government. The faculty of JNU, in association with several public intellectuals, delivered a series of lectures on nationalism and created a public debate. The lectures were filmed and made available online. People immediately started commenting on these videos on social media. JNU professor, Gopal Guru (2017), whose lecture initiated the series, questioned if government's 'nationalism' was territorial nationalism. The space where these protests and speeches were held—in front of the administration building—quickly became known as 'Freedom Square'. Thus, to counter the existing narratives, students chose protest and debate as a form of resistance. Until Kanhaiya's release from jail, students held massive protests and rallies in New Delhi during the day, and every evening, they convened with professors for debates on nationalism to counter what they saw as the media's propaganda to defame JNU. These month-long protests were, as Professor Nivedita Menon (2016) of JNU writes, 'militant but utterly non-violent', true to the ethos of the university.

The anti-national debate opened up many avenues to understand the evils of Indian society. Scholars and students questioned and debated who and what is nationalist and anti-national. Being liberal, gay, feminist, and secular are all anti-national, they concluded. Indian public intellectual and Nobel laureate Amartya Sen commented that caste itself is anti-national, as 'it divides the nation'.[5] A version of nationalism that places cultural commitments at its core is usually perceived as the most conservative and illiberal form of nationalism. Historically, nationalism has been a major force behind political generational movements from nineteenth century onwards. The rise of intellectual ideas, cultural forms, and political ideologies has also stimulated the formation of political generations (Braungart 1984). It promotes 'intolerance and arrogant patriotism' (Tamir 1993: 95). Indian scholar Mehta (2017) concludes that 'most nationalism is poisonous for intellectualism'.

Scholars and activists expressed their concern over the government's silencing of opposition at universities, condemning it as an attempt to 'depoliticize the campus'. Students burned an effigy of the then minister of human resource and development (MHRD), Smriti Irani, who had been a popuar actress in the well-known television series, *Kyunki Saas Bhi Kabhi Bahu Thi* (Because mother-in-law was a daughter-in-law once). A writer at *The Telegraph* penned his reaction to the JNU incident in an article, '*Kyunki Mantriji Kabhi Student Nahi Thi*'[6] (Because the [education] minister has never been a student), criticizing actions taken by Irani, who allegedly does not have any higher education qualifications. Interestingly, the article was blocked online immediately after gaining popularity on social media, as it evoked common sense knowledge as a tool of resistance. The article also carried a statement by Amartya Sen about intolerance. The identity of the university student became central to the intellectual's argument of student agency and one's 'lived experience' as a part of an institution. JNU students' cause resonated across the globe, gaining support from international academia, from Berkeley to Yale, from Columbia to Cambridge. More than 100 scholars, including Noam Chomsky, Orhan Pamuk, Judith Butler, Arjun Appadurai, Partha Chatterjee, and Homi Bhabha released a public statement in solidarity with JNU and freedom of expression in India.[7] Student unions and university intellectuals questioned why student politics is seen negatively by the government and the masses. Several government ministers remarked against JNU. Messages like 'JNU produces anti-nationals and terrorists. You should get out of the country. Long Live India, shut down JNU' and 'Shoot Anti-National JNU Students & Profs' went viral on social media (*Huffington Post* 9 March 2016; Telegraph 15 February 2016). It was rumoured that a proposal surfaced to change the name of the university to disassociate it with its legacy of student activism.

After the anti-national incident, JNU as a public institution was compelled to prove its 'nationalist' credentials, and hoisted, for the first time, the national flag at the administrative building. To further instil the feeling of nationalism among students, JNU vice-chancellor (VC) Jagadish Kumar requested the Indian Army to install an artillery tank as a memorial for the country's martyrs. At the same time, the University Grants Commission (UGC) ordered a new admission policy for research universities to limit student intake. Several activists were given rustication notices by the administration. Students showed their resentment by rallying together against the policy, saying that this policy would kill the spirit of an 'inclusive university'.[8] Later, the administration implemented a new policy of marking students' compulsory attendance—an unprecedented move for JNU. In Foucauldian terms, it is 'disciplining the bodies', which is a strong practice in schools, but university ethos stands against such rules. Predictably, the announcement met with strong protests by teachers and students alike. Compulsory attendance in universities in general, and in research universities in particular, does not appear to be rooted in academic wellbeing of the students, says Swain (2017), an alumnus. With 'no problem of mass absenteeism', JNU professor, Pathak (2017b), questions the new rule: 'Not everything, the administration should know, can be accomplished through surveillance, CCTV cameras and the registers of documentation, classification and hierarchization'. What makes a university is not how it behaves but what it produces. Ultimately, JNU is experiencing a battle of two cultures: the long-standing liberal campus culture is at odds with the conservative culture of the mainstream education system represented by a VC who is neither a product of JNU nor in sync with the campus culture.

The common sentiment among JNU faculty and student activists was that a university's role is to research and explore the meaning attached to the symbolic aspect of nationalism, not to accept any given meaning. Many argued that the university as a space of engaged learning was increasingly being pushed towards policing and disciplining the mind. JNU professor, Avijit Pathak, stated, 'In the present emotionally charged environment we are confusing political sensibility with political indoctrination' (Pathak 2017a). Professor Janaki Nair (2017: 39) alluded to 'a toxic mix of state, military, and neo-nationalist cultural power that wishes to confine, if not eradicate, freer forms of thought and expression'. Student activists from the Left questioned the right wing: 'Does your idea of nationalism also include those millions of mothers who work tirelessly under the worst conditions with hungry stomachs only to feed their families? … Does it also include those Dalits, tribals and Muslim women who suffer due to patriarchy?' In short, many students took a critical stand against the abstract idea of 'Mother India', and continued their struggle to save the free space their university was known for.

In the following months, the effect of Rohith's death and the Azadi campaign dominated public consciousness and led to a wave of caste and communal upheavals across the country. Obscene messages were directed at female JNU student leaders. Umar Khalid and Shehla Rashid[9] were to be panellists at an academic conference at Ramjas College of University of Delhi, but the venue was attacked by ABVP, abruptly ending the event.[10] One after the other, incidences of bans and violence occurred. The staging of Mahashweta Devi's *Draupadi* at the Central University of Haryana was opposed by right-wing organizations, who deemed the play to be anti-national.[11] Among other incidents were the Dadri lynching,[12] the ban on Wendy Doniger's book on Hinduism,[13] cancelling the screening of Sanjay Kak's documentary, *Jashn-e-Azadi*, at Symbiosis University and Anand Patwardhan's *Ram ke Naam* at Indian Law Society College, and the murder of Kannada literary scholar M.M. Kulbargi, who posed critical questions to his community about idol worship. Similar acts of 'intolerance' towards others' identity (that is, religious, caste, gender, ethnic, and national) became commonplace in villages and cities alike. As a form of protest to the right-wing government's inaction, more than 30 prominent artists, writers, and scholars, including university professors, returned awards bestowed to them by the government.[14] Intellectuals initiated an 'intolerance debate' to engage and educate the masses. The ruling powers rejuvenated and strengthened right-wing student politics, resulting in proscription of certain groups and events across university campuses. For example, the administration at the Indian Institute of Technology (IIT) Chennai banned the Periyar Study Circle established by scheduled caste (SC), scheduled tribe (ST), and other backward class (OBC) students, resulting in student protests in Chennai and New Delhi. The administration at the University of Hyderabad laid down new rules regarding protests.[15] With these major recent incidents, university campuses found themselves at odds with the public, media, and politicians. In Hyderabad, activists questioned the university's higher authorities, referring to Rohith Vemula's death as an institutional murder[16] and demanded the VC resign.[17] At the annual UoH convocation, one student refused to take his doctorate degree from the VC. The impact of Rohith's suicide was much deeper than what the administration had anticipated. Similarly, the Azadi campaign united the Left and liberal students at JNU against fundamental forces.

UNIVERSITY AS A SITE OF RESISTANCE

The incidents at Hyderabad and New Delhi reflect how public university education is not only about personal gain or career development in a competitive age, but also about social justice and creating an intellectually vibrant space. Students' activism compels us to contemplate how and why universities and institutions of higher learning become sites of resistance. The past century shows ample evidence of student resistance across the globe. Radical change emerged from university campuses and challenged authoritative rules to ensure a society of liberal and free ideas. A wave of social movements arose in Europe and the United States of America in the 1960s and 1970s. Thousands of students catalysed the anti-war movement, particularly, against the Vietnam War. In the 1960s,[18] campuses such as Berkeley, Columbia, Princeton, and many others greatly influenced historic European student resistance at universities in France, Germany, Italy, Poland, and the former Czechoslovakia.[19] Commenting on that period, Chomsky (2013: 29) notes that 'students [were] suddenly asking questions and not just copying things down'. Issues relating to the environment, race, gender, and sexuality were raised in an unprecedented fashion. Martin Luther King Jr.'s fight for civil rights and Malcolm X's 'Black Power' movement marked the arrival of an era for alter-native voices to be heard. Decades earlier, students in nineteenth- and early twentieth-century France, Germany, and Russia adopted 'renunciatory personal styles, including long hair among men and short hair among women, colored spectacles, dirty clothes and life style, and a stress on obscene language' (Lipset 1971).

Since the advent of the twenty-first century, the world has been witnessing a significant increase in the number of student protests,[20] despite the sentiment that the youth is disengaged and politically apathetic. The most intense have occurred in the UK, Germany, United States of America, Canada, Chile, and more recently, South Africa, and are united by similar causes against education budget cuts and university fee increases. Recent student activism has not been limited to higher education issues, as demonstrated by the Occupy Wall Street movement in United States of America, the Arab Uprisings, the 2013 protests in Turkey against tightening government policies, and the Umbrella Revolution[21] in Hong Kong. In 2015, thousands of university students from South Africa protested fee hikes and their anti-establishment slogans became viral on social media.[22] Black students, in their agitation against apartheid's legacy, removed the statue of British imperialist Cecil John Rhodes from the University of Cape Town.[23] In United States of America, the 'Black Lives Matter' movement against violence towards Blacks has spread across the country and become a global network. An important addition to the contemporary student protests is the tremendous growth of social media, as Brooks (2016) highlights. Enabled by online resources, contemporary student politics is symptomatic of the era of resistance. Students are not content with accepting the status quo, and engage in several ways to counter what they perceive as injustices on any scale.

INDIAN UNIVERSITY ACTIVISM: CHANGING CONTOURS

Western student politics has had a profound influence on the student politics of the global south as well. In his study of the period from 1960s to 1980s, Altbach (1984: 646) draws comparisons between the West and the rest of the world. He found that social science students in nearly all countries have the most liberal and radical views on social issues. He observed that student leadership was comprised of cosmopolitan, affluent, and exceptional academic backgrounds. Altbach's (1966, 1968, 1969) pioneering work also highlighted the contribution of the left movement. Interestingly, after his study, there is neither any global discussion nor any analysis available on Indian student activism after 1980 (Ciotti 2006; Jeffrey 2008, 2010; Jeffrey and Young 2012; Jeffrey, Jeffrey, and Jeffrey 2004, 2005; Kumar 2012). Nevertheless, scholars of social movements have highlighted the contribution of the university campus behind such resistances. A space for ideological activism exists, which students use to enlarge their space for freedom and autonomy leading to critical thinking, radical ideas, and activism. Since the past two decades, there has been a major shift in the way student unionism has taken shape on university campuses. Though many student organizations played a significant role in the independence movement, including the first (Leftist) ideological student group, the All India Student Federation (AISF), political parties showed little interest in student politics post-independence. The popular words of the first prime minister, Jawaharlal Nehru, 'Go back to studies', prove the fact that political parties had no desire to cater to students' demands. In fact, post-independence phase, studies[24] describe issues as campus or student 'unrest'.[25] The nature of this activism was different than that of pre-independence India. Under colonial rule, the suppression by the British government was violent in nature. In 1904, Lord Curzon had announced a *New University Act* by which all initiatives and liberty[26] were withdrawn from the university (Joshi 1972: 16). Boycotting 'foreign' education was one of the defining features of the student movement. With his return to India, Mahatma Gandhi influenced university students on non-violent civil disobedience. Joshi (1972: 17) states, 'The students who were first perturbed and mystified by his strange and irrational ideas were thrilled by the Champaran struggle'. As a result, students campaigned en masse in Gandhi's

Non-Cooperation Movement in the 1920s. Almost all provincial and district congress workers were student workers in their early 20s, who had left college. By the 1930s, students were leading at every front. In 1936, the first AISF was born, which inculcated the feeling of nationalism among youth in the quest for independence.

Post-independence India has a few noted universities, such as Banaras, Allahabad, Lucknow, and Patna, which are historically well known, not only for the quality of education but also for their activism. However, Desai (2008: 80) alleges that some of these university campuses have become 'nurseries for breeding mafia-politicians in their student and teachers' union', and that 'lumpen behaviour is sanctioned by senior party leaders since they took upon university and teachers' unions as effective weapons to be used in the vote bank war' (Desai 2008). One of the reasons behind this, he cites, is that the student composition in the majority of Indian universities is local or regional (Desai 2008). On the other hand, the best western universities seek to draw students and faculty from all over the world. Guha (2008) gives the example of '*viswabharti*', the idea initiated by Nobel laureate Rabindranath Tagore, to set an example of a global university. Universities in Gujarat started the *Nav Nirman* agitations under the JP (Jaiprakash Narayan) movement. A minor agitation concerning the increased fees at the hostel's canteen turned into a nationwide movement against price hikes and corruption.

Though Indian higher education is seen to be primarily publicly funded (Agarwal 2009: 46), now under the neo-liberal rubric, 'education has been moving out of hands of educationists and into those of politicians, bureaucrats and cultural and religious organisations with strong political agendas' (2009). The arrival of economic liberalization in 1991 has led to a mushrooming of national and international NGOs. These NGOs redefined the state and civil society, and 'crowd[ed] out some of the more protest-oriented forms of organizing' (Ray and Katzenstein 2005: 9). They argue that the fragmented political field of the 1970s and 1980s, marked by deinstitutionalization, has been replaced by a new institutionalization, coupled with twin ideologies of the market and Hindu nationalism (Ray and Katzenstein 2005: 9). Currently, there are more than 800 universities in India. These include 47 central universities, 366 state universities, 122 deemed-to-be universities, and 279 private universities. The present challenge facing institutes of higher education is to strike a balance between state control and the market driven economy.[27] The dominant notion nowadays is that 'universities are supposed to be market friendly' (DeSouza 2015: 94) and serve as a skill factory rather than a space for critical ideas. This new pragmatism, according to Pathak (2017b) destroys the idealism of a university. Two key words, ranking and quality, have become performance indicators for higher education. Each institution markets itself to compete with others on similar standards. This race, on the one hand, leads to 'institutional homogeneity' (Nair 2017), and on the other, undermines the power of academic disciplines which are not market-oriented. The emphasis on the 'production' driven success remains the prime agenda of 'innovation universities' (Nair 2017). This is a serious challenge, not only to the autonomy of the university but also to the goal of university. If autonomy is challenged, then it restricts freedom and expression, the arenas where students' resistance is possible. Theoretically speaking, the university has the 'onus or obligation in the training of critically minded students, who can synthesize, see connections, evaluate argumentations and determine the root cause of things' (McLaren 2005: 273). In other words, the pedagogy in the universities should have emancipatory goals with a freedom to be critical.

THE UNIVERSITY AS A DEMOCRATIC INSTITUTION

The history of global student activism shows that the university has been fighting for its existence and autonomy while challenging existing traditions in the form of knowledge production. Despite the intervention of the state, the community of scholars constitutes one of the longest surviving democracies in the world (Visvanathan 1999: 51). A range of scholars (Apple 1996, 2011; Bernstein 2000; Giroux 1983; Habermas 1967) understand the university as a democratic institution that instils liberal values of justice, enables ethical/moral and political agency. To make such an institution possible, we must problematize the traditional notion of 'democracy' and its long-standing educational cognate, 'equality', as Giroux et al. (1988) suggests. Among the masses, there is a tendency to look at university life as detached or aloof from reality—a bubble that is often referred to as 'utopia', where one is lucky to spend a few years before venturing out into the 'real world' for a career. In contrast, Indiresan (1999: 152) argues that 'campuses cannot remain insensitive to the happenings in society around them'. Campus politics is the space to understand how mainstream politics works and the internal mechanisms and processes involved. Movements and activism are about challenging existing politics. Therefore, it is rare for a student movement to be fully campus-based and concerned mainly with university issues (Altbach 1984: 637). As Touraine (1971: 332) states, 'the university is not a reflection of society; it is society, because it is from now on at the centre of society's change'.

Universities have been, as Visvanathan (2016a) defines, 'the litmus of crisis and democracy'. No democracy can survive without the roots of ethical and philosophical imagination (Visvanathan 2016b: 10). This is the democratic aspect of a knowledge society where 'discipline and dissent have strange a relationship'. Visvanathan (1999) emphasizes exploring the relationship between the university and liberal democracy. He believes that the 'creative power' will emerge from these two. Student politics, their activism, and resistance keep this spirit of democracy alive. In Giroux's (1991: 502) words, the university is 'a site of political and cultural contestation'. Thus, ideally, the university imparts to students' humanistic values from a humanistic approach to form a global community.

As an institution or organization, the university works as the 'form of mediation between theory and practice' (Lukács 1968: 299). There is a 'symbiotic' (Pant 2008: 171) and 'reciprocal relationship' (Heredia 1996: 66) between university and society.[28] The university stands in a close relationship to practical life and to the needs of the state, since it is always concerned with the practical affair of training the younger generation (Humboldt 1970: 248; Giroux 1977: 263). Thus, universities do not exist in a vacuum; they are very much part of society. All in all, the university serves as a site of freedom of thought, social resistance, and through its activism, textures the traditional fabric of society and brings about social change.

Newman, Blehl, Bombogan, and many others have discussed the liberal role of the university. Newman (1982: 15), in his popular book, *The Idea of a University*, writes that 'the very name of the university is inconsistent with restrictions of any kind'. Therefore, 'it is a mistake to make virtue or religious training the immediate aims of the university' (Blehl 1963). There is a real necessity for this 'universal teaching in the highest schools of intellect' (Newman 1982: 15; Culler 1965: 261).

Habermas presents a critique of the fundamental idea of the German university and breaks away from the tradition of Kant-Humboldt-Jaspers' faith in the 'idea' of university, and offers a critical renewal of this very idea. He puts forward the renewal of the idea of the university in terms of 'shared self-understanding' (Habermas and Blazek 1987: 5). The university, states Bhushan (2016: 39), is a place where the force of rationality will spread among the narrow- and broad-minded; self-reflection or philosophizing, if not philosophy, becomes the unifying forces of all sciences.

India, the world's largest democracy, has more than 37,000 institutions of higher education, with 32.3 million students and 1,367,535 faculty members.[29] The country produces roughly three million graduates every year and places third in the largest higher education system in the world, behind United States of America and China (Pant 2008: 170). With the arrival of neo-liberal policies in the 1990s, Indian education has been experiencing new socio-political churning. Scholars have debated whether, under the neo-liberal model, the challenges in the fields of finance and public–private partnerships (Bhushan 2013; Chattopadhyay 2012; D'Souza 2004; Kumar 2002; Patnaik 2007; Prakash 2007; Tilak 2013a) and autonomy, access, equity, and quality and excellence (Chattopadhyay 2009; Khora 2015; Kumar 2016; Lall and Rao 2011: 26; Prakash 2011; Tilak 2013b) and exclusion (Guru 1995; Neelakandan and Patil 2012; Attewell and Thorat 2007) explain how education is becoming a commodity in the present age of market liberalization and teachers are becoming 'Traders of Knowledge' (Pathak 2017b). By 'giving away' their responsibilities to the private sector, governments directly problematize the notion of democracy, a process which Jessop (2002: 199) refers to as 'de-statisation'. On the other hand, burning issues such as academic corruption, the unregulated mushrooming of universities, and the growing role of middlemen in 'arranging' degrees and diplomas have devalued higher education, and made it a commodity which can be purchased by those who can afford it. Moreover, nepotism, bribing, academic corruption, and hiring alumni or one's personal connections all create a kind of parochialism, explains Guha (2008: 9). Whether based on identity, ideology, or institution, these varieties of parochialism have had a corrosive effect on university life, and such parochialism has 'undermined the quality of teaching, narrowed the range of subjects taught, and polluted

narrow-mindedness.

the general intellectual ambience' (Guha 2008: 9).[30] Thus, with such problems and changes in policies, higher education has become an inaccessible and expensive 'commodity'. This shift from being a public good to private good has deeply impacted the society.

UNIVERSITY AS A SITE OF IMAGINATION

The university is a 'community of teachers and scholars' (derived from the Latin *universitas magistrorum et scholarium*) that serves as a link between other social institutions and helps find a solution to the social, economic, and political problems through its research. The Latin words *alma mater* used for one's university or college literally mean 'nourishing mother' or 'fostering mother', suggest an educational institution that provides intellectual nourishment to its students. Bombongan (2008: 483) states that the 'university is the womb' where 'human beings are well nourished'. Similar phases are found in other cultures as well. In India, the goddess of education, Saraswati, is affectionately known as '*Maa Saraswati*' (Mother Saraswati). Many universities in India have temples on campus dedicated to Saraswati, and many university logos include her image.[31] The history of Indian education and the nature of the educational institution is rather sacrosanct with its origin from the *Guru–Shishya* tradition of the past (Government of India 2016: 1).

Lynch, Crean, and Moran (2010: 297) state:

> [T]he university is one of the few institutions in society where there is an opportunity for people to think critically and to document that critique in writing and teaching. Thapar (2015: 35) defines the university as a place 'where existing knowledge is assessed and, if need be, revised, and certainly brought up-to-date and where new knowledge should be created'. It is a space where one can exercise intellectual autonomy ...

Addressing the International University Congress in 2016 in Havana, Argentinean sociologist Altilio Borón stated that 'the university must be the centre of critical thought. It's not easy. We must ensure it is the centre for tolerance of the ideas being discussed, of dialogue, of debate'.[32] Tierney and Sabharwal (2016: 9) suggest that the 'university should be a noisy conversation where individuals are encouraged to argue with one another'.

Recent literature on student politics at Indian university campuses highlights various incidents from the past decade where Dalit, Tribal, and OBC students adopted a new kind of activism by using their identity and caste culture as a medium of assertion (Pathania 2016). In 2006, the Dalit student union at the University of Hyderabad planned to serve beef in the annual university food festival, *Sukoon* (Gundimeda 2009). In reaction to the ban by the university administration, Dalit students organized several protests and challenged how consuming chicken was considered 'secular' while beef consumption was portrayed as 'religious and anti-Hindu'. Gundimeda (2009: 131) presents this move by Dalit students as 'a step towards equality in representation'. Students argued that beef is consumed publicly outside the university campus, where it does not appear to create tension between consumers and non-consumers. According to Dalit students, the intention was not to create a divide between vegetarians and non-vegetarians, but to make the campus more inclusive, wherein everyone's cultural dimensions, including their food habits, would be respected and understood in the larger context of the country's diversity. Such resistance may work against the existing cultural hegemony and signal the emergence of a new kind of politics on campus, as Pathania (2016) argues. Dalit students did not naively take the question of beef as a purely cultural sentiment but used it for political provocation to gain control over public space.

Years later, on 16 April 2012, national newspapers covered the story of how Dalit students at nearby Osmania University (OU) in Hyderabad had organized a 'Beef Festival', which led to physical violence when opposed and attacked by right-wing students. At the same time, in JNU, a student group called The New Materialists (TNM)[33] also fought against the 'Brahminical' mould. They organized various talks and debates on food culture in India. A joint 'Committee for the Democratic Right to Choice of Food' and TNM issued a pamphlet on organizing a beef festival on 17 September 2012 on campus to commemorate Shaheed Bhagat Singh's birth anniversary. The university administration, along with the New Delhi Police, prohibited the event from taking place, but the issue did bring a taboo subject into daily conversation. Similar debates on beef were also initiated in the Tata Institute of Social Sciences (TISS), Mumbai.[34] To oppose students' activism, some prestigious IITs and IIMs were directed by the government to open separate canteens for vegetarian students.[35] However, merely 5 per cent of students are vegetarian (400 out of 8,000 students).

Thus, according to Dalit activists at IIT Mumbai, this 'food *diktat* is trying to dictate the agenda for the remaining 95 per cent'.[36] Pant (2008) writes that 'Indian higher education has ended up becoming another instrument for serving myriad socio-political goals and has lost sight of its true purpose, relinquishing any vision of the role of education in a liberal democracy' (2008: 173). Professor Sukumar of University of Delhi writes about the discrimination and animosity he and other Dalits faced, while he was as a student at University of Hyderabad:

> Comments like 'Bakasura and Kumbhakarna tables' are commonly made by the non-dalit students and mess workers.... Dirty comments are scribbled on such posters in hostels to insult them. Abusive comments like 'pigs', 'government's son-in-laws', 'bastards', 'son of god', 'beggars', etc., and comments which question paternity are quite common. In 2002, a miscreant (a PhD student) scribbled 'bastard' on B R Ambedkar's poster in the social science building. (Sukumar 2008: 17)

The university hostel, therefore, serves as a site for both the putative national culture and unrepresented food cultures. Persistently ignoring such food diversity symbolizes hegemony of a specific culture over others (Pathania 2016: 265).

Another example of student resistance against the establishment occurred at the English and Foreign Language University (EFLU) in Hyderabad. For the first time in the history of Indian student activism, the harvest festival of Onam was boycotted in 2012 by marginalized students. A pamphlet[37] issued by a number of student organizations argued: 'Dalits and Adivasis work from dawn till dusk to fill your granary. Why should we celebrate your harvest festivals when it always left us landless, poor and deprived?' Such examples point to a palpable change in the nature of student activism in India. Whereas earlier it had ideological roots, identity-based activism is the new norm (Pathania 2012). Rather than idolizing Gandhi, marginalized students hailed Jyotiba Phule as the 'Father of Nation'. B.R. Ambedkar, Periyar, and Birsa Munda became the most powerful icon of campus politics. Leftist parties in Kerala, who rejected the role of caste organizations in the process of social formation, are now using caste icons such as Sree Narayana Guru, Ayyankaali, and Chattambi Swamy in their party conventions.[38] Both OU and EFLU celebrated Savtiri Bai Phule's birthday on 3 January as National Teachers' Day. Professor-activist

Kancha Ilaiah started celebrating his own birthday as Dalit-Bahujan English Education Day on OU campus. In Hyderabad, for the past few years, students at OU have paid homage to a Dravidian warrior, Naraka Shoora, traditionally projected as an evil character who was killed by Aryan invaders. A new narrative of *Moolnivasi*[39] dominates the Dalit-Bahujan discourse, which argues that Dalits were the original inhabitants of this country. Such are the new voices and themes characterizing student activism in India.

On many campuses across the country, Dalit student assertion has been a reality for the past decade. At the JNUSU presidential debate of 2007, a Bahujan Student Front (BSF) candidate compared the Hindu god Rama to Satan.[40] His speech provoked the right wing and violence ensued. Furthermore, since 2010, the All-India Backward Students' Forum (AIBSF) has been organizing a Mahisasur Martyrdom Day (*Mahisasur Shahadat Diwas*) at JNU to counter the highly popular Hindu festival, *Durga Puja*. Burning the popular Hindu text *Manusmriti*[41] also symbolizes rejection of upper caste Hindu cultural hegemony and catalyses the debate on democratic and liberal space of the campus. These are but a few examples of university students challenging the norms and paving the way for inclusion and freedom of expression. New narratives countering the status quo have evolved and buoyed marginalized students' causes. From university campuses in Kerala to Hyderabad to Delhi, Leftist and Dalit student organizations are countering the communist *lal salaam* (red salute) with *neel salaam* (blue salute) or *Jai Bhim-Lal salaam*[42] (salute to Ambedkar and Marx). Such narratives have questioned the sacrosanct image of educational spaces as *vidya ke mandir* (temples of learning). Through education, Dalit and other marginalized students not only understood the cultural agenda of the state but also devised their own agenda to counter the existing one. Dalit students now occupy spaces which they were denied access to for centuries. In addition to caste, there has been a reflection on the legacy of untouchability in public institutions (Jaoul 2006; Shah et al. 2006; Sooryamoorthy 2008), including education. Education in general, and higher education in particular, is the arena in which Dalits were denied access. Before education, Dalits led movements to gain access to other public spaces. For example, in 1927 in Maharashtra, 'untouchables', under the leadership of Dr Ambedkar, embarked on *Mahad Satyagraha* to access water from a public tank (see Kumar 2007). That day is now observed as Social Empowerment Day in India. In 1930, Ambedkar led a temple entry movement known as *Nashik Kalaram Temple Satyagraha*[43] to claim the right to enter the temple. A similar movement for temple entry, known as *Viakom Satyagraha*, occurred in Kerala in 1924–5. These are just some examples emblematic of the daily struggle many lower-caste Indians face that have inspired Dalit activists today.

University space is rife with narratives and counter-narratives created by student activists to counter existing narratives. There are many such narratives of cultural assertion which have produced new symbols and icons to challenge the traditional caste hegemony in education. This is a new narrative of identity resistance politics. In a few campuses, the strong emergence of Dalit-Bahujan groups (such as Birsa Ambedkar Phule Student Association (BAPSA) in JNU) presents new a *Bahujan* narrative, and calls on Dalits, OBCs, and religious and sexual minorities to create a collective political voice. During the elections, such narratives (anti-national, anti-reservation, and caste-based), evoke an individual's identity and the history attached to it. They play a decisive role in defining their agenda, politics, and ideology to counter their political opponents, especially during elections. These narratives serve as instruments of dissent and create a counter-discourse. They challenge the roots of existing history, construct and deconstruct our identities, and define us based on our histories and ideologies. They are cultural resources of political parties and gradually transform themselves as part of their ideologies. University campuses are the breeding grounds of such ideologies; therefore, it is the responsibility of the university and its intellectuals to provide its students new epistemic tools to debate these narratives as well as imagine new ones. With this in mind, one should consider the questions: what is universal about university education? What is universal about ideology?

The 'contemporary social conflicts are not just political, since they affect the system's cultural production' (Beckford 1989; Melucci 1985; Offe 1985; Touraine 1985). Melucci suggests the NSM areas are 'increasingly autonomous' from political systems. Their form is quite distinct from that of older political organizations, and Melucci argues, the form is the message. Beyond modernization and beyond innovation, movements question society on something else: 'who decides on codes, who establishes rules of normality, what is the space for difference, how can one be recognized not for being included but for being accepted as different, not for increasing the amount of exchanges, but the affirming another kind of exchange?' (Melucci 1985: 810).

IDENTITY RESISTANCE POLITICS

Student politics in India today reveals that class politics has been on the decline while identity politics or identity resistance politics has been on the rise (Pathania 2017). Leftist parties have long simplified the complexities of caste by projecting them as class politics (Pathania 2017). They have not yet honed a clear-cut strategy to understand these social complexities unique to India. Moreover, projecting the class notion undermines the anti-caste agenda that democracy demands to create an egalitarian society. On the other hand, Centrist forces and the right wing use cultural politics as a tool to address these issues, which appeal to the masses. However, ideologies must break the habit of thinking that 'culture is encyclopaedic knowledge whereby an individual has become a mere container of data … this form of culture is truly harmful, especially to the proletariat' (Giroux 1999).

The ongoing resistance in education should be analysed through an angle where students from marginalized communities are producing a counter culture to the existing dominant culture. For Gramsci, any analysis of education could only be understood in relation to existing social and cultural formations and the power relations they imply. Gramsci emphasized that schooling constitutes only one form of political education within a broader network of experience, history, and collective struggle. Given Gramsci's view of political education, it is difficult to reduce his view of teaching and learning to a form of positivist reductionism, in which a particular methodology, such as rote learning, is endorsed without questioning whether such pedagogical practices are either implicated in or offer resistance to the mechanisms of consent, common sense, and dominant social relations (Giroux 1999). Such moments carry with them the potential to incorporate a caring and critical pedagogy that meaningfully engages both teacher and student in cultivating an understanding of our own places in systems of oppression.

The university, and the residential university in particular, is a site of transformative encounters, with radically different forms of living, food cultures, and religious practices. In post-independence India, the hostel has shed some of its sectarian characteristics, particularly in the public university, and enabled all manner of new opportunities (Nair 2017: 38). According to Sukumar (2016), 'education is supposed to be the instrument with which to usher in radical social transformation and liberation, enabling oppressed communities to overthrow centuries old social-cultural burdens'. In this regard, present-day student activism (of students from marginalized communities) on university campuses in India offers a 'new epistemic understanding of the existing hegemony of a particular belief system', and demonstrates that 'the realm of academia is no longer restricted to space of learning "traditions", but has itself become a site for counter-hegemonic assertion' (Pathania 2016: 271–2). More than the classroom, perhaps, it is the hostel that amplifies these possibilities and predicaments. The everyday cultural politics of caste, religion, and community within a putatively secular space illuminates the contradictory dynamics of producing modern secular citizens in India (Lukose 2006: 44).

Since independence, there have been several regional identity movements taking shape across the country. Andhra Pradesh, Tamil Nadu, Assam, Punjab, Haryana, Uttar Pradesh, and many other subregions in India have a history of struggles for separate statehood based on language, ethnicity, and economic and social marginalization. Many north eastern Indian tribes have been leading ethnic wars to claim their region based on their tribal identities. Similarly, university students from Bihar played a vital role in the popular anti-corruption movement led by JP in the 1970s. The All Assam Students Union (AASU) emerged in local universities in Assam in the 1980s and produced an intense student movement, which later brought political power to its student leader. Nagaland[44] and Manipur have also faced similar agitations.

The decade of 1980s has opened global avenue and opportunities for Indian economy. Agriculture-based economy was gradually shifting towards industrial economy. LPG (liberalization, privatization, and globalization) became the buzzword. Socio-cultural tension has slowly been mounting since early 1990s. In 1992, the demolition of Babri Mosque by Hindu fundamental forces revived Muslim student organization like SIMI (Students Islamic Movement of India) and thereafter a new identity politics took shape in Indian politics. Thus, the decade of the 1990s paved the way for Hindutva—the 'political imagination' of the BJP, as Nandy (1997) calls it. With the additional effect of neo-liberal policies in the early 1990s, the sphere of education became a contested political site in the knowledge economy. Globalization has led to greater economic, social, and educational inequalities (Apple 2001; Carnoy 2000; Rikowski 2002; UNDP 1999) and this is true for India. Ball (2004), Apple (2001), and other scholars have highlighted the increasing 'commodification' of education under the market economy. Access, democratization, and the politicization of education, has become the core issue of contemporary higher education (Heredia 1996: 57). Marxist scholar Peter McLaren (2005: 24) expresses his concern over the neo-liberal economy that 'education has been reduced to a subsector of the economy, designed to create cybercitizens within a tele-democracy of fast-moving images, representations, and lifestyle choices powered by the seemingly frictionlessness of finance capital'. He calls the relation between the economy and the states as an internal one and defines it as a 'neo-liberal dictatorship' (McLaren 2005: 29).

In 1990, to include a section of historically marginalized people in the job market, the Indian government introduced a 27 per cent reservation for OBCs. The policy became known as the Mandal Commission. The new policy stirred up student unrest and political expression (Chaitanya 1994; Kumar 2005; Mishra 1993; Thorat 2004). For months, students protested the government's decision of 'imposing' a reservation policy only to 'play [caste] vote bank politics'. Another policy of guaranteeing 27 per cent reservation for OBCs in higher education admissions was implemented in 2006. This decision met with anger and resentment among upper-caste students, especially those in the technical and medical disciplines[45] (Lukose 2010: 208). A group of students from IITs and IIMs formed Youth for Equality (YFE), and boycotted the decision. Yet, the quota was implemented and gradually, a large contingent of OBC students gained access to higher education. By 2010, the formation of the AIBSF added a new dimension to campus politics. A large section of OBC Muslim students formed unions such as Pasmanda Students' Forum. Amidst this backdrop, contemporary student movements or campus activism in India largely took shape. Therefore, the issues of neo-liberalism, Mandal, and Mandir–Masjid (popularly known as '*Kamandal*') are crucial in understanding Indian student activism. The political confluence of caste, ethnic, and regional identities structurally influenced university campus activism and gave birth to identity politics.

Gradually, these caste-based student organizations developed into more nuanced and culturally based identity politics movements. This, in turn, prompted academic interest in Dalit studies (Rege 2006, 2010; Satyanarayana and Tharu 2011). Extended reservations exposed the problem of the 'contemporaneity of caste' as 'a live force in modern Indian culture and politics' and revealed many contradictions in Indian society, especially regarding ways of thinking about castes (Satyanarayana and Tharu 2011: 9–10). However, Indian society and politics have largely rejected reservation and the existence of caste. Supporters of Mandal reservation policies, usually lower-caste citizens, are regarded as casteists (supporters of caste discrimination), whereas anti-reservationists tend to project themselves as defending national interest and regard themselves as meritorious citizens. As a result, caste per se tends to be associated with lower-caste groups. The general category world of upper castes, on the other hand, is essentially seen as casteless (Deshpande 2013; Satyanarayana and Tharu 2011: 11). Thus, there is a tendency among scholars to look at universities, intellectual circles, and urban areas as places where caste has almost lost its relevance.

At universities, where studies have been conducted, caste discrimination is not explicit, in contrast with other social environments, such as rural areas, where social hierarchies and modes of interaction are based on caste identities. Prestigious Indian universities (such as EFLU and JNU) attract students from culturally diverse regions and states. In such multicultural environments, the expression of caste differentiation becomes more complex because regional caste interaction models lose their significance. At universities, students enter, at least formally, a secular environment where they must overcome caste barriers by sharing hostels, canteens, and classrooms. Inevitably students broaden their social networks. On the other hand, an argument can be made that 'the university environment hardly allows one to be caste-anonymous' (Garalyte 2015: 59–60). Lower-caste students in the universities are labelled as '*quota-wala*' throughout their student lives. The shared experiences by Dalits 'aptly describes how caste discrimination is manifested within the university setting' (2015: 60). Gopal Guru, a leading Dalit political science scholar, described a Dalit experience at university as follows: 'The strict observance of a language code, protocols, body language and ground rules effectively converts seminar halls into a hostile structure that very often inflicts humiliation on the Dalits, who then feel too nervous or intimidated to enter such structure ...' (Guru 2012: 20).

Language appears to be one of the most significant factors through which Dalit identity represents itself. Most Dalit students come from illiterate families and attend state schools where the language of instruction is a local regional language. Once at university, where English is the dominant language, and by extension, a symbol of higher-caste/upper-class status, Dalits face severe difficulties in dealing with language barriers. Even after Dalits master some English, not infrequently their pronunciation and way of expression exacerbates their difference to students from English-medium private school backgrounds. Due to their limited exposure to English, Dalits and other subaltern students do not feel confident enough to express themselves publicly in English. As a result, public speaking becomes dominated by students from upper-caste/class backgrounds who are at ease in English. In the classroom, the English language along with sophisticated intellectual jargon becomes a major obstacle for Dalits to articulate themselves (Harinath 2013; Kumar 2005; Paik 2016; Pathania and Tierney 2018; Sukumar 2008: 15).

UNIVERSITY AS A SITE OF CULTURAL POLITICS

'The educational system is intended to level people, make them passive, disciplined and obedient.'

Chomsky in an interview with Meyer and Alvarado (2010: 12)

Chomsky defines education as enlightenment, which is to foster the impulse to challenge authority, think, and enquire critically. He define opposing concept of education as indoctrination.[46] Giroux (1981: 109) calls it reproductive process that not only serves the interest of dominant but also contains the seeds of conflict and transformation. A university's role is to promote critical thinking, to analyse society's 'common conscience', and to question given truths (Abraham 2016). Thapar (2016), like other scholars, emphasizes the need for critical pedagogy[47] to make the university a site of social change, an agency of modernization, as well as radical change. We derive from Giroux's 'radical pedagogy' expressions of hope, critical reflection, and collective struggle (1989: 113) that is not divorced from politics. For him, being critical entails political engagement of teacher constraints and possibilities. Rather than rejecting the language of politics, critical pedagogy must link public education to the imperatives of a critical democracy (Dewey 1961; Giroux 1989). Giroux (1989: 32) refers to teachers as 'transformative' and schools as public places 'to reproduce the idea of critical democracy as a social movement that supports individual freedom and social justice'. By viewing schooling as a form of cultural politics, educators can bring the concepts of culture and differences together to create a borderland where multiple subjectivities and identities exist as part of a pedagogical practice that provides the potential to expand the politics of democratic community and solidarity (Giroux 1991: 516).

The past decade of student activism shows a cultural deconstruction of power. Dalit students demanded space and equality for self-representation and the right to the availability of beef in the university mess or at least the right to eat beef in public during the 'Beef Festival'. The beef debate reached a broader public when Dalit groups started writing about it (Chandran 2012; Gundimeda 2009; Shyamala 2013) and launching cultural programmes, including singing and poetry readings to express the significance of beef in the lives of the untouchables. As Dalit student activists acquire cultural capital through university education, they revive their historical identity that emerged from the tradition of struggle and sacrifice to devise a new language of resistance against the dominant tradition.

Urban India is experiencing new forms of identity assertion, and the geographical location of universities plays a crucial role in changing the social landscape of the city. In December 2012, a brutal gang rape in Delhi led to country-wide protests, largely led by female university students. These protests made the public aware of power structure of the traditional 'malestream' mind rooted in culture and tradition. Activists raged against patriarchy: 'Respect the sex which gives you birth'; 'I live in a country where a girl is neither safe inside the womb nor outside it'; and 'Don't harass women, they are your lovely mothers, sisters and daughters'. There was distress and pity for women, and anger and shame for the state. Some other posters read: 'Black Day—I am ashamed to call myself Indian'; and 'You can get raped but not protest against rape: #WorldsLargestDemocracy'. Protesters carried candles and wore black, their mouths bound with black cloth. This display was a challenge to the traditional and patriarchal argument that girls' short and tight attire provokes sexual urges among boys. Slogans such as '*Kapde chhote nahi, tumhari soch chhoti hai* (our clothes are not short, your thinking is)' asserted women's rights to live freely. One very contentious slogan, 'Better to chop "it" off than to rape', shows the intensity of public anger. Referring to the victim of the 16 December rape, one poster read, 'She is not dead, she has gone to the place where there is no rape'.[48] What is new in these slogans is the radical tone. Unlike previous protests against rape, these slogans challenged male and masculine notions of a patriarchal society (Pathania 2015: 286). In the preceding year in Delhi, hundreds of female university students started a campaign called '*Pinjra Tod*' to fight against gendered hostel rules.[49] For the past few years, activists are also organizing Gay Pride parades in Delhi. There are many women's groups in many cities across the country, which closely work with university students and are trying to create a counter-discourse to patriarchy. In September 2017, women led protests against an incident of sexual assault at Banaras Hindu University (BHU), a central university in Uttar Pradesh.[50] The uniqueness of these protests was their diversity, as they, in Butalia's (2012) view, were not merely 'women's issues', but a symbol of the deep-seated violence that women and other marginalized people experience every day in society. With the continuous expansion of higher education and access through reservation policies, the class, caste, and gender profiles of universities has been changing significantly but not without tension. For example, Richa Singh, the first female president of the Allahabad University Student Union 'battled the entrenched patriarchy of the Hindi-belt campuses' (Menon 2016), to become an inspiration for students who come from socially and economically marginalized families.

These events question the 'hegemonic oppressive Brahmanical nationalist Hindu culture' and seek publicity for the 'counter culture of ex-untouchables usually through the means of oppositional symbolism' (Hardtmann 2009: 236–7). In their social movement, Dalits have created a broad counter-public sphere 'where the politics of difference can articulate itself, and caste can emerge as a legitimate category of democratic politics' (Pandian 2002: 25). Similarly, when Dalit literature became a legitimate and popular category in the recent past, it started with a never-ending debate that 'literature cannot be Dalit'. Yet, as literature is the mirror of society, if society is characterized by caste inequality, then it is obvious that corresponding literature would evolve. But the emergence of Dalit literature was not limited to criticizing caste but its origin as well, and it found Hinduism to be a system based on structural hierarchy. It not only challenged the religion but questioned the existence of caste. It has been argued that that since Hindu culture is dominated by religion, the intellectual entrapment of the Dalit cannot be eased unless a large-scale rewriting of the Hindu holy texts takes place (Ilaiah 2001: 57).

India's university-educated class[51] lives in a paradox. While it projects itself as anti-caste, anti-patriarchy, progressive, and so on, it still takes pride in using caste surnames for introductions and marrying along caste lines. One can experience this paradox while reading the morning newspaper from any corner of India. Matrimonial advertisements highlight caste, sub-caste, region, and religion. This hints that we need to look at higher education critically. How does the university inculcate this parochial thinking among its students? According to Beteille (2007: 447), 'If caste has dug its roots deeper into the university today, the main responsibility for that lies in the way in which politics has come to be organized'. Therefore, the challenge of the twenty-first century is to realize the cultural potential of those who have remained at the margins of society for ages. It is possible by diversifying our classrooms through inclusion of every caste, tribe, and language in the classroom. Democracy 'has to be judged not just by the institutions that formally exist but by the extent to which different voices from diverse sections of the people can actually be heard' (Touraine 1997: 190). Its raison d'être is the recognition of the other. It has been observed, with much justice, that 'the relationship between identity and inequality lies at the heart of secularism and democracy in India' (Tejani 2007: 265).

As more of India's university student population has grown to reflect the diversity in society, so have the issues of debate and contention. The university is a 'futuristic institution that makes innovative use of the past' (Visvanathan 1999: 50). If the past is characterized by social contradiction and animosity, one should expect from these institutions to correct the historical wrongs. Various reports and committees have suggested several measures to handle discriminations in universities but there is no measurement of indirect discrimination. David Mosse (2012) concludes that caste has turned inward and now resides as a 'feeling inside the mind/heart'. Thus, the existence and persistence of caste is deepening in the minds. There is no mechanism to capture this. Khora (2016), responding to Rohith Vemula's suicide, suggests 'periodic discrimination audit' in educational institutions.

FOCUS OF THE BOOK

With a focus on the aspect of regional identity, this book provides an ethnographic account of the movement for Telangana's statehood—one of the longest student movements in India—which developed as a protest movement at OU in 1969. This movement is a distinct example of the cultural assertion between two regions that speak the same language, Telugu, but with different accents. After Indian independence, the Telangana region was merged with the Andhra region. This merger incited the demand for a politically separate Telangana. The idea of a separate state was first initiated by Telangana government employees but OU students took up the issue and spearheaded a movement in 1969. Their year-long protests created bedlam in the state. During this agitation, hundreds of students lost their lives in police firings. Students who sacrificed their careers turned radical, left the university to join extremist groups, and took up arms and continued their struggle against state authorities. After two decades of 'anti-state' activities, many students realized that to achieve Telangana, they had to find a democratic alternative. They put their trust back into the electoral process and formed a new party, the Telangana Rashtra Samiti (TRS) in 2001. This gave rise to a renewed aspiration for power among new activists. The period from 2009 to 2014 served as the second phase of the protest movement.

After almost a half-century-long struggle and countless sacrifices made by students and peasants, Telangana was formed on 2 June 2014 as the 29th state of India. As the government announced Telangana's formation, demands for separate states across India were reignited (that is, Gorkhaland from West Bengal, Bodoland from Assam, and Vidharbh from Maharashtra). Many of these demands were raised on university campuses. What is interesting is to understand the origin of these demands among youth. What are the backgrounds or circumstances under which such demands turned into agitations and movements on campus? In the case of the Telangana movement, how did regional identity traverse through campuses to the masses and vice-versa? How does regional identity shape the political understanding of university students? Such conceptual questions are important to understand the outcomes we experience in the form of protests, agitations, and movements. Rao (1972), Weiner (1978), and Suri (2002) highlight the role of the students, non-gazetted officers, and politicians in Telangana movement.

The purpose of this book is to examine how university space fosters student activism and raises identity consciousness for a specific goal, in this case the formation of the most recent Indian state. It seeks to illustrate how students mobilized, networked, and strategized on and off campus to produce one of the protracted social movements in India. How do a public university and its members navigate and negotiate with the state in a time of extreme privatization of higher education? In this context, the volume argues that it is imperative to study the changing nature of student activism to understand the impact of larger social movements. It argues that university space continues to be a resource for resistance and collective action.

STRUCTURE OF THE BOOK

With a conceptual debate between old and new social movements, the first chapter titled 'Telangana Movement: A Cultural–Political Discourse' offers theoretical insights on culture as a site of politics, social domination, marginalization, and resistance. It understands the 'problem of Telangana' within the framework of 'internal colonialism', the term used by the first State Reorganisation Commission (1955: 105). It tries to understand the activists' experience and the larger forces that shape their motives, ideas, and identities. It establishes that the movement evoked various local cultural symbols such as language/accent, food, dress, festivals, arts, theatre, and music as forms of resistance to spur a popular movement against the 'dominant' culture of Andhras, whom Telangana people referred to as 'outsiders', 'non-*mulki*' or 'settlers'. Chapter two, titled 'Osmania University: Academics, Culture, and Politics', provides activists' narratives of the past five decades of activism at OU. It illustrates how a 'culture of resistance' and 'culture of activism' were created by 'organic intellectuals' (students and teachers) and produced generations of campus activists. Chapters three and four, titled 'Campus Networks and Agitations: The Making of a Student Activist' and 'Learning from the Past, Imagining the Future' respectively, draw upon ethnographic observations, insights from informal and formal discussions, and interviews with student leaders. They also explain how the existing culture of campus activism helped produce and maintain various networks and how these networks were instrumental in the movement's success and in the making of OU as the movement's epicentre. Additionally, chapter four provides a comparison of the 1969 agitation to that of 2009. The concluding chapter, 'New State, Old Narratives', sheds light on the current state of affairs in Telangana. It briefly covers the nature of the ongoing struggle led largely by OU students and alumni due to the continued lack of political representation and high youth unemployment. It argues that the movement for separate statehood became a mass movement due to students' inclusive approach to mobilizing at the grassroot level.

NOTES

1. Available at http://indianexpress.com/article/india/india-news-india/dalit-student-suicide-full-text-of-suicide-letter-hyderabad/, accessed 24 November 2016.
2. The Home Minister of India stated in the media: 'If anyone raises anti-India slogans and tries to raise question on the nation's unity and integrity, they will not be spared'.
3. As a liberal campus, JNU has been popular for its joint struggle (teacher–student–employees). In 2017, for the first time in the history of any Indian university, the teachers' union of JNUTA called for a public enquiry against its own VC, Professor M. Jagadeesh Kumar, for allegedly violating various conventions of the university.
4. In their study of 39 central universities in India, Marisha, Banshal, and Singh (2017: 2205) found that DU and JNU as the best performers in social sciences research.
5. Available at http://www.hindustantimes.com/india-news/caste-is-anti-national-as-it-divides-india-says-amartya-sen/story-Hbk4R-PLejo0XEgpM-bEO4rN.html, accessed 5 January 2017.
6. Available at https://www.telegraphindia.com/1160213/jsp/frontpage/story_69079.jsp#.WIMWWFN97IU, accessed 5 August 2016.
7. Available at https://scroll.in/latest/803722/top-academics-including-noam-chomsky-judith-butler-condemn-centres-action-at-jnu, accessed 5 August 2017.
8. UGC Gazette Notification: Death of the Idea of an Inclusive University, organized by the Committee of Suspended Students for Social Justice. 15 February 2017 at the Freedom Square, JNU. 4:30–6:30 pm.

9. JNU students who were associated with the controversial Afzal Guru march that landed Kanhaiya Kumar and Umar Khalid in jail.
10. Available at https://thewire.in/111181/delhi-university-ramjas-abvp/, accessed 5 April 2017.
11. Available at https://thewire.in/68869/abvp-central-university-haryana-draupadi/, accessed 27 November 2016.
12. The mob killing of a Muslim man who was suspected of consuming beef on 28 September 2015 in Dadri, Uttar Pradesh.
13. See https://www.theguardian.com/world/2014/feb/13/indian-conservatives-penguin-hindus-book.
14. See https://www.theguardian.com/books/2015/nov/05/arundhati-roy-returns-award-protest-religious-intolerance-india-bollywood-modi-government-violence.
15. Available at http://www.sify.com/news/hyderabad-varsity-students-not-satisfied-with-new-protest-rules-news-national-rhpdJohig-baec.html.
16. Available at http://sanhati.com/articles/15951/.
17. Dilip Menon questions the 'structure of administration, pedagogy and structure of scholarship' that are highly dis-criminatory in Indian higher education. Available at https://theacademiccitizen.org/2016/07/06/12-the-state-of-higher-education-in-india/, accessed 9 October 2017.
18. Explaining his experiences of the 1960s, American educationist Peter McLaren comments that the 'youth counter-culture of the sixties served as the ideological loam that fertilized my pedagogy. I had learned the rudiments of a middle-class radicalism that was preoccupied with the politics of expressive life and avoided examining in a minded and a critical manner the structural inequalities within the social order' (McLaren 2015: 11).
19. Self-immolation by a university student in Czechoslovakia in 1968 led to a massive agitation known as the Prague Spring. Neighbouring Poland experienced revolt where students challenged Communist party control over universities and cultural production (Bischof, Karner, and Ruggenthaler 2010). See Zubok, V. 2010. 'Soviet Society in 1960s', in *The Prague Spring and the Warsaw Pact Invasion of Czechoslovakia in 1968*, ed. G. Bischof, S. Karner, and P. Ruggenthaler, pp. 76–101. Lanham, MD: Lexington Books.
20. See http://www.universityworldnews.com/article.php?story=20160510173152311 and https://www.theatlantic.com/education/archive/2015/05/the-renaissance-of-student-activism/393749/.
21. Available at https://www.theguardian.com/world/2014/sep/30/-sp-hong-kong-umbrella-revolution-pro-democracy-protests.
22. 'I am no longer accepting the things I cannot change, I am changing the things I cannot accept' was the slogan students adopted against university authority and government's unfulfilled promises.

23. Available at http://www.bbc.com/news/blogs-trending-34125297.
24. Indian scholarship is vast in the area of student politics up to the 1970s: Altbach (1966, 1967, 1968, 1968a, 1968b, 1969, 1970a, 1970b, 1972, 1982, 1984, 1987), Damle (1966), Dasgupta, Bhattacharjee, and Singh (1974), Deshmukh 1968), DiBona (1966), Dhangare (1983), Jafar (1977), Jayaram (1979), Kakkar and Chowdhury (1969), Gupta (1968), Metta (1967, 1970), Mishra (1967), Reddy (1969), Ross (1969), Oommen (1974, 1985), Shils (1959, 1961), Srinivas (1966), Singhal (1977), Vidyarthi (1976), and Vinayak (1972).
25. Studies on the pre-independence history of student movements highlight the debate between nationalist and liberal ideologies: Chandra (1938), Curran (1951), McCully (1940), Nurullah and Naik (1962), Reddy (1949), Sakrikar (1946), Singh (1942), and Spencer (1967) have contributed to the understanding of student movements in India.
26. For example, at Rangpur in Bengal, the entire student body was fined four aanas each for singing *Vande Mataram*.
27. Growth of financially independent private institutions has been the most significant development over the past few decades. Such institutions have proliferated all over the country over the years, but faced with financial constraints, the government has had little option but to reluctantly allow their entry (Agarwal 2009: 22).
28. University education expands one's way of thinking by sensitizing one about others in our social environment. If any education system in the world is not doing that, then it is a matter of concern. Indeed, scholars of pedagogy (Apple 2010; Bernstein 2000; Giroux 1983; Habermas 1967) have also defined the role of university education beyond merely imparting knowledge. Indiresan (1999) asks a critical question: 'we must ask whether there is something wrong with our education system, that it trains only the head without touching the heart' (1999: 148).
29. Statistics are from Government of India. 2015. 'All India Survey of Higher Education 2013–14'. New Delhi: Department of Higher Education, Ministry of Human Resource Development.
30. Explaining the history of Indian universities, Guha defines three forms of parochialism: (a) identity; (b) ideological; and (c) institutional.
31. Available at https://en.wikipedia.org/wiki/List_of_university_mottos.
32. Available at http://en.granma.cu/cuba/2016-02-25/the-university-must-be-a-center-for-critical-thought, accessed 4 July 2016.
33. The group is made up of Dalits, tribal, backward, and Leftist students and bases its ideologies on Marx, Periyar, and Ambedkar.
34. 'Beef and Pork Politics Divides TISS Students', *Mumbai Mirror*, 9 August 2014.
35. On 28 November 2014, a national newspaper covered a story titled 'Shuddh Vegetarian in IIT Delhi: RSS Activists Spur Smriti Irani to Dictate

Hostel Food'. After this, IIT Delhi decided to *play safe* by only serving vegetarian food in campus.

36. Available at http://www.firstpost.com/living/shuddh-vegetarian-in-iit-delhi-rss-activists-spur-smriti-irani-to-dictate-hostel-food-1825509.html, accessed 4 December 2014.

37. Cited from a pamphlet jointly published by the Dalit Adivasi Bahujan Minority Student Association (DABMSA), the Telangana Student Association (TSA), the Progressive Democratic Student Union (PDSU), Bahujan Student Forum (BSF), and Telangana Vidyarthi Vedika (TVV) at EFLU on 15 August 2012.

38. Available at http://www.countercurrents.org/2016/09/16/confrontations-and-scope-of-identity-politics-observations-on-left-politics-of-jnu-and-kerala/, accessed 26 September 2016.

39. 'The original inhabitant' refers to a group of students who consider themselves as part of Dravidian civilization, not the 'outsiders' Aryans.

40. Available at http://www.hindustantimes.com/delhi-news/5-hurt-in-jnu-clash-over-ram-s-existence/story-wDxFUeqNuL5suteYo-PDMpM.html, accessed 30 March 2016.

41. Available at http://economictimes.indiatimes.com/news/politics-and-nation/what-is-wrong-in-manusmriti-burning-jnu-students-to-varsity/articleshow/51499704.cms, accessed 30 March 2016.

42. Popularized by Dalit students in agitations after Rohith Vemula's suicide and also from speeches by Kanhaiya Kumar. Available at https://thewire.in/25435/from-lal-salaam-to-jai-bhim-lal-salaam/, accessed on 27 December 2017.

43. Available at https://drambedkarbooks.com/2016/03/02/2nd-march-1930-in-dalit-history-nashik-kalaram-temple-satyagraha-started/, accessed 20 October 2016.

44. The Naga Hoho, the apex civil society body of the Nagas, strives for a unified Naga identity. Several factions of Naga militias divided along tribal lines or factional loyalties that override ethnicity.

45. Available at https://timesofindia.indiatimes.com/india/United-against-quota-Students-hold-countrywide-protests/articleshow/1512585.cms?referral=PM, accessed 30 October 2016.

46. Interview, Jones, L. 2012. 'Noam Chomsky Spells out the Purpose of Education'. Open Culture. Accessed 4 June 2017. http://www.openculture.com/2012/11/noam_chomsky_spells_out_the_purpose_of_education.html.

47. The notion of critical pedagogy as a recognized concept is a relatively new phenomenon that emerged particularly from the thought of Paulo Freire and others (Kincheloe 2008; McLaren 2000). Critical pedagogy is an empowering way of thinking and acting fostering decisive agency that does not take a position of neutrality in its contextual examination of the various forces that impact the human condition (Kirylo 2013: xxi).

48. Available at http://www.thehindu.com/opinion/op-ed/life-rape-and-death-in-an-indian-city/article5125290.ece, accessed 30 October 2016.
49. Campaign by female students for freedom of hostel curfew and other 'sexist' restrictions. Available at http://indianexpress.com/article/cities/delhi/pinjra-tod-student-campaign-exhorts-women-to-oppose-sexist-hostel-rules/, accessed 29 October 2016.
50. Available at http://www.firstpost.com/india/watch-bhu-fears-more-protests-varsity-shut-till-3-oct-no-girl-here-who-hasnt-been-molested-say-students-4078173.html, accessed 28 October 2017.
51. Desai (2008: 68) calls it 'New social class'.

1 Telangana Movement

A Cultural–Political Discourse

The available literature on the Telangana movement offers historical, political, and economic perspectives that define Telangana as a 'backward' region and the movement as an offshoot to this backwardness. The backwardness generally discussed pertains to the economic standing of the people of Telangana. From the vantage point of a fresh perspective, this chapter uses regional culture to understand the emergence of the mass movement. It explores the context in which the idea of statehood for Telangana took shape and discusses how the movement can be understood as a new social movement. The chapter also attempts to understand the contours of the movement's history in terms of how the culture of Telangana was marginalized, and how Telangana activists, especially employees and students, mobilized against the dominant Andhra culture, leading ultimately to widespread, robust cultural assertion.

DEBATING THE TELANGANA MOVEMENT AS NEW SOCIAL MOVEMENT

Social movements lead to social transformation (Frank and Fuentes 1987: 1507). After the proliferation of the Civil Rights Movement in the United States of America in the 1950s and 1960s, university students around the world launched various counter-cultural movements and became agents of social change. In the spring of 1966, a group of Black students at San Francisco State College (now University) organized the nation's first Black Student Union (BSU), demanding a more inclusive higher education system. The 'Black Power' movement spawned the term 'student power' (Ross 1969: 245). Topics such as the psychology of love and the social significance of drugs were the major attraction among university students who formed a group called Young Americans for Freedom (YAF). As literature highlights, similar agitations were led in Italy, Germany, and France (Brand 1983, 1985; Friberg and Galtung 1984; Paris 1981; Roth 1984; Rucht 1982; Touraine 1981, 1985). Scholars such as Alain Touraine (France), Alberto Melucci (Italy), Jurgen Habermas (Germany), and Manuel Castells (Spain) realized that the existing 'ideological' Marxist[1] class paradigm was unable to provide a convincing explanation as to why students had become the vanguard of protest (see Lee 2007: 52).

One of the central figures of the 'New Left' was the Columbia University sociologist, C.W. Mills. His 'Letter to the New Left' (Mills 1960) became the manifesto for student organizations who criticized the Left and classical Marxism. The 'New Left' questioned the notion of universal Marxism and tried to compose a 'surrogate universal' (Gitlin 1995: 313). The idea of universal mass movements was rejected as students claimed that 'mass movements were nothing more than sectoral movements for themselves' (Gitlin 1993, 1995). The scholarship of Touraine, Melucci, Habermas, and Castells explains the emergence and character of these new movements and locates contemporary student movements as New Social Movements (NSMs) in a global context. Contrary to the (working) class base and ideology of old social movements, NSMs of the 1970s drew their support from a different social class base, such as gender, age, race, sexuality, ethnicity, and region (see Melucci 1980, 1985, 1989) made up of new social actors.[2] The women's movement, anti-nuclear protests, environmental movement, gay rights, animal rights, minority nationalism, and ethnic movements were all considered NSMs. In short, according to Crossley (2002: 10), NSMs arose from a contradiction between Marxist and Hegelian tradition of the philosophy of history. This, according to scholars, marked the beginning of a distinction between old and new forms of movements, and became a fresh addition to social movement literature. Thus, scholars have sought to break down the conventional theoretical distinction in the field between political process, resource mobilization, and NSM theories (Ferree 1992; Johnston and Klandermans 1995;

Meyer 1999; Morris and Mueller 1992; Polletta 1999). NSMs arise within the sphere of 'cultural reproduction of social relations, symbols and identities' (Melucci 1980) and are 'specific to history and social structure' (2001: 40). According to NSM theorists, identity movements seek to transform dominant cultural patterns or gain recognition for new social identities by employing 'expressive' strategies (Cohen 1985; Melucci 1985, 1989; Touraine 1981). According to Kriesi and Giugni (1995: xxi) the development of NSMs is 'ultimately rooted in structural and cultural transformation that characterize all Western and European countries'.

Identity has an ontological and epistemological status (Somers 1994: 606). Cultural identities—religious, national, regional, and ethnic identities—are more fluid and may be either public or private depending upon historical context. Duncombe[3] (2002: 5) explains, 'culture is used, consciously or unconsciously, effectively or not, to resist and/or change the dominant political, economic, and/or social structure.' He points out that some forms of cultural resistance can be dismissed as an 'escape from politics and a way to release discontent that might otherwise be expressed through political activity' (2002: 6). However, there is an emphasis on both macro and micro historical elements. Resistance based on culture explains the use of such categories.[4]

Political process theorists are increasingly coming to realize that cultural dynamics are central to the origin and development of social movements.[5] Culture, ideas, belief systems, rituals, oratory, emotions, and grievance interpretation are central to social movements. Social movement scholars analysed cultural processes as elements of political opportunity (Ferree et al. 2002; Meyer et al. 2002; Gamson and Meyer 1996; Steinberg 1999). Polletta (2004) also theorizes the role of culture in mobilization. Like Goodwin and Jasper (2003), Polletta (2004: 97) believes that we can usually adopt a 'less anaemic conception of culture than some political process analysis has done without making actors, interests, strategies, and resources simply figments of a culturalist imagination'. For example, scholars raised questions about who we are, how we live, and who is accountable, rather than demanding fair remuneration and improved working conditions (Habermas 1981; Klandermans, Kriese, and Tarrow 1988; Melucci 1985). In short, the core characteristics of NSMs are derived out of lived experiences, which are very much rooted in the culture of everyday life. In their work on contentious politics, McAdam, Tarrow, and Tilly (2001) argue that, at most, there is a fine line between social movements and the politics of everyday life.[6] Laraña, Johnston, and Gusfield (1994: 7) call it the 'democratization dynamics of everyday life'. Habermas uses 'life-world' to describe this everyday phenomenon.[7]

According to Buechler (1995: 458), there are two versions of NSM theory: political and cultural. He states, 'The cultural version emphasizes the symbolic explorations and expressions of identity that precisely challenge the instrumental logic of systemic domination'. The political version of NSM is pro-Marxist and draws upon the most promising work in neo-Marxist scholarship, seeking to build upon the strength of this tradition.

Buechler (1995: 457) argues that the political version of NSM is more concerned with strategic questions and instrumental action as the ultimate goal of social movements while recognizing the importance of identity formation, grievance definition, and interest articulation as intermediate steps in the process of movement activism. Table 1.1 outlines political and cultural versions of NSMs.

Since the social construction of identity always takes place in a context marked by power relationship, Castells (1997/2001: 7–8) proposes a distinction between three[8] forms and origins of identity building: legitimizing identity, resistance identity, and project identity. Social movement theories tend to view power as state centred and rooted in the political and economic structure of societies. Polletta (2004: 98) argues that when political opportunities are seen as structural and not cultural, activists' capacity to take advantage of those opportunities is cultural. Culture provides a structure and context which helps in expressing our behaviour, our identity, status, and emotions. Therefore, understanding a movement from the cultural angle unfolds deeper realities of lived experiences. Scholars (Bernstein 1997, 2005; Polletta and Jasper 2001) establish a link between identity and social movements through cultural identities. Identity exists in the social structure which might be dignified, stigmatized, or derogatory according to contexts. Identities are integrally related to structure and interest (Bernstein 2008: 287).

NSMs do not arise from relations of production and distribution of resources but from within the sphere of cultural production and the life world, and from the need to 'create cultural alternatives in everyday life that seek to escape from the state, not influence or seize it'

TABLE 1.1 Political and Cultural Version of New Social Movement Theories

Issue	Political Version	Cultural Version
General orientation	Pro-Marxist	Post-Marxist
Representative Theorist	Manuel Castells	Alberto Melucci
Societal Totality	Advanced capitalism	Information society
Image of Power	Systemic centralized	Diffuse, decentralized
Level of Analysis	Macro, Meso-level, State-oriented	Meso-, micro level, civil society, everyday life
Movement Activity	Retains role for instrumental action	Eschews strategic concerns in favours of symbolic expressions
First Debate: View of New Movements	Recognizing their role without rejecting the role of working class movements	Regards new movements as having displaced working-class movements
Second Debate: Movement Orientation	Potential for progressive orientations if allied with working class movements	Sees NSMs as defensive or rejects category of 'progressive'
Third Debate: Evaluation of Movements	Sees political movements as most radical, cultural movements as political	Sees cultural movements as most radical, political movements as co-optable
Fourth Debate: Social Base of Movements	Analyses in class term via contradictory locations, new class or middle class	Analyses in terms of non-class constituencies or issues and ideologies

Source: Buechler (1995).

(Melucci 1996: 27)..They are linked to the survival and reproduction of culture, social relations, symbols, and identities. Scholars (Calhoun 1993; Castells 1978; Edward 2009; Habermas 1984, 1987; Melucci 1980; Scott 1990; Singh 2001; Tarrow 1991; Touraine 1985) claim that NSMs' engagements are less about material reproduction and more about cultural reproduction, social integration, and socialization.

Following Western scholarship, the Indian debate on NSMs began almost three decades later. Omvedt (1993, 1994), Oommen (2010),

Shah (2004), and Singh (2001) have debated a conceptual shift in social movement literature. They all agree that NSMs question the relevance of both the functionalist as well as the dialectical Marxist models and 'reflect the cultural and democratic representational crisis of society' (Singh 2001). Oommen (2010) takes a clue from movement scholars (Cohen 1985; Klandermans, Kriesi, and Tarrow 1988; McAdam 1988; Melucci 1989; Offe 1985), and highlights some major points to explain NSMs—that (*a*) they cannot be characterized in terms of ideology as they represent a variety of ideas and value; (*b*) their participants have structurally diverse backgrounds; (*c*) they breed new identities or reinvent old ones; (*d*) they often represent counter cultures; (*e*) they struggle to reclaim their past through the intimate aspects of human life such as dietary practices, dress patterns, sexuality, and the like; and (*f*) they interrogate the legitimacy and style of the functioning of traditional political parties and may give birth to new types of political parties. In a comparative study of Egypt and Tunisia, Beissinger, Jamal, and Mazur (2012) found that corruption and unemployment motivated protests that kicked off uprisings across the region known as the 'Arab Spring'. Pathania (2015), Sitapati (2011), and Thakur and Rai (2013) see a similar case in India in 2010 when the 'India Against Corruption' movement led to countrywide agitations.

The NSM framework offers a fresh way to analyse the Telangana movement. Functionalist and dialectical Marxist frameworks assume the identity of individuals and their action and subjectivities in favour of a formalized non-human structural image of society (Singh 2001: 157). The subnational movement in Assam and the demand for Jharkhand are examples of NSMs, according to Singh (2001: 206). Three major themes emerge which help us understand the regional movement for a separate Telangana state. One theme is identity, second is culture, and third is the decentralized nature of the movement with the emergence of civil society. These themes are appropriate to understand the Telangana movement as a cultural movement. Scholars (Pingle 2014; Rao 1997; Reddy and Sharma 1979; Simhadri and Rao 1997; Thirumali 2013), who studied Andhra–Telangana problems, centre their arguments primarily on 'social and economic backwardness' of Telangana. According to them, this is an important reason behind the emergence of the movement. These scholars have adopted the term 'internal colonialism',[9] which was first used by the first State

Reorganisation Commission (SRC) in 1955 (1955: 105). There has been a tendency to view the *internal colonialism* and *son of the soil* theses only in the context of economic deprivation. But in the process of colonialism, there is also 'a loss of identity and the formation of a new, forced identity. The marginalization and, in some cases, even irretrievable loss of indigenous knowledge systems is also a part of this process' (Panikkar 2007: 21).

Applying the NSM framework, the next section highlights how different phases of the movement were essentially a struggle between two cultural identities. As Lisa Mitchell (2010: 96) argues, 'cultural identities—whether defined by language or any other foundation—are central to the functioning of politics in India today'. This book takes this view further and divides the Separate Telangana agitations into three phases. The first phase (1953–72) lies in the cultural deprivation and humiliation of the Telangana people in the wake of the merger with Andhra. The movement's second phase, from 1973 to 2000, was a lengthier phase marked by intense cultural mobilization in the region. The third phase, from 2001 to 2014, is one of cultural and political assertion. The movement evoked various local cultural symbols such as dialect, food, dress, festivals, and the arts, as forms of resistance against the so-called *dominant* culture of Andhras, a political identity. The Telangana movement defines this culture as the culture of the 'outsider', 'non-Mulki', or 'settler'. Thus, the feeling of a unique Telangana identity emerged against the *other* identity of the Andhra.[10] The 'son of the soil' argument can also be better understood through the cultural thesis. Thus, the movement reinterpreted, or in Bernstein's (2008) language, *deconstructed*, cultural representations such as language, dress, food, and literature.

A BRIEF BACKGROUND ON INTER-REGIONAL DIFFERENCES

The Telangana region was part of the Hyderabad state, ruled by Nizam Osman Ali Khan. It constituted a large part of present-day Maharashtra and Karnataka. That it was never ruled by the British makes Telangana historically distinct and unique. During the Nizam's rule, Urdu was the official language of Hyderabad state (Zahir 2008: 2), despite the widespread presence of Marathi, Kannada, and Telugu. As a result, these languages became heavily influenced by Urdu. Telangana Telugu became a mixture of Urdu and Telugu, and Hindi (*dakhini* Hindi or Hyderabadi Hindi) became a mixture of Urdu and Hindi. Various versions of Telugu were spoken across the region. With the establishment of the largest educational institution in the city of Hyderabad in 1918, Osmania University (OU), the Nizam aimed to provide higher education in Urdu.[11] In his quest to promote language and Islamic tradition, he encouraged the establishment of more than a dozen Urdu dailies.[12] Thus, Telugu remained underutilized during the Nizam's rule, and later became a point of contention after the merger with Andhra. Hence, the Nizam's patronage established a distinct political culture in Hyderabad.

As much of the Andhra region had been part of the Madras Presidency under British rule, a large portion of Andhras were exposed to and educated in English. In contrast with the Telugu of Telangana, Andhra Telugu maintained its Sanskrit base. Such variations in Telugu further amplified the difference in the two main accents spoken within the region. The Telangana accent came to be considered inferior in the eyes of the growing Andhra population in Hyderabad, who dominated the city culturally and politically after 1953.

The roots of Telugu unity can be traced to the beginning of the twentieth century. On 20 May 1913, the first *Andhra Mahajana Sabha* was created, which coined the idea of *Telugu Talli* (Mother Telugu). B.N. Sharma, who later became member of the Viceroy's Executive Council, was instrumental in the formation. Another organization called *Andhra Jana Sangam* was formed which was the public forum for Telugu separateness from Madras Presidency. The *Andhra Maha Sabha* was formed in 1930 and dominated by the communists (CPI) in the mid-1940s (Mantena 2014: 351). Later, the formation of *Visalandhra Maha Sabha* in 1949 by P. Sundarayya promoted the idea of a 'greater Andhra'. Andhra activists began to promote language as the neutral bond that would be cultivated to create a political community in the region. Mantena (2014: 356) argues that 'regionalism was endorsed by both the CPI and Congress leaders in Hyderabad and his ultimately led to calls for severance of the state along linguistic lines as the best political situation to a monarchical modernity that reached its limits and ultimately demise'. Thus, to many, Telangana's merger with Andhra began on unsecured footing (Mantena 2014).

As India gained independence, 500 small kingdoms and princely states were merged to create Union of India with the efforts of the then home minister, Sardar Vallabhbhai Patel (see Map 1.1 depicting Hyderabad state before its merger with Indian union). However, his negotiations did not yield anything in the case of Hyderabad and Kashmir. Kashmir was ruled by a Hindu, Raja Hari Singh, and was not given much attention. The government focussed more on Hyderabad because of its Muslim ruler. Patel ordered the Indian Army to impose military action in the city on 17 September 1948. This forceful attempt to merge Hyderabad state with the Indian government was known as 'Operation Polo'. Thousands of Muslims were killed, looted, and raped

MAP 1.1 Hyderabad State before Its Merger with Indian State in 1948
Source: Chaturvedi, 1956, *A Descriptive Atlas of Hyderabad State*, p. 6.
Note: This map is not to scale and does not represent authentic national and international boundaries. It is provided for illustrative purposes only.

by Hindus and the Indian Army[13] (Noorani 2001; Thomson 2013). After the merger, the Telangana region remained under Indian military rule from 1948 to 1952 after the annexure of Hyderabad state to the Indian union.[14] Before any general elections took place, the central government appointed M.K. Vellodi as chief minister[15] of Hyderabad. Telangana activists claim that during his rule, there was rampant migration to Hyderabad, as Andhras quickly filled the need for English-speaking employees. Thirumali (2013: 79) states: 'There was a huge migration from Andhra region after 1950s which strengthened the Andhra form of politics in Hyderabad. Their sectarianism reinforced the regionalism to keep them apart'.

According to Simhadri and Rao (1997), 'Approximately 70,000 people were registered in the employment office in 1952 in Hyderabad state'. The Andhra peasant castes acquired lands in and around Hyderabad and other parts of Telangana. The Andhras 'occupied crucial positions in the administration, particularly in the secretariat, judiciary and education' (Thirumali 2013: 80), which left locals at a competitive disadvantage for employment. Thus, a 'native *vs.* outsider' agitation began known as 'mulki *vs.* non-mulki'.[16] A mulki was defined as one who was born in Hyderabad or whose father had completed fifteen years of government service 'in the Hyderabad State at the time of his birth' (Reddy and Sharma 1979: 318). To be considered for government service in the city, one had to prove 'mulki' status. Thus, there were rampant cases of producing fake mulki certificates. According to Alam and Khan (1972: 61), more than 25,000 'bogus' mulki certificates were produced, as the administration was run largely by Andhras. The number of migrants rapidly increased after 1961, contributing to the unemployment of locals.[17] The city of Hyderabad became an industrial hub as it had the necessary infrastructure. Andhra settlers successfully competed with other business communities from other parts of the country, such as Gujaratis, Marwaris, and Punjabis. Gradually, the traditional economy transformed into a capitalist economy. Table 1.2 shows the migration pattern from Andhra and Coastal Andhra to Hyderabad.

In the span of a decade, there was an 80 per cent increase in migration of Andhra population to Hyderabad. 'It was a case of the periphery taking control of the centre', state Alam and Khan (1972: 228). Telangana employees faced humiliation as their culture was considered 'inferior' and their Telugu accent ridiculed. Telangana ideologue and professor,

TABLE 1.2 Migration from Coastal Andhra to Hyderabad District (1961, 1971)

Districts	1961	1971	% increase
Srikakulam	1,500	1,800	20
Vishakhapatnam	3,200	4,600	44
East Godavari	8,400	16,000	90
West Godavari	7,700	12,500	62
Krishna	12,500	23,000	84
Guntur	10,700	19,000	78
Nellore	4,600	6,000	30
Ongole	–	4,000	–
Total	**48,600**	**86,900**	**79**

Source: Chandra Sekhar, A., 1961, *Census of India: Volume 2—Andhra Pradesh, Part I-A 9 (i)*; Census of India 1971.

Harinath,[18] explains, '*Mulki* [certificates] gave them [Andhras] ethnic character. This ethnic character helped them in securing political positions as well'. Incidents of insult and humiliation of Telangana employees by Andhra employees (who considered themselves the best Telugu speakers) became commonplace (also see Srinivasulu 2002: 10). The continuous discrimination in government jobs led to several protests in the state in 1952.

Students of OU in Warangal carried out a five-day agitation on 26 June 1952, chanting 'Non-mulki go back!'.[19] Telangana mainstream political leaders, Marri Chenna Reddy (henceforth MCR) and Konda Venkata Reddy supported the movement. Professor Jayashankar, former Vice-chancellor of Kakatiya University, who is considered one of the founding fathers of Telangana movement, recalls: 'Khammam district experienced protests for two days against giving preferences to other states in employment and admissions into schools and colleges. From then onwards there were several spontaneous movements'.[20] On 8 August 1952, nearly a thousand students marched down the streets of Warangal again, demanding the non-mulkis leave. On 26 August, the students in Hyderabad and Secunderabad went on strike by not attending their classes, and the same scene was repeated over the next few days with a growing number of protesters. On 30 August 1952, the police carried out a lathi charge (cane beating) on the group of students who were conducting a peace gathering in Hanamkonda. During these agitations, Reddy, Velamma, and Vyshya hostels were used as a place for Telangana activists' meetings.

After experiencing continuous opposition by the masses, the Indian government appointed a SRC in December 1953, consisting of Justice Fazal Ali as chairman, and H.N. Kunjroo and K.M. Pannikar as members to investigate the problems of the Telangana region. The Commission worked for 22 months and presented its report in October 1955. The SRC expressed the fear that 'Telangana itself may be converted into a colony by the enterprising coastal Andhras' (SRC Report 1955: 105). Interestingly, Nehru expressed the same fear, and suspected that the Andhras would occupy the land, jobs, and educational institutions. In a press meeting in October 1953, he stated, 'Visalandhra is an idea bearing a taint of expansionist imperialism'.[21] Nevertheless, on 1 November 1956, the Government of India formed the new state of Andhra Pradesh by merging the 11 districts of Andhra and nine Telugu speaking Telangana districts of the princely state of Hyderabad. It became the first state formed on a linguistic basis (Map 1.2 illustrates the united Andhra Pradesh by merging three Telugu-speaking regions: coastal Andhra, Rayalaseema, and Telangana). The merger was supported by many promises and constitutional safeguards, such as the Gentlemen's Agreement, signed on 1 February 1956. The agreement was a promise to make equal development and socio-political representation between Telangana–Coastal Andhra and Rayalaseema. According to the agreement,[22] the five-year term of chief minister should be shared by both Andhra and Telangana equally. However, in the entire state ruling of 56 years and six months (from 1 November 1956 till 2 June 2014), only four Telangana chief ministers served the state. To quantify this, out of 20,212 days of rule, a total of 2,298 days were given to Telangana. While chief ministers from the Andhra region (Coastal and Rayalaseema) ruled for 17,914 days, for the remaining 433 days, the state remained under President's rule. The chief minister and the most powerful portfolios in the cabinet were given to Andhra People. Chief Minister N. Sanjeeva Reddy (from Andhra) formed his cabinet without a deputy chief minister from Telangana, as promised in the Gentlemen's Agreement, to which he was a signatory.[23] Thus, the Gentlemen's Agreement was ignored (Jadhav 1997: 8; Pingle 2014;

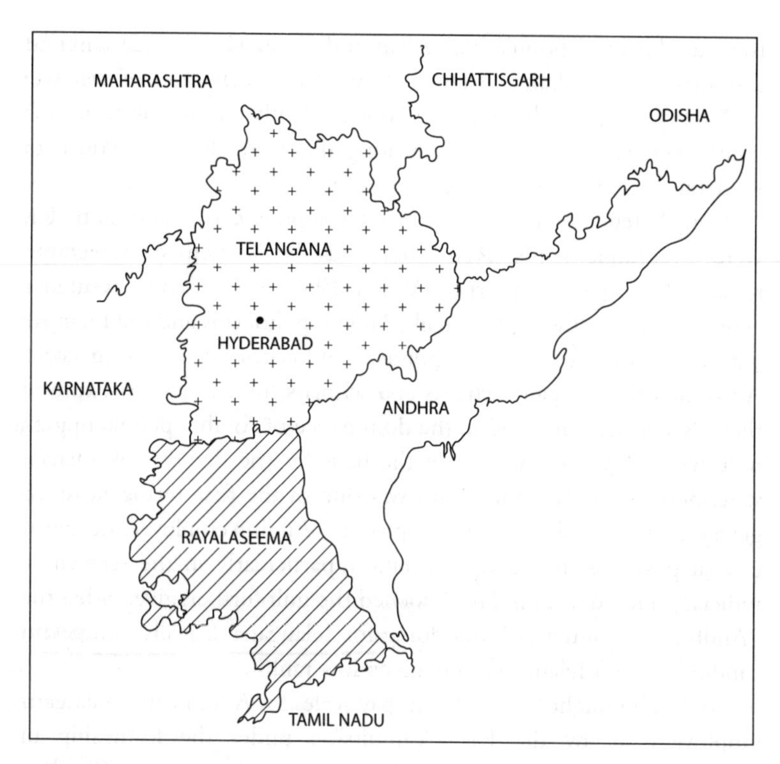

MAP 1.2 United Andhra Pradesh
Source: Map by Monika Batham.
Note: This map is not to scale and does not represent authentic national and international boundaries. It is provided for illustrative purposes only.

Rao 2009; Thirumali 2013). Subhash[24] explains the Andhra 'prejudice about Telangana people':

> History repeats itself. Andhra people had English education and exposed to all kinds of shrewdness. They knew the historical Gentlemen's agreement between the United States and Japan in 1907–08. That is why they chose this term but our innocent people from Telangana had no idea that this agreement was a trap. This was an agreement of slavery to Andhra people … (*laughs*) you know, our poor Telangana people haven't even seen the 1947 hit Hollywood drama called 'Gentleman's Agreement'. Andhra will never be gentle to us.

Andhra colonies' in Hyderabad, according to Weiner (1978: 228), soon became the 'symbol of government's discriminatory policies towards the local population'. Alam and Khan (1972: 142) describe a similar state of affairs: 'After 1956, with the formation of the state of Andhra Pradesh, thousands of jobs explicitly meant for Telangana youth were given to Andhras. Among the 8,000 Reserve Police of Hyderabad, 'the majority were non-locals'.[25]

Many 'safeguards' to ensure equal development to Telangana region were never implemented (Rao 1969). Thus, the Gentlemen's Agreement remained 'a rhetoric flourish' (Welch 1980: 319), leaving Telangana economically backward. Gradually, Andhra politicians and their culture started dominating the social, political, and economic life of the state. According to Telangana activists and scholars, 'non-implementation of these "safeguards" resulted in the dominance of Andhra people in jobs, industry, and politics, which set the basis for the demand of separate statehood.' Mr K.R. Amos, who was one of the first Telanganaites to get a job in Hyderabad in 1952, explains:[26] 'Andhra employees occupied crucial positions in the administration, particularly in the secretariat, judiciary and education. This widened the gulf further, given what the "Andhra administration" was doing for Telangana. Equally competent candidates from Telangana were given low ranks'.

Studies highlight how different pay scales for Andhra and Telangana employees set by the Pay Commission under the leadership of K. Brahmananda Reddy created permanent grievances (Bhushan and N. Venugopal 2009; Hyderabad Forum for Telangana 2009, 2010; Ramulu 2007; Simhadri and Rao 1997; Thirumali 2013). Gradually, through government policies, Telangana's culture and people became systematically disenfranchised. Government offices became sites of cultural contentions as public sector Telangana employees were disregarded or ridiculed by their Andhra counterparts. Mr Amos shares his experiences of exclusion and humiliation:

> I was the only one in my office who was from Telangana in Hyderabad. Imagine, surrounded by Andhra people. Although, I was working as an officer but in daily office routine, to get signature from my boss, I had to request a peon or a clerk to get any work done. If I dare to meet him directly, he would shout at me and throw the file out of his office. We could never sit together as colleagues. They used to laugh at Telangana Telugu. A similar situation was happening to many other employees. All the Telangana employees used to meet and discuss these issues—that they have no say in their offices.

> Our presence had no meaning in our own offices. High positions were given to Andhra people. The behaviour of the Andhra employees working in the secretariat and the daily humiliation forced us to come together in one platform and form an association called Telangana Non-Gazetted Officers' Association.

Culture acts as an 'authoritative zone that sets goals and standards for individuals' (Taylor 1978: 157–9). If one culture does not fit in such standards, it is looked or judged with some prejudices or stereotypes. Dr G. Ram Reddy (1967: 2213), in his study of Block Administration in Telangana, explains the role of the Block Development Officer (BDO): '[The] BDO held a strong prejudice against the Telangana employee and commented that they were lazy, backward and intellectually inferior to the people of Andhra Region'. Explaining the Andhra attitude, Jadhav (1997: 8) writes, 'Telangana language is no Telugu, Telangana people are lazy, they are also fools and criminals at the same time: such was the officially sanctioned Andhra attitude. While the entire country lauds Hyderabad and its way of life the Andhra rules are never tired of saying that Telangana people are uncultured. Thus the suicidal attempt to subjugate Telangana permanently continues'.

In *The Myth of Lazy Native*, Syed Hussain Alatas (1977) demonstrates how, under colonial influence, from the sixteenth to twentieth century, workers in the rubber plantations in Southeast Asia came to believe in their own laziness. That colonial subjects developed 'a sense of inferiority and dependency' complex is generally recognized. How they came to acquire them falls within the domain of culture as much as psychology (Panikkar 2007: 22). That is how the construction of social identity occurs which is 'strongly influenced by the past' (Sen 2009: 97). They are constructed through attaching labels that put themselves or others into categories (Williams 2011: 130), as in the eyes of Andhras, Telangana people are 'lazy'. In common parlance, words like 'Nawab' and 'Nizam' are used to make fun of Telangana people which is also reflected in modern films (Nag 2011: 101).

The idea of the *native* unleashed a new spirit to the movement and the ideology of *son of the soil* started taking hold (Oommen 2005: 70; Weiner 1978). Political circumstances engendered by a constricting employment situation for the Telangana middle class and the psychological need to find a difference between Telangana and the rest of the state necessitated the search for a distinctive cultural identity

(Weiner 1978: 247). Thus, gradually, the movement for implementing special safeguards for Telangana turned into a 'native *vs.* settler' issue. This started formation of a separate identity. Weiner also observed that the 'search for a distinctive cultural identity formed a significant feature of the Telangana movement' (Weiner 1978: 237). Thus, there is a complex relationship between regional autonomy, political viability, and the cultural and political consolidation within a more democratic, plural, secular, and developmental politics in contemporary India.

In many ways, the regions of Telangana and Andhra represent two different life-worlds. Yet, one of their main commonalities is the Telugu language. Thota (1969: 4) claims that language acted not only as a binding force but also a separating one. According to Thirumali (2013), a kind of 'ethnocentrism exists between these two regions in the name of language and culture'.[27] Scholars also highlight how Andhra's dialect, culture, and festivals dominated mainstream media and became part of popular culture. Thus, the Telangana–Andhra association represents a hierarchy and exploitation in the name of language which manifested itself politically. Maringanti (2010: 35) provides historical detail:

> Notwithstanding formal protections for *mulkis*, these migrant communities insinuated themselves into structures of governmental power and yet maintained cultural boundaries with the local people. In agriculture, for example, in many of the irrigated areas in Telangana one sees villages known as 'settler camps' or 'Guntur *palle*' [villages]. By the early 1960s, much of the grape cultivation around Hyderabad was in the hands of such migrant farmer-investors. Similarly, particular segments of government jobs both departmentally and hierarchically came to be occupied by migrants. For example, teaching jobs especially at the college level, were occupied by Andhra migrants.

The socio-economic conditions and historical context behind the emergence of the mass movement for Telangana statehood cannot be ignored. The cultural struggle occurred on two different grounds: (*a*) among Andhras to strengthen their Telugu identity; and (*b*) an internal state struggle of Telangana[28] *prajanikam* (people) against Andhra to protect their regional dialect and culture. Lisa Mitchell (2010: 130) explores the new role of *culture* within education that emerged in the twentieth century, and concludes by arguing that language not only provided a medium for the acquisition of that which was accepted in the twentieth century as *knowledge*, but also began to act as a marker for cultural identification. She further argues that making language the most important object of education has transformed language into 'foundation stone for language-cultures' (Mitchell 2010: 155). From 1998 onwards, every edition of *Pedda Bala Siksha* (primary school textbooks) contained a statement on the back of the book (and the only English used in the entire book) proclaiming, 'This book is designed based on the concept of Cultural Literacy' (Mitchell 2010: 155).

THE TELANGANA MOVEMENT AS A CULTURAL MOVEMENT

The student movement for Telangana became a mass movement where students, with their diverse forms of activism, engaged civil society to make it a cultural movement. In this sense, we may safely argue that the Telangana movement is not just political (as it is projected), but also civil and intellectual in orientation, which manifested itself onto the political platform. The movement's group of intellectuals have been trying to rewrite the history of Telangana to emphasize its culture in contrast to Andhra culture. Analysis of the movement's debate in light of the discussion on NSMs establishes that cultural politics is at the heart of identity building for Telangana activists. Cultural mobilization that occurred through micro-level social and political events turned into cultural radicalization within existing institutions like universities, schools, art, and folk traditions. With various ideological contours, the Telangana movement gained political maturity. Table 1.3 offers an analysis of the Telangana movement through old and new social movement's frameworks.

As per the framework outlined in Table 1.3, the Telangana movement shares more characteristics with NSMs than traditional social movements. In this case, university teachers seem to be the critical group of intellectuals supporting and participating in the Telangana movement right from the beginning of the movement in 1953. For instance, the Telangana movement has come to be identified for several decades primarily as a student movement sustained as well by teachers and intellectuals of OU, most of them OU alumni. Thus, OU has become synonymous with the Telangana movement and has often been hailed as 'Telangana University' or the 'nerve centre' of the movement.[29]

TABLE 1.3 Understanding the Telangana Movement as a New Social Movement

	Old Social Movement	New Social Movement	Telangana Movement
Aim	Social/political/cultural	Socio-cultural	Socio-cultural-political
Base	Class specific/Proletariat Class/ Worker Class	Civil Society—educated elite-led organization and middle class and new middle class	All social groups across class; not state-sponsored
Mode of Resistance	Traditional	Anti-traditional	Revival of neglected language, music, folklore, and literature
Organization	Formal	Formal and bureaucratic	Both formal and informal
Orientation	Against political structure or class	Non-political/less political	Trust in democracy
Perspective	Class and political ideology	Identity based	Identity based
Membership	Face-to-face intimacies among activists	Local global/borderless	Local–global and social media support
Location	Region or institution specific, for example, industrial workers	Civil society/beyond boundaries	Civil society and common masses
Interests	Fixed interests and relations	New social interests—new social relations	End numbers of stakeholders
Vision	Socialism	Historic-specific new forms of identity	To empower the masses of Telangana

Source: Author.

Telangana Activists' Assertion against the Andhra Culture

The cultural aspects of the Andhra–Telangana problem overshadow political and economic ones. However, there has been a general tendency to focus more on the political aspect of the movement. According to Reed and Alexander (2007), usually politically engaged sociologists limit their activism to defending people who are unequivocally oppressed. No doubt, this is a final goal but cultural sociology can offer another one. They suggest 'we need to ask how people talk and act in everyday situations, in which they balance their own judgements regarding what should be denounced against what should be maintained, what should be ignored against what should be said' (Reed and Alexander 2007: 94). Thus, cultural sociology has both the potential and responsibility to contribute to democratic theory.

Cultural Symbols and Festivals

Culture maintains and sustains itself through history. It is kept alive through building monuments, making art, writing books, and producing and maintaining other artefacts. The pride of a community, region, or culture is preserved through celebrations and eulogizing history. In the case of Telangana–Andhra, there was much strife on these issues—who and what to celebrate and commemorate. Explaining culture as 'honour' and 'self-respect', senior activist V.K. Rao (2010: 183) states that 'the artistic and poetic talent of Telangana youth was so much neglected as to be not on par with the youth in the other region, where many such events (such as *Andhrabhuydaya Utsavalu*) are encouraged in many ways'. Yet, culture can be used as a source of domination. The merger of a distinct cultural region triggered a series of discontented voices among the educated in Telangana. 'To understand the cultural politics, one needs to be not only educated enough but also conscious enough', declares Professor Rao.[30] To make people conscious about their humiliation and discrimination, Telangana employees and students formed new associations and reached out to villages. Towards the middle of 1968 the NGO Association demanded implementation of safeguards. The founder of *Telangana Jagruthi* states, 'After all, the whole movement has been about the reassertion of the cultural identity of the people of this region. I hope the government will realise this, and I will do whatever it takes to ensure that the culture of Telangana is not only restored, but also researched' (Kavitha 2014).

V.K. Rao (2010: 185), in his submission to the Sri Krishna Commission wrote, 'The People of Telangana region ask for separation as strongly on cultural grounds as they demand on political and economic grounds'. Krishna Sagar Rao, another activist, cited 'emotional oppression' (K.S. Rao 2010: 89).

The national award-winning filmmaker B. Narsing Rao notes how theatre also changed over time, becoming more involved in the movement: 'As a child, I grew up watching and listening to folk music such as Gollu Sudhi, Oggu Kathalu, and Gotralu'. In the 1970s, Gollu Sudhi and Oggu Katha merged together and new forms emerged. The traditional drum (called *dappu*) became the symbol of resistance and the beat of the movement. In every movement, agitation, or strike, the dappu played a central role. There are students at OU who are researching the role of dappu in the movement and the community who plays dappu. The word dappu symbolizes the 'life-world' of a lower caste which has been on the margins for ages. The guiding force behind the 2009 movement has been the enormous amount of literature published by OU students and alumni.

There are popular incidents of state repression, which became part of everyday life of the Telangana activist. Learning about fellow artists is important to understand the emotional attachments among activists. The story of the murders of activists Belli Lalita and Ravinder Reddy[31] are narrated in common parlance. Such brutal incidents aggravated Telangana activists against the state, which they referred to as 'Andhra government'. After their murders, their art and music gained even more popularity and they were revered as martyrs. Books and literature banned by the state government nevertheless spread to rural Telangana by youth activists. Balkishan's *Dhoom Dhaam* performances portrayed the struggle and exploitation in the region.

Gaddar's revolutionary genre breathed new life in music. Popularly known as *Gadaranna* among common masses, his live performances attracted masses from every walk of life. He brings various elements of Telangana culture to the forefront, which served as symbols of identity assertion. He was instrumental in establishing an organic linkage between oral and written tradition. P.K. Kumar (2010: 66) highlights his contribution: 'Gaddar stands as a culmination point of culture, literature, politics, life and struggle of oppressed people'. It is not an exaggeration that literary artists call the pre-set age in Telugu poetry as 'age of Gaddar'.[32] His revolutionary songs inspire Dalits and women's movements in Telangana. He has been critical of Dalit movements and its strategies. He served as an intellectual communicator between Naxalite and Dalit movement in Andhra Pradesh. His songs 'Dalit Pululamma' (Dalit Tigers) and 'Chunduru Dalitanna' (Dalit Brothers of Chunduru) became symbols of assertion during Karamchedu and Chunduru massacres in 1985 and 1991 respectively. Dressing like a poor shepherd of Telangana, he remains half naked, wearing a *ghochi* (loincloth) and a blanket on his shoulder; he holds a red kerchief in one hand and ties *gajelu* (ankle bells) to his legs. His theatrical performances are a mix of his songs, poetry, dialogues, and satire of landlords and political class. The Andhra Pradesh government took up various initiatives in an effort to keep the state united. The celebration of Telugu festivals like *ugadi, sankranti*, and *yeruvaka* became ritualistic to bring about homogeneity among Telugu-speaking people (Thirumali 2013: 30). However, Telangana activists were not convinced of the value of such initiatives. To oppose this 'unity', they criticized the idea of 'Telugu Talli'.[33] Activist Sudarshan[34] claims: 'It [Telugu Talli] does not represent Telangana. As we are losing our resources, jobs, especially our pride in the joint state, we can't linger any longer in such sentiments. We are being treated as second class citizens in our own region, so we don't accept "Maa Telugu".'

Telugu Talli was soon replaced with the concept of 'Telangana Talli'. During the 2009 movement, Osmania student activists used the Telangana flag in every function they organized. Many of them changed their vehicle number plates from AP (Andhra Pradesh) to TG (Telangana). Citing further cultural differences, Dr Chiranjeevi explains: 'We are closer to the north on matters of religion. Our main religious festivals are *holi* and *dassara* [festivals of northern India] while the Andhras celebrate *pongal* [a Tamil festival]. Similarly, we have lots of Urdu words in our Telugu. On the other hand, Andhra Telugu has more words of Sanskrit, thus closer to Madras.'[35]

Festivals[36] also became a site of debate and resistance. For example, *Batukamma*, which is primarily celebrated in the Telangana region, was never recognized as a state festival (Nag 2011: 99). According to Shyam Mohan, 'Textbooks for school perpetuate the Andhra culture as if there was never any Telangana culture'. As a result, 'generations of youth of Telangana were sought to be kept in the dark about their culture, says the representation submitted by the newly spawned Telangana *Jagruthi*' (Nag 2011: 98–9).

In academic discourses, Telangana intellectuals referred to the 'inferior status' that the Telugu literary establishment gave to Telangana poets such as Pothana, Kaloji, and Dasharathi and absence of their status at the Tank Bund monument in Hyderabad. As with *Bharat Mata* (Mother India) in the British era, Telugu Talli is presented as a victim of colonial domination (Srikanth 2013: 42). A senior OU doctoral student's paper, entitled 'Telangana Women Designed the Indian National Flag?', was rejected by the conference, *Interpreting Deccan History*,[37] organized by OU's history department. Activists of the 1969 Telangana Movement Founders' Forum (TMFF) reacted with a press statement[38] offering an explanation: 'The convenor of the conference is an Andhra settler, she could not digest the reality and recognition of Telangana people especially of Muslims'. It also stated that the *Jai Hind* slogan was coined by Abdul Hasan Safrani and the Indian national flag was designed by Mrs Surya Tayyabji. The press release concluded with an appeal to the Telangana people 'to fight nail and tooth to expose the malafide intensions of these Andhra settlers'.

Language and Dialect

As stated earlier, Andhra Pradesh was the first Indian state formed on the basis of language by merging the Telangana and Andhra regions. Thirumali (2013: 27) believes that the real strength of Andhra has come from standardizing the Telugu language. Thirumali observes that the emergence of print culture established its superiority over the spoken, and thus a standard *Andhrabhasha* (Andhra language) was established through the spread of education and formation of the middle class in the Andhra region. This changed the vocabulary and created a wide gulf between the educated and illiterate. The trend brought in use of the typical middle class respectable terms like *andi* and *garu* (to give regard). These terms spread among various subregions, dividing the people vertically along class or cultural lines.

Andhra intelligentsia spoke and recited Telugu culture in the native language to present how they were culturally different from the other linguistic groups (Thirumali 2013: 30). Thirumali highlights the ethnocentrism existing between these two regions in the name of language and culture.[39] Telangana activist Kaloji Narayan Rao (1914–2002) underscored how children were also discriminated against in terms of language and the way they spoke (cited in Mitchell 2010: 215). In a popular children's radio programme, 'one would never hear the voices of children from the Telangana region of Andhra Pradesh because their dialect was considered non-standard' (Mitchell 2010). Language became a basis, not simply for new cultural identities, but also for the articulation of unique political identities and forces us to consider changes in what it means to be 'political'. Due to the heavy influence of Urdu, 'Telangana Telugu speakers describe themselves as more gentle in their speech and manners, more cordial to guests, more leisurely and less aggressive than the people of Andhra' (Weiner 1978: 240). Explaining it further, Dr Sanjeev,[40] the co-convener of the 1969 TMFF, states, 'Telangana Telugu is a mixture of Telangana Urdu and other languages. In Andhra Telugu language we find lots of Sanskrit terminology. We can find Telangana Telugu has many words from *Pali-Pakrit* language. Then the problem comes how to identify a word whether it comes from Sanskrit or Pali language. They both look alike but they have much difference'.

Thus, the Telangana dialect is not merely the question of *language* but became an issue of identity and representation. As the movement for a separate state gained momentum, Telangana activists projected their dialect as a 'defiant statement of identity in the face of standardization and false homogeneity of the universal Telugu identity promoted by all media industries, including cinema' (Prakash and Vemmireddy 2015: 7). The dialect which was denigrated in various ways in Andhra-dominated media was consciously chosen as the language of resistance by Telangana activists. A hallmark of the movement, the Telangana dialect was aestheticized positively to a great extent. Student groups and cultural troupes constantly produced new arguments and rhetoric against the alleged cultural aggrandizement of the Andhra–Telugu culture. The 'Dhoom Dhaam' and other cultural festivals provided ample space for creative usage and development of new aesthetics based on the Telangana dialect (Prakash and Vemmireddy 2015). This way, the language became the medium of assertion. Local language, according to Habashi (2014: 326), is a direct result of the 'dialectic relationship between global and local political discourse'. However, in the case of the Telangana movement, these dialectics worked in such a manner that the local discourse has contributed in creating *inferiority* of Telangana accent, and global discourses have helped the people of Telangana to overcome such feelings. According to Reddy and Sharma (1979), this also became the 'basis of their cultural differences'. When a 'hostile attitude towards a region' develops among masses, it is more because of cultural reasons, and language is an essential element of the reflection of this attitude (Reddy and Sharma 1979).

Food

Similarly, food habits are also an important element of a culture and an individual's identity. Generally, when two cultures confront each other, food (after language) becomes a major issue. Migration to a new place or culture often forces an individual to adopt alternative food practices, which, in many ways, challenges one's individual identity. Yet, studies have shown that food habits are one of the last cultural traits to change in the context of migration and ethnic minority cultures (Charon 2004; Spiro 1955). Bhushan (2009: 58) adds that 'there has been little acknowledgement of the fact that the Telangana movement advanced not only by means of cultural assertion but also through cultural rejection of the other as evidenced in slogan such as '*idli sambhar ve-nakki po*' (*idli sambhar* go back), referring to Tamil and Coastal Andhra people, and '*Gongura pachadi*'[41] go back'. During student protests of city colleges and Nizam College at Hyderabad, 'Jobs to Telangana people only' and 'Hyderabad for Hyderabadis' were popular slogans focussing on the rejection of the culture of Andhras. Feelings of humiliation and discrimination were channelled through opposing the cultural symbols of 'idli-sambhar', 'gongura pachadi', and others.

During the 2011 agitations, Kalvakuntala Chandrashekhar Rao (henceforth KCR) used the cosmopolitan culture of Hyderabad to criticize Andhra culture and to gain support of the Muslim population concentrated in Hyderabad. On 31 January 2011, KCR remarked that 'the biryani prepared by people in Andhra Pradesh tasted like cow dung'.[42] He further mentioned that '[p]eople from Andhra who came here without even footwear are claiming that they have taught us how to make biryani'. He claimed, 'Hyderabadi Biryani is the best'. KCR used food as a strategy to gain political mileage, which is the part of cultural politics or resistance. Scholars like Duncombe (2012: 6) would argue that politics is essentially a cultural discourse, a shared set of symbols and meanings that we all abide by. When one culture makes fun of another, it can expect to receive counter criticism. KCR's statement had charged up Andhra leaders and activists. To counter KCR's statement, Vijayawada (Andhra) women stated: '*Sherwani*, *qubani* [a sweet made of dates] and *biryani* are what we in Hyderabad have known for ages'. Some women from Guntur and Vijayawada reportedly sent a parcel of Andhra-style biryani to KCR's home in Hyderabad, asking him to 'taste it and then talk'. Dr Chiranjeevi shares his opinion on the rival food cultures: 'The worst food in the world is Andhra food. Because they eat polished rice in which vitamins totally washed out. In their *rasam*, there is only vitamin C and nothing else. They eat lot of curd, which creates heaviness. On the other hand, Telangana food such as *sajjalu*, *ragulu*, *jonnalu*, *sankati*, *ghatkas* and *ambali* is very nutritious.'[43]

However, it is not about the nutritious value of the food but the ethnic element of culture that makes food a political subject.[44] Andhra food culture dominated Hyderabad cuisine. According to Thirumali (2013: 29), 'With a changing scenario, new generation of Andhra people has developed a taste for *brinjal* and lentils called *pappucharu*. They eulogized eating various pickles'. In every corner of Hyderabad, Andhras established their hotels popularly called 'Andhra Tiffins' and 'Andhra Meals'. Popular media presents Andhra culture and food as ideal. Gramsci (1971) offers us an image of society in which the cultural realm is a central location for the exercise of social power and hegemony. On the other hand, as an important part of culture, food can be a binding force. On a lighter note, Srinivasulu[45] states, 'Seeing the current food politics, I think "pickle" is the only thing which connects the entire Andhra Pradesh'.

Film and Media Industry: 'There Is No Telangana in Telugu Cinema'

Film is another cultural medium to promote or dispel social prejudices and biases. Generally, these are easily internalized by the masses and satisfy one's existing set of beliefs. The Telugu film industry, popularly known as Tollywood,[46] is one of the largest in India. According to Professor Jadhav (1997; Elavarthi and Vamierddy 2015), the arrival of local film making marked the dawn of yet another avenue to generate callous stereotypes: 'The regional discrimination which Telangana was facing since the 1950s on the basis of language now started appearing on the big screen. There was no representation of Telangana people in Tollywood. Heroes would speak only "Andhra dialect" as de facto standard and villains and comedians would be speaking in the Telangana accent.'

At this stage, the Telangana dialect ceased to be a question of *mere language*, and became an issue of identity and representation.[47] The ubiquitous presence of Andhras in films, print, and electronic media led to a kind of cultural domination (Janardhan and Raghavendra 2013: 555). Government media (that is, Doordarshan and All India Radio) were used as vehicles to ridicule the language and culture of the people of Telangana. Professor Jayashanker, an ideologue of *Telangana Rashta Samiti*, asserted that the demand for a separate state was to protect the self-respect of the people of Telangana. 'Although we respect the culture and dialect of other regions, our dialect and culture is being ridiculed, particularly in mass media. We can preserve it only through self-governance'.[48]

Professor Jadhav highlights another example with the 2013 movie *Mondi Mogudu Penki Pellam*, whose main characters are a police officer and his wife. Prakash and Vemmireddy (2015) comment that 'the film is suggestive of the strange relationship between the two regions, where one region is ashamed of being with the other and wants to reform it to meet its standards'. They further explain:

> Except her character, no major character speaks her dialect in the film. Her behaviour and language are ridiculed and used to generate comedy. Even though he loves her, her police officer husband is always ashamed of her language and makes sure that she does not speak in front of his colleagues and friends. When she speaks before a colleague in the first scene, he feels embarrassed and covers it up by saying, 'she is doing research in Telangana dialect'. Even a few months before the bifurcation, Andhra politicians and supporters of unified state were using the analogy of wife and husband to suggest that the dispute is internal and does not require outside intervention.

Activists debated the 'hegemonic structure of the film industry'.[49] The movement responded to Telugu cinema's mocking of Telangana by attacking the industry and its links to the political apparatus dominated by Seemandhra. Activists argue that the film industry was given prime land at heavily subsidized prices, besides production subsidies, soft loans, and tax incentives by successive governments to facilitate the shift of the industry from Chennai to Hyderabad. 'Telugu cinema stood as a sore example for the cultural supremacy thesis of Andhras,' state Prakash and Vemmireddy (2015: 8). The cultural politics happening at the national level repeated the same way at local level.[50]

Mamidi Harikrishna, in his article titled '*Noorella Therapai Telangana Atma*' (The Soul of Telangana: One Hundred Years of Screen) declares, 'There is no Telangana in Telugu cinema' (cited in Thatha 2015: 406). He argues that the special ways of life and conditions in Telangana have influenced and contributed to parallel and cross-over cinema in India.[51] As Telangana opened up as a new market, Telugu cinema now addressed Telugus as a single unified community, even claiming to speak for the Telugu nation, although Srinivas believes that this was only an 'unintended consequence' (Reddy 2014).

Hyderabad City as a Site of Cultural Expression

The city of Hyderabad also played a decisive role in cultural change and expression. Starting in 1999, the government of Andhra Pradesh, under the leadership of Chandrababu Naidu (the then chief minister) planned to rebuild Hyderabad and brand it as a global city (Kamat 2011: 188). The effect of the neo-liberal economic policies of the 1990s was already clearly felt and visible in the city due to the wealth and industry of Andhras. Sociologist Biao (2007: 32) broadly describes the character and growing trend of the resident populations in many upscale residential localities in Hyderabad: '[People in these localities] have lands in Andhra, have a house in Hyderabad and have a job in America'.

By 2008, the number of technology and software companies grew rapidly. It is interesting to note that as one part of the city was developed to be known as 'Hi-tech City', attracting 'the best' technical minds, students at the OU were in the process of leading a movement for the deprived masses in the region. They also use technology to connect with each other. All of this was possible because they were living in Hyderabad, the cosmopolitan state capital.

The government's plan of rebuilding Hyderabad was occurring more at an economic level. The Gachibowli area soon became Hi-tech City. Multinational companies (MNCs) and major software companies including Microsoft, Computer Associates, Infosys, and Wipro set up their branches there. Naidu wanted to compete with the nearby 'Silicon Valley', Bangalore. As Hyderabad attracted the global market, thousands of new jobs were created. Yet, the 'native people' of Telangana could not easily access the new opportunities. In the words of Suresh, an Osmania activist:

> When I shifted to Hyderabad from Jagityal, I was in urgent need of a job. Those days there were plenty of jobs. After 15 interviews, I realised that they will not take me because I am from Telangana. They recognise it through my accent. I started practising more of Andhra accent and words. But even then, I could not get any chance because then they reject me because my certificate shows my Telangana identity.

A similar story was also expressed by students who completed professional degrees yet struggled for employment. What it highlighted is a kind of 'ethnocentrism existing between these two regions in the name of language and culture'[52] (Thirumali 2013: 30). Explaining the transformations throughout the 1980s and 1990s, Maringanti (2010: 36) states:

> New cultural codes have been inscribed into Hyderabad through the naming of housing colonies, installation of statues and sculptures, renaming of places and institutions, construction of flyovers, development of new exclusive housing lots and most importantly through cinematic representations of particular locations in Hyderabad which reworked popular imaginations quite significantly. Many of these refigurements of Hyderabad visage pushed its cosmopolitan cultures inherited from the multi-lingual Nizam state aside and imposed a narrow parochial 'Telugu' culture on it.

By 2000, almost every hospital, mall, multiplex, MNC, software, and service industries in Hyderabad were owned by Andhras. The new post-industrial economy is, therefore, very different from the industrial economy: it is somehow all encompassing, according to Touraine, in that it controls not just the production of material goods, but the production of a symbolic world of meaning (in other words, culture) as well. One can see the erection of statues of Andhra dominance in the city of Hyderabad (Rao, Reddy, and Rao 2014). Though the city had a legacy of the Nizam and Telangana martyr, there was little to show for it. Amar expresses an activist's predicament: 'Isn't it ironic that many times we had to go to Andhra businessman to publish our pamphlet and poster for our anti-Andhra protest, because he has big printing establishment. This is a question to ask why we [natives] were not given equal representation in business by the government. Are we lazy or are they afraid of us?'

Such issues are discussed among Telangana activists. During their meetings, they sadly joke, 'After this meeting, we have to eat in an Andhra hotel', 'Where are Telangana people in Hyderabad?'. This kind of questions provokes Telangana activists to debate and spread awareness on the ownership of resources.

During agitations in 2011, a programme called the Million March was organized by Osmania University-Joint Action Committee (OU-JAC). This march is a prime example of cultural resistance. During the march, activists damaged an ATM of Andhra Bank as it was associated with Andhra. They dismantled many of the statues of famous Andhra personalities (freedom fighters, politicians, and artists) situated on the main road, Tank Bund, by Hussain Sagar Lake. Armed with nylon ropes, sickles, and other instruments, the activists demolished 12 of the 33 statues and threw 11 of them into the lake. Even the statue of Sri Sri, a revered Andhra poet of earlier generations of students, was not spared. While dismantling the statues, student leaders stated to the media: 'Today, we made it clear. This is our capital. Your statues are not welcome here anymore. You cannot impose them onto us. Sooner you realize the better it is for all of us. A movement becomes violent only as a reaction to oppressive methods used by the ruling regimes'.[53]

This echoes the sentiments of students who defined the destruction of statues as 'cultural renaissance of Telangana' or 'de-Andhraization of Telangana'. A group of Telangana Rashtra Samithi Vidyarthi Vibhagam (TRSV) activists said, 'We are in the middle of a revolution—maybe we can call it Pink Revolution because we see pink flags everywhere'.[54] A popular slogan of students' march was: *Telangana Jago, Andhra Bhago* (Telangana wake up, Andhra go!). It raised a kind of consciousness which could be understood as symbolic of the identity politics between the two groups. Social movements are specific to culture, history, and social structure (Singh 2001: 40). This, according to

Melucci (1980), defines NSMs and the cultural reproduction of social relations, symbols, and identities. Cultural symbols are reproduced to reclaim the past through which collective cultural identity is recalled. The organizational form has a self-referential quality (Buechler 2011: 170). 'A feeling of the time has come when people should belong first to Telangana and then to their parents' (Reddy 2009: 165). Regional unrest is broadly articulated on the lines of nationalities and cultural and economic spaces (Bheenaveni 2013). As mentioned earlier, Telangana student movement was largely led by Dalit students and the cultural revivalism was also going along the movement, for example, boycotting Hindu upper-caste culture, challenging caste structure, celebrating Ambedkar, Jyotiba Phule, Savitribai Phule, Shahuji Maharaj, Periyar, Komaram Bheem, and Chakali Ilamma. Thus, the political representation and issues of regional imbalances were further elaborated and accentuated by the caste alliance and it made upper castes to form their own organization. Kamma, Velama, Vaishya, Brahmin, and many other caste-based organizations appeared in Hyderabad, projecting and eulogizing their caste culture and contribution. The goal of these organizations was to represent their caste and be part of bargaining process in movement. Landowning castes like Kapus were devising ways to get other backward class (OBC) status and reservation.[55] They represented their demand through mainstream political parties such as Telangana Rashtra Samithi (TRS) and Congress. As opposition, political parties have regional pockets of influence almost compel them to swing on the tide of regionalism. Narain (1976: 911) calls regionalism in India 'psychic phenomenon' and 'emotional overtone gets easily attached to regionalism which, in turn, can be traced to its cultural moorings and economic roots'. He concludes that regionalism in India is a complex amalgam of geo-cultural, politico-economic, and psychic factors. It is difficult to decipher which component has ascendency (1976: 913). Interestingly, Telangana movement adds a mix tone of caste culture to the regionalism. Venugopal (2009: 38) also emphasizes that 'regional inequality, as a concept, cannot be understood without understanding 'cultural roots and dimensions'. Statistics would merely present the growth in terms of profit and loss. He summarizes his arguments:

> Neglect of sub-regional aspirations, cultural oppression, internal colonialism, exploiting a region as hinterland for resources—raw

> material and cheap labour, exclusion of locals from centres of power and decision making structures, promoting a section of the locals with comprador nature as minor partner and co-opting and using them as show-pieces, exercising brutal forces against local elements that effectively articulate the concerns of the region—all these are evident symbols of the discriminatory state policy against Telangana. (Venugopal 2009: 46)

Thus, tension between migrants and 'sons of the soil' manifested itself not merely economically but also deeply in a cultural way. The conflict between Assamese and Bengalis in Assam and the Shiv Sena's slogan of 'Maharashtra for Maharashtrian' illustrate a similar cultural notion. Without unpacking this notion, it is not easy to understand the underlying current of any regional movements.

DISCUSSION

At every social front, Telangana cultural manifested itself by rejecting and boycotting 'Andhra' culture. From 'idli sambhar go back' to boycotting Andhra Tiffins and Andhra movies, the Telangana movement gained a cultural consciousness which is reflected in the literature produced by its activists. This chapter highlighted the emergence of the Telangana movement, outlining a brief history and the political consequences in both regions of Telangana and Andhra. A vast migration from Andhra to Hyderabad for government jobs diminished the scope for employment among Telangana youth. Using their influence, Andhras acquired 'mulki' status to own land and resources. Gradually, this spawned a cultural hegemony of Andhra culture over local Hyderabadi and Telangana culture. Cultural humiliation of Telangana government employees was rampant. Excessive unemployment and cultural humiliation collectively created resentment among youth led to a year-long agitation in 1969 and culminated in the formation of a political party that produced many revolutionary leaders. By the end of 2000, activism spilled across India and the rest of the world through the Telangana diaspora. During this phase, cultural symbols, ethos and identities, food, festivals, and films were instrumental in creating a contentious politics and asserting Telangana identity and its history. In 2009, students reignited the movement with the help of other activists to reach out to the masses. In this phase, the assertion of Telangana cultural symbol were asserted and propagated in an effort to boycott Andhra culture. In other words, the Telangana movement gained momentum not only by cultural assertion but also by creating a counter-culture of the *other*. This signified a cultural confrontation between Telangana and Andhra that reflected in group formation, mobilization strategies, slogans, and the manner of protests for Telangana statehood.

There was a time in early twenty-first century when Chandrababu Naidu did not want to hear the word 'Telangana' in the legislative assembly. But by the end of 2010, Telangana became the buzzword in Andhra politics. For KCR, food became a powerful tool to play cultural politics. How language plays a vital role in construction, diffusion of contentious politics, argues a movement scholars Professor Sidney Tarrow, 'The deployment and diffusion of contentious language respond to both cultural and strategic incentives through the constitution of actors who draw upon a battery of language to describe their identities, their claims, their opponents, and their forms of action' (Tarrow 2013: 20).

Compared to the 1969 agitations, the 2009 period was much more enriching in terms of ideological and movement strategy. In 2009, countless debates and ideologies were at work. Three major ideologies worked in the movement after 2010, namely (*a*) Geographical Telangana, (*b*) Democratic Telangana, (*c*) Dalit-Bahujan Telangana/ Socially Inclusive Telangana. These three concepts were backed by various political parties. The demand of Geographic Telangana was raised by TRSV, All India Student Federation (AISF), National Student Union of India (NSUI), Telugu Nadu Student Forum (TNSF), and Akhil Bhartiya Vidyarthi Parishad (ABVP). Its aim was to promote and ensure Telangana statehood through democratic, non-violent methods. Their primary focus was to achieve a state first and then deal with social issues later. On the other hand, Chaithanya Mahila Sangam (CMS), Progressive Democratic Student Union (PDSU), Telangana Student Organisation (TSO), Telangana Madiga Vidyarthi Sangam (TMVS), Telangana Student Association (TSA), and Telangana Vidyarthi Sangam (TVS) supported the notion of 'Democratic Telangana'. Organizations not affiliated to any political parties but to caste groups and others working with Ambedkar's and Phule's ideology were the Dalit-Bahujan Telangana/Social Inclusive Telangana. Groups adhering to this concept were Bahujan Student Forum (BSF), Madiga Student

Federation (MSF), schedule caste (SC), scheudule tribe (ST) students' union, Backward Castes Students Union, Telangana Madiga Student Federation (TMSF), Girijana Vidyarthi Sangam (GVS). The idea behind Dalit-Bahujan Telangana was to ensure social justice within the constitutional framework. However, these ideologies culminated from the existing ideologies of Communists, Maoists, and Dalit activists.

In 2007, Dalit students, under the banner of BSF, organized various programmes with political parties and called upon Dalit and OBC leaders such as Mayawati and Sharad Yadav to promote the Dalit and OBC agenda in the movement. Their massive rally for Telangana State Bahujan Students (*Prachar Yatra*) carried the slogan: '*Mayawathi Pradhan Mantrini Cheddam; Telangana Rashtranni Saiddhum*' (If Mayawati becomes the prime minister, we will get our Telangana state).[56] They organized talks and seminars in commemoration of Ambedkar, Jyotiba Phule, Savitribai Phule, Periyar, Narayna Guru, Chhatrapati Shahuji Maharaj, Komaram Bheem, and Kanshi Ram. Later when MSF was founded, they included pictures of Babu Jagjivan Ram, Chakali Ilamma, and other local leaders in their pamphlets.

In her discussion on identity movements, Bernstein (2008: 287) uses the term 'deconstructive movements' and explains that such movements may target the state, institutions, and more general cultural practices. What Bernstein means by *deconstructive* is basically that movements change the meaning of existing identities and add new meaning to them. Therefore, exposing the social basis for these categories by deconstructing them undermines the cultural and political bases for oppression (Bernstein 2008: 288). Struggles for recognition are, and have been, a struggle for political voice (Hobson 2003: 265). This struggle, whether for social or cultural recognition, would manifest in some or the other form of politics. However, Bernstein (2008: 289) raises critical questions around recognition which need to be addressed: how are deconstructive movements linked to movements of recognition? Can deconstructive movements emerge in the absence of movements for recognition? If so, under what conditions do such movements emerge (Bernstein 2008: 288)? How do movements negotiate identity for empowerment when the identity around which the movement is organized is also the basis for grievances (2008: 289)?

There has been a tendency to tag any movement for *recognition* as an 'identity movement'. Sociologists *demystify* culture (Reed and

Alexander 2007: 21). By *demystification*, Reed and Alexander (2007: 21) mean they explain the form, meaning, and existence of culture quite directly by the social structure or power, terms that refer to 'demystifying projects to social force that exists apart from symbolic mediation, the hard stuff of social life'. They conclude that 'cultural conflicts are therefore identity conflicts' (2007: 229). For Bernstein (2008: 289), 'movements that seek to challenge the stigma associated with a given identity may change the practices of institutions or the knowledge that is produced by these institutions'. What we can derive from this discussion is that the source of oppression lies and reflects in the cultural practices of the group that was subjugated, discriminated, and humiliated. Therefore, defining economic basis (as most scholars have emphasized) takes us back to the Marxist theory of class that undermines the centuries of caste oppression.

NOTES

1. Scholars have different views on defining the category of student. According to Pinner (1972: 83), 'Students share certain characteristics with intellectuals or others in academic settings but their position sets them apart'. Other scholars (Aspinall 2005; Emmerson 1968; Lee 2005) have also debated student identity as workers, military leaders, and so on. In Marism, students do not constitute a class (Weinberg and Walker 1969: 82).
2. Although there is no consensus on the question of class in NSMs, this debate offers some important insights.
3. He characterizes the trajectory of cultural resistance as moving along three spectra (political consciousness, social unit, and results) that begin at the level of unconsciousness, the individual, and survival, and end at consciousness, the entire society, and complete revolution, respectively. In such a framing, theories of cultural resistance may also subscribe to teleological conjectures of change, according to Duncombe (2002: 7–8).
4. It describes a state of being as well as a category of social knowledge and classification. In an ideal universe, political identities merge emotional attachment and institutional categories. 'I am Indian' and 'we are Indians' would be both ontological and epistemological statements.
5. Much of the recent theorizing on culture and movements was actually formulated by critics (Fantasia 1988; Goodwin and Jasper 1999; Jasper, 1997; Johnston and Klandermans 1995; Morris and Mueller 1991; Snow et al. 1986) or in response to challenges raised by critics.

6. It is within the context of social movements, however, that the indeterminacy of culturally embedded identities is heightened and new possibilities are explored. It is not so much that political movements have come to identify a layer of more 'cultural' injustice flourishing alongside the economic injustice that were the staple of an earlier socialist politics.

7. In Habermas' scheme, there are three structural components: culture of the particular tradition of a community, the network or solidarities or society and, finally, process of socialization or personality development that formulates identities.

8. Castells proposes three forms and origins of identity building:

Legitimizing identity: A set of logic and meaning introduced and propagated by the ruling powers, in order to rationalize, reproduce, and expand existing rule.

Resistance identity: Constructed in response to devaluation and stigmatization; where social actors build 'trenches of resistance' in opposition to the ruling norm. This formation leads to communes or communities of resistance.

Project identity: The construction of a 'new identity that redefines their position in society and, by doing so, seek the transformation of overall social structure' (Castells 1997/2001: 8).

9. Adding to this debate while defining the nature of the movement, the perception of the people of the region that they are treated as an 'internal colony'.

10. During everyday interactions, conversations contain a sense of regional pride which is also sectioned by the local or regional proverb. Meier-Dallach (cited in Raagmaa 2002: 61) believes that regional identity may also lie in deliberate emphasis on local cultural or regional peculiarity or even express itself in political and cultural actions. Scholars (Passi 2003: 477; Peterson and Anand 2004) have recognized regional culture and identity as *key elements* in the making of regions as social and political spaces.

11. The Nizam invited scholars from Europe and the Middle East to translate science subjects into Urdu.

12. The famous *Golconda Patrika* had to be so named because the government prohibited the use of the word 'Andhra'.

13. The findings of the report were not disclosed until 2013 when they were made available at the Nehru Memorial Museum and Library in New Delhi. See Thomson (2013).

According to Noorani (2001), 'The lowest estimates, even those offered privately by apologists of the military government, came to at least ten times the number of murders with which previously the Razakars were officially accused ...'.

14. Major general J.N. Chaudhuri took over as military governor of Hyderabad and stayed in that position till the end of 1949. In January 1950,

M.K. Vellodi, a senior civil servant, was made the chief minister of the state and the Nizam was designated *'Raj Pramukh'*.

15. Mr M.K. Vellodi, a civil servant, was appointed as the chief minister of the Telangana state from September 1948 to 1952. His period is known as Vellodi rule. He was appointed by the central government in Telangana state before forming democratic government by people through elections.

16. The history of the anti-mulki protest can be traced back to 1910 when Maharaja Sir Kishan Prasad took up the struggle of Mulkis. Mulkis fought against the Non Mulkis' domination and suppression. In 1919, The seventh Nizam, Mir Osman Ali Khan, passed an order (*Firman*) that Mulkis were exclusively eligible for government employment.

17. In addition to job opportunities in Hyderabad, the arrival of the Green Revolution accentuated the migration process. Though the Green Revolution created surplus in coastal Andhra, the region 'could not ploughed back into agriculture as capital absorption by agriculture, unlike industry, is inelastic'. As Haragopal (2010a: 53) argues, 'The coastal capital in search of greener pastures started moving to those areas of Telangana region wherever there were sources of irrigation, particularly tanks or river water'.

18. From an interview with Professor Harinath on 31 May 2013.

19. The slogan was given by Ramchari who had earlier worked in the Nizam's administration. He also formed the *Hyderabad Hitha Rakshana Samithi* in August 1952.

20. Available at https://www.telegraphindia.com/1130804/jsp/7days/17193418.jsp.

21. *Indian Express*, 2 October 1953.

22. In agreement with national leaders G.B. Pant and Jawaharlal Nerhu, Andhra leaders like B. Gopala Reddy (CM), N. Sanjeeva Reddy, Gothy Lachanna, A. Satyanarayana Raju, and leaders from Telangana like B. Ramakrishna Rao (CM), Dr M. Chenna Reddy, J.V. Narasinga Rao, K.V. Ranga Reddy, and J.V. Narasinga Rao were signatories.

23. Chief Minister N. Sanjeeva Reddy denied the post of deputy chief minister to Telangana person as was agreed in the Gentlemen's Agreement. This movement lay on the foundations of the failure of implementation of Gentlemen's Agreement and lack of employment opportunities to the people of Telangana.

24. Interviewed on 19 September 2013.

25. Also see Adiraju (1969).

26. He was interviewed on 23 June 2013 at the Congress Bhawan, Hyderabad.

27. However, when we speak of diversity in the region, one can find around 30 different dialects of Telugu in the state of Andhra Pradesh and almost half of them are present in the Telangana region.

28. The Fazal Ali Commission recognized the consequences of uniting a developed area with a backward area and recommended that Telangana be kept as a separate state.
29. Universities in many developing nations are in capital cities and thus close to the seat of power. In this geographical environment, it is relatively easy to organize a demonstration which can be seen—and perhaps felt—at the seat of government (Altbach 1984).
30. Interview with Professor P.L.Vishveshwar Rao, September 2013.
31. Lalitha was a popular singer and leader in the movement before her murder in 1999.
32. Prajashakti Publications. 2002. *Neekochina Bashalo Rayi Neevimuktikosam Rayi*, Interview to Prasatanam, p. 127. Hyderabad: Prajashakti Publications.
33. Available at http://www.thehindu.com/todays-paper/tp-features/tp-educationplus/maa-telugu-talli-to-be-or-not-to-be/article665963.ece.
34. From the interviews of Sudarshan, a PhD scholar and senior Telangana activist.
35. From the interview of Dr Chiranjeevi on 19 June 2013.
36. Referring to the Kakatya Dynasty (between eleventh and fourteenth centuries), Pandu Ranga Rao from Kakatiya Heritage Trust claims that Bathukamma and Sammakka festivals find roots here. Available on http://www.deccanchronicle.com/140601/lifestyle-offbeat/article/telangana-brush-history, accessed 11 October 2017.
37. Osmania University Notification letter Lr. No. 05/Sem/Hist/2013 dated 22 April 2013. The seminar held on 28–9 June 2013.
38. A press handout was released during a press conference at Zen College at *Lakdi-ka-Pul* in Hyderbabad on 1 July 2013.
39. However, when we talk about diversity in the region, one can find around 30 different dialects of Telugu in the state of Andhra Pradesh and almost half of them exist in the Telangana region itself.
40. Interviewed on 8 January 2013 at his residence.
41. Sorrel-leaves.
42. Available at http://timesofindia.indiatimes.com/city/hyderabad/KCRs-remarks-trigger-biryaniwar/articleshow/7411639.cms, accessed 15 June 2014.
43. Interview at his residence.
44. Tuomainen (2009: 548), in his study of Ghanaians settlers in England, concludes that 'the importance of the maintenance of ethnic food ways as a marker of ethnic identity among migrants, often portrayed by the prompt establishment of food-related businesses, such as among the Chinese in the UK. The case study of Ghanaians, nevertheless, shows that the initial reaction after migration differs among migrant groups'.
45. Interviewed on 19 June 2013 at his residence.

46. During N.T. Rama Rao's period, Tollywood was shifted from Madras to Hyderabad in 1994.
47. Available at http://www.anveshi.org.in/telangana-and-language-politics-of-telugu-cinema/.
48. For detailed interview, see Rajiv 2009.
49. In a seminar held on 10 September 2014.
50. To the grossly under-explored field of Telugu cinema, S.V. Srinivas's *Politics as Performance: A Social History of the Telugu Cinema* is a significant contribution. As one of the first works on the topic, it is likely to gain historical value and become a reference book.
51. He lists Angrez (2005), Ankur (1974), Baazaar (1982), Hyderabad Blues (1998), Hyderabad Nawabs (2006), Mandi (1983), Nishant (1975), Susman (1987), and how despite being made in non-Telugu languages, they reflect the region, its uniqueness and flavour.
52. However, when we talk about diversity in the region than one can find around 30 different dialects of Telugu in the state of Andhra Pradesh and almost half of them exist in the Telangana region itself.
53. Available at http://missiontelangana.com/toppling-our-masters-and-statues/.
54. From a meeting among activists and Telangana intellectuals over the movement's goal at Arts College on 25 October 2013.
55. Since 2009, Kapus had high hopes in politics under the leadership of Chiranjeevi, the popular Telugu Star. Chiranjeevi had no clear political stand on the separate Telangana demand.
56. BSF pamphlets on 14 November 2007, 14 April 2008, 17 September 2009, and many other pamphlets of each year where date is not mentioned.

2 Osmania University

Academics, Culture, and Politics

For the past five decades, Osmania University (OU) has regularly made headlines due to the robust participation of its students in the movement for Telangana statehood. The university has produced several activists who later became part of mainstream politics and university faculty. Due to its constant student activism, OU has popularly been referred to as 'Telangana University'. The widespread notion that the 'movement is the business of Osmania' is explained here, highlighting Osmania's role throughout the various phases of the movement. The Srikrishna Commission Report (SCR) on the question of bifurcation notes that OU and Kakatiya University became 'trouble spots' and 'trouble creators' during agitations (Srikrishna Commission 2010: 51–2). OU has been the nerve centre for every agitation, strike, meeting, or debate for a separate Telangana. Lipset (1968) argues that 'intellectuals and students have a major potential mass base for new revolutionary movements, and they remained a source of radical leadership and mass support while other elements of society have not'. Here, the word 'intellectual' has a wide connotation and this chapter explains how, due to the movement for separate Telangana, intellectuals established organic linkages with the poor working classes through their art, music, writings, and speeches. This chapter illustrates how a culture of resistance was created by intellectuals (students, alumni, and teachers) and how their activism made the campus the epicentre of a mass movement. Focussing primarily on out-of-the-classroom ethnographic material, this chapter discusses the influence of campus education and (un)learning: how university spaces and interpersonal relations make individuals more cognizant of their regional identity, and how this identity assertion translated into a mass movement.

OU CAMPUS: A SITE OF DISSENT

OU is an open, residential campus in Hyderabad, adjacent to the twin city of Secunderabad. The campus shares a border with the English Foreign Language University (EFLU). The main road that connects EFLU to nearby Vidya Nagar is around 3 kilometres long and passes through OU, in which there are five bus stops. Most of the university departments and hostels are situated along this road (see the route on Map 2.1 below). OU is a multidisciplinary university, heavily devoted to the social sciences. As the oldest and largest university in the region, its alumni have served in nearly every sector, from journalism to politics, law, engineering, education, and medicine. The history of the movement shows a large participation of social science students studying at Arts College who had actively and vibrantly responded to the state's social and political issues. Most of the political leaders in Telangana were 'produced' by this campus. The Narmada Research Scholars (NRS) Hostel, also known as Dr B.R. Ambedkar Hostel, has been the 'hallowed abode' of student leaders (Pathania 2015). The college became the 'sacred' place for activists, where students pay homage to the sacrifices made by their predecessors. It is a common saying among students that 'once you are part of Arts College, you will be a Telangana activist for life'. From the 1950s, students have contributed to the movement as alumni or as faculty, by guiding and motivating successive generations. How and why the university served as a site of regional Telangana identity assertion is central to this chapter.

OU was established in 1918 by the seventh Nizam of Hyderabad state, Nawab Osman Ali Khan, and the university was named after him. It is the seventh oldest university in the country and third oldest university in South India. The Nawab believed that higher education must have its foundations deep in national consciousness and national integration, which he found a tangible reality. While establishing the university, his administration felt Urdu to be the appropriate medium

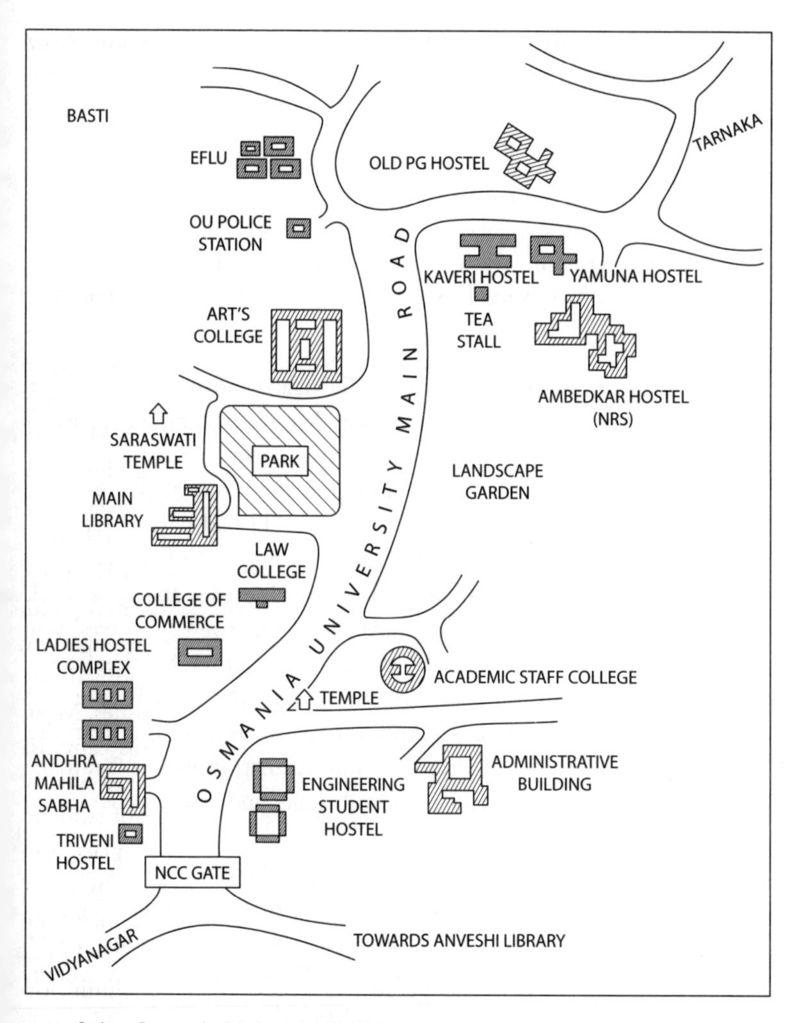

MAP 2.1 Osmania University Route Map
Source: Map by Monika Batham.
Note: This map is not to scale and does not represent authentic national and international boundaries. It is provided for illustrative purposes only.

of instruction 'as it was the official language of the state'. Yet, this contrasted with the supremacy of the English language that ruled India. Nevertheless, it became the first Indian university to use an Indian language, Urdu, as the medium of instruction (Geiger 2009: 154–5; Elliot 1972: 274). In his letter to the Nizam, Nobel laureate

Rabindranath Tagore praises Osmania's initiative and dedication to impart education in the vernacular:

> I have been long waiting for the day when, freed from the shackles of a foreign language, our education becomes naturally accessible to all our people. It is a problem for the solution of which we look to our native States, and it gives me great joy to know that your State proposes to found a University in which instructions are to be given through the medium of Urdu. It is needless to say that your scheme has my fullest appreciation.[1]

One of the founding fathers of the Telangana movement, Professor Keshav Rao Jadhav (popularly known as 'Mr Telangana), whose fore-fathers from Maharashtra migrated to Hyderabad in late nineteenth century, states, 'The Nizam had hired English and Urdu translators from Europe and the Middle-Eastern universities. He had natural sciences translated into Urdu. I studied physics, chemistry, and mathematics in Urdu script'.[2] The Nizam hired teaching faculty from abroad as well. The academic excellence of the university, Professor P.L. Visweshwar Rao claims, 'can be appreciated by the fact that until 1980, there were 25 professors from abroad teaching at Osmania'. Professor Rao smiles while recalling, 'My own guide, Professor Krishnamurthi was from the University of Pennsylvania. Professor Shiv Kumar, Professor Gautham Mathur were from University of Cambridge, and many other great scholars in their areas used to teach us'.[3]

From its inception, the university campus had been a fertile site for liberal ideologies. For example, in 1940, the Communist Party of India (CPI) played an important role in making the Telangana armed struggle—a peasant uprising against the Nizam—a mass movement. Many Marxist thinkers such as George Reddy and Javed Alam have had an association with Osmania. According to senior activists, the spread of Arya Samaj was received well in Hyderabad and a section of Hindu students at Osmania became active members. Students were also influenced by the magnetic personality of Swami Ramanand Teerth, the founder of Hyderabad State Congress. His thought-provoking lectures on the Mackenzie Report and on the evolution of democracy on the day of *Janmashtami* (birthday of Lord Krishna) were delivered at OU in 1936.

During the Indian independence movement, *Vande Mataram*[4] was a popular song praising 'Mother India'. The song was banned by the

Nizam on 28 November 1938. The same day, some Hindu students at OU went to the prayer hall and sang the song. When students were exiting the prayer hall of B hostel, the warden and other officials of the university collected signatures of the students who had violated the university order (Hugar 2015: 31). On 29 November, the students were literally kept under house arrest—they were asked not to leave the hostels and not to attend the college until further notice. Ultimately, students were asked to leave the hostels. In retaliation, they formed an action committee of the Vande Mataram strikers with K. Achyut Reddy as president, P.G. Puranik, Narsing Prasad Jaiswal, D.M. Deshmukh, and a few other members to take necessary action depending on the situation. The committee decided to continue the movements until their demands were met.[5] Emphasizing the autonomy of the university, Elliot (1972: 274) states that the 'Osmania case demonstrates how the university's development as a separate institution with its own vital interests and values helps to generate a propensity to resist incursions from outside'.

The phrase Vande Mataram was used as initial or common greetings by the patriots while calling the names of freedom fighters. During the accession movement, the people started to greet each other on their first sight with the words 'Vande Mataram' instead of saying 'Good Morning' or 'Namaskar'. This was part of a movement called the Vande Mataram movement, which has a unique place in the history of students' movement in India—it cracked the citadel of the Nizam Kingdom. It has profound impact on the minds of a whole generation of young men of the days. During the Vande Mataram Movement (1933–9), a leader called Ramachander Rao (popularly known as Vande Mataram Ramchander Rao) was arrested and jailed for uttering Vande Mataram.[6] To support him, students of OU and its colleges at Warangal and Aurangabad also participated in the national independence movement and sung the same song. In 1938, a large section of Hindus, sang Vande Mataram instead of the prayer song[7] that praised the Nizam in their morning prayers. Consequently, 350 students were given official notice not to sing Vande Mataram. Explaining the event, Jadhav[8] recalls:

> Order prohibiting the recital of Vande Mataram in the university hostels, having been violated by certain students, their names had been removed

from the hostels and they have been suspended from attending the colleges. Scholarships and free-ships granted to them have been cancelled. They were asked to settle their accounts with the hostel wardens and to be ready for eviction.

This led to an intense debate between the university administration and students. One student, Venkata Rao Vakil, wrote an appeal to Mr Akbar Hyder, vice-chancellor (VC) of OU, stating, 'It was very difficult to find a prayer for various sects of the Hindu students which could be acceptable to Shaivaites, Vaishnavaites, Lingayats, Shaktaites, and so on. Hindu religion had numberless sects and sub-sects and hence the choice of *Vandemataram*' (Adiraju 2009: 14). The VC replied to the letter stating that he agreed that Vande Mataram was a secular choice; however, it did not change his official stance. This reply invoked a discussion among faculty and students and points to a liberal campus culture of debate at the university. Bourdieu (1983), DiMaggio (1991), and Daenekindt and Roose (2015) explain the gradual process of such hegemony of the state by stating that celebrations such as classical music, prayer, literature, and dance, which a child learns through his school curricula and are sponsored, celebrated, and diffused by the state, thus granting them a high degree of legitimacy[9] and consecration.

The campus also contributed to making leaders such as P.V. Narasimha Rao, who played an active role in state as chief minister and in national politics, and who later went on to become the prime minister of India. Keshav Rao Jadhav claims that 'student activism has always played a prominent part of the Telangana movement since 1957, as they [students] were most affected by the discrimination'. Hyderabad state was merged with the Andhra region forming the state of Andhra Pradesh in 1956, shifting the nature of the movement and focussing it on inter-regional issues.

Osmania has been a hotbed for every kind of activism from all spectrums of ideologies to non-violent and radical resistance. Classroom teaching played an insignificant role, if at all, in the formation of this cultural resistance. Rather, it was primarily the non-academic environment that contributed to a campus culture of activism for a separate Telangana. As Suvaram Sudhakar Reddy, who is currently the general secretary of the Communist Party of India, recalls his student days at Osmania in 1965, the time when Naxalite movement was starting out due to split in Communist movements:

> Being an Osmanian, I learnt ten times more than what I learnt in the classroom. My outlook had become much wider, broader and I certainly gained from my stay on the campus. Comrade Aziz Pasha and Sadanand were student leaders of other colleges then but later joined the OU campus. 'We used to organise study circles at YMCA all at Narayanaguda and Young Men's Club at Sultan Bazar. Comrade Rohit Sen was a popular speaker in our meetings. (Reddy 2017)

An inspiring student leader in the 1969 struggle, Dr Sridhar Reddy contributed to the literature on the movement by publishing several books. During the agitation, he left his studies and dedicated himself to the movement, taking an oath that he would not cut his beard until Telangana became a state. Later he completed his doctoral thesis on student politics in Osmania and published various books on Telangana. He left his studies and dedicated himself to the movement, taking an oath that he would not cut his beard until Telangana became a state. Later he completed his doctoral thesis on student politics in Osmania and published various books on Telangana.[10] OU alumni, Dr Kasim, who had been part of the Maoist movement, started the magazine *Poru Telangana* in 2010 to contribute to the movement as a writer-activist, and later became a faculty member at Osmania. He guided the movement through his ideological writings. Another activist-writer, Mr B.S. Ramulu, took an oath publicly to publish a book every month until Telangana state formed. In all, he published 150 story books and six novels. He explains, 'They (Andhra) made fun of Telangana Telugu, I decided to popularise our Telugu and I keep writing and see now I have a wide readership of common masses'.[11] Intellectual work, according to Shils (1959: 403), whether it is scholarly, scientific, literary, or artistic, must be concerned with problems which arise from the situation it confronts, and it must be carried on within an intellectual tradition; the standards of aspiration and judgement that guide it must likewise be conjoined to the situation and the tradition. Intellectuals must recognize the significance of political processes in developing their understanding and critique of the existing social-political order (Kothari 2012).[12]

Several forums were organized for critical debate on Telangana issues. During agitations from 2009 to 2013, the writings of Kancha Ilaiah (then professor of Arts College) revitalized the movement. Later, when the Telangana movement gained momentum, Ilaiah initiated a discourse on the topic of Dalit-Bahujan Telangana. Unlike others from the region, he did not subscribe to the notion that a separate Telangana would bring about any change. Instead he focussed on the education of Dalits and Other Backward Classes. He emphasized the importance for lower castes to learn English, claiming it as the only source of their emancipation in a neo-liberal era. He started celebrating his birthday as 'Dalit Bahujan English Education Day'. His slogan 'Read, Write and Fight' inspired scores of Osmania students. Speaking on his birthday in 2013, he stated, 'I am not saying that things will drastically change if you learn English. Today English is the language of rulers, if you want to rule, you have to learn' (translated from Telugu).[13] Ilaiah is an ideal for many Telangana students at OU. Thus, OU and its intellectuals, through their critical understanding of socio-political issues of Telangana, gained a grand reputation among the masses, media, and activists.

THE ROLE OF OSMANIA INTELLECTUALS IN TELANGANA MOVEMENT: 1969 PHASE

> *'What is the role of intellectuals when the state or the nation is faced with a crisis?'*
>
> Satyanarayan (1969)

This question was part of the opening speech delivered by OU VC, Dr Ravada Satayanarayan at the convention for 'Telangana University and College Teachers' held on 20 May 1969. Osmania teachers, under the guidance of the VC, organized the convention to debate issues facing Telangana. His remarks became the foreword of a research volume, 'The Telangana Movement: An Investigative Focus':

> ... after certain amount of introspection, I came to the conclusion that, as the various problems involved in the Separate Telangana agitation are not clear to many person—even to those very deeply involved on either side of the movement—it would be appreciated as a useful service by all concerned if the teachers of the colleges take up on themselves the work of clarifying the issue. (Thota 1969)

Osmania intellectuals spent a considerable time studying and understanding the regional problems so as to make a strong and valid political position. Dr Satyanarayana argued that intellectuals should play a dynamic role and cautioned them against the consequences of inaction. He called for members to express their views clearly and plainly. In an obvious reference to safeguards for Telangana, the VC observed, 'I detest the word safeguard; it is a humiliation—either live together on mutual trust or better separate' (cited in Thota 1969). He encouraged other Telangana activists and argued, 'if the organizations do not discharge this much obligation, it is a sin' (1969). The convention concluded that the 'socio-cultural exclusiveness' of Andhra is at the 'root of the exploitation of Telangana automatically, administratively and politically' (1969). They described the Telangana movement as a 'revolt of the youth against all exploitation', specifically focussed on ending regional exploitation (1969).

A similar situation occurred during the 1990s. Before forming the Telangana Rashtra Samithi (TRS), intellectuals examined the Telangana problem, new data was collected, and various seminars were held in OU between 1992 and 1997 that conceptualized the issue from various angles. The proceedings were published by the Centre for Telangana Studies in 1997 in an edited book, *Telangana: Dimensions of Underdevelopment*, which became a catalyst thenceforth.

With a sad look on his face, Chiranjeevi utters, 'Andhras will not understand our pain. Now, in the presence of media, every week OU students are committing suicide, but Andhras are calling it a political move or political suicide. And some of our Telangana leaders are also speaking their language'. Going back to the history of 'dignified politicians', Chiranjeevi recalls how on 15 May 1969, the ex-deputy chief minister of Andhra Pradesh, Konda Venkata Ranga Reddy, and the VC, Satyanarayana, resigned from their posts when they learned that government had killed thousands of innocent students. Konda Luxman Bapuji was the first state minister to resign from office. University intellectuals, in such crises, did not surrender, but rather used their autonomy: the VC passed a resolution for students to boycott classes until the demand for a separate state was conceded. The university relayed a strong message to the government that staff, students, and teachers were united in their concern and expressed their solidarity with the movement against the 'hegemonic' power of the Andhra state. Dr Rao explained the student–teacher unity: 'We were fully aware of the fact that students have a genuine cause. It was not them but the entire Telangana was suffering due to the exploitation by the Andhra region. Even Arts College faculty was dominated by the Andhra region.'

Expressing a similar opinion, Professor Rakesh, who led the Teachers' Association, explained how teachers watched after and enabled the movement through students:

> Many times, we had no money for students' bail but then our union of Telangana teachers was so cooperative and within no time, we used to collect money. When Andhra teachers' saw us, they started lobbying and supporting the United Andhra demand. It was their media, their government, so their small strikes used to appear on the front page of the newspaper.[14]

Teachers not only supported the students but also advised them how to counter the Andhra student lobby on campus. 'It was because of our teachers' guidance we could understand the political agenda and strategies of Andhra students',[15] claims Krishna, a 1969 activist. Two of the popular founding fathers of the movement—Professor Jaishankar and Professor Keshav Rao Jadhav[16]—had been the guiding force behind the student movement. Similarly, Sri Sri's poetry influenced the youth and students in 1969. Students formed poetry and theatre clubs and various other platforms for mobilizing students. Each event and group added strength to the fibres of Telangana activism.

Students served as frontrunners, while professors and alumni served as the movement's guiding force. University employees were mobilized as well. The OU community decided to commemorate 1 May 1969 as 'Telangana Demand Day'. Thousands of students and employees gathered in Hyderabad holding a banner that read, 'Telangana Demand Day'. As the communist movement remained popular since the 1940s, the intelligentsia's perspective of the movement was influenced thus. They related to the history of Telangana as part of the peasant revolt against the landlords. Therefore, they chose 1 May, International Labour Day, to commemorate the day they made their historic appeal.

Some radical Left ideologues such as Gaddar, Andhesri, Goranta, Narayan Rao, Sri Sri, Varavara Rao, and many others formed *Virasam* (*Vipalava Rachayitala Sangham* [Revolutionary Writers Association])[17] in 1970, and *Jana Natya Mandali* (JNM) as a cultural group was founded in 1972. The Progressive Writers Association (*Arasam Abhyudaya Rachayi-tala Sangham*) gave a new direction to literature and people's arts. All these forums provided platform for Dalits and other lower-caste writers, artists, and poets of society. JNM and *Virasam*, along with the Revolutionary Democratic Front (RDF) and *Srujana*, made a profound impression on educational institutions that became centre for spreading the revolutionary culture and ideology inspired by the Naxalbari movement. Gaddar[18] explains: 'The idea was to tell the common masses that all human beings are capable of writing and through his writings he can write bring social change. With a collective effort, Virasam motivated young writers from different class and caste backgrounds.'

Gaddar's singing performances attracted rural youth and the labour class. Students from OU also started writing for Virasam-run journal, *Aruntara*. In October 1974, Andhra Pradesh Radical Student Union (APRSU) formed on the basis of radical ideology of Marx, Lenin, and Mao. This organization, among many others, was formed by communist ideologues who led the anti-feudal struggles.

The programme of the *Gramalaku Taralandi* or 'Go to Villages' campaign, undertaken by the Radical Student Union (RSU), Radical Youth League (RYL), and the cultural front JNMs spread the message of agrarian revolution attracted these youths.

These organizations were consolidated through the establishment of the *Rytu Coolie Sanghams* (RCS, the organization for peasants/landless poor). By the end of 1978, the RCSs were established in most parts of Karimnagar district, specifically Sircilla and Jagityal (Srinivasulu 2002: 20). RCS united farmers and labourers for Jattra Yatras (Victory Marches). One of the largest march took place on 7 September 1978, in which people from 150 villages marched together to Jagityal town. Gaddar, a popular balladeer and Telangana activist, recalls:[19] 'I joined OU right after the agitations. In 1971–2, to oppose the Andhra movement, I became a cultural activist and joined Arts Lover Movement on campus. It was run by fine art student intellectuals. The idea I learnt is that art should be for people's sake. It should be for the annihilation of caste.'[20]

Gaddar kept the movement's spirit alive with his revolutionary songs, some of which were featured in the film *Jai Bolo Telangana*. His song *Podusthunna Poddumeeda* became the voice of common masses.

Many OU youth were inspired by him and joined full-time art and cultural activities. A lot of them went on to become singers, poets, and writers. Commenting on sustaining the movement, Gaddar states that 'intellectuals burn like paper but activists are like coal that burns with the ideological spirit and keeps the movement charged'.

In 1990s, dozens of new groups emerged on campus supporting the separate Telangana movement. There were groups who explored the history of Telangana and boycotted everything related to Andhra Pradesh. In 1999, to oppose the AP formation day on 1 November, a student activist Sanghishetty Srinivas, climbed up the Arts College building and hoisted a handmade Telangana flag. He recalls:

> Like all other government offices in the state, our university administration was also full of Andhra people. It used to celebrate all the state sponsored festivals. Andhra Pradesh State formation day had become the part of the official state cultural festivals therefore to oppose the existing State Day was not just opposing the state but rejecting all the historical and cultural celebrations glorified by the state. It was a shame for us to celebrate Andhra Pradesh formation day in the premises of Arts College whose hundreds of students were killed by the same Andhra state.[21]

What Shetty Srinivas tried to oppose was the 'cultural hegemony' of the state, which, according to him, is reflected in the socio-political and cultural life of the state. Shetty was arrested by the police and later released. However, this incident motivated him to dedicate his life to the movement. He has written almost 40 books and translated dozens of volumes on Telangana. He also became the main pillar of the Telangana Resource Centre. Without a doubt, his efforts inspired OU students in their activism. After the year 2000, student activists founded magazines such as *Campus Voice* which enjoyed a wide readership among hostel students, especially those in NRS hostel.

After serving in radical groups, Telangana student activists became disillusioned.

> We were struggling against issues like capitalism, imperialism, feudalism, etcetera and we worked against the state. But after decades we realised that Telangana has never become the primary agenda of all these radical groups. Scholars have different views on why Naxalites or other radical Left parties did not highlight the caste issue. In many ways the 1980s has

been the most important phase in the history of Andhra Pradesh. This decade was also rife with caste violence in the Andhra region where the 'Red' and 'Green' revolution was strong.

Srinivasulu (2002: 33) argues that 'if caste violence is symptomatic of the rising aspirations of the downtrodden and disadvantaged strata of our society and their challenge to the historically inherited and established structure of socio-economic, cultural and political dominance, then the violence is also an expression of resistance to these aspirations by the dominant power-that-be.

According to both Srinivasulu's (2002: 2) and Damodaran's (2008: 94–5) studies of caste relations in Andhra Pradesh, the Andhra region has been economically and politically dominated by two land-owning castes, the Kammas and the Reddys, who formed just 6.5 per cent and 4.8 per cent of the population, respectively. Caste has largely defined both political power and entrepreneurial dominance, as the Reddys dominated the political space and the Kammas the entrepreneurial space (Srinivasulu 2002: 7). The class-oriented struggles of the communists did help Dalits, according to Srinivasulu. It helped in providing or increasing their daily wage and also in their acquisition of land. They received education and had a social space to articulate their grievances. Dalits were certainly closer to the Naxalite party than any other political party. Therefore, there was no contention between Naxalites and Dalits (Patil 1992: 30). Naxalites established *sangams* (associations) in the name of caste in some parts of Telangana. In Nizamabad and some parts of Medak district, *Chillara Kulhala Sangam* or *Ambedkar Yuvajana Sangam* were organized (see Laxamaiah 2007).

Lower-caste politics began to rise to the surface in late 1980s. Marginal communities like *Chakalis* (*dhobhis*), *Nayibrahmins* (barbers), *Kummhari* (pot makers), *Katikaparlu* (a caste that buries the dead), and Dalits (particularly Madigas) have not only participated in the movement but in fact formed many organizations and protested. 'Caste-Based Telangana' (*Kula Sanghala Telanganam*) became ubiquitous headlines of the local newspapers. The decade witnessed the mushrooming of caste-based organizations. The decade witnessed the mushrooming of caste-based organizations such as *Telanganalo Samajika Prajarajyam* and caste organizations like *Madiga Dandora*, *Kuramgolla Doludebba*, Democratic Forum for Dalits and Minorities

(DFDM), *Telangana Jana Parishad*, and *Telangana Mahasabha*. Along with caste organizations, these organizations have created a cultural discourse through their political activism for Telangana movement. In creating these different discourses, Osmania intellectuals played a key role. In fact, the idea of forming these organizations has a close linkage with OU.

To carry forward the legacy of Telangana activism on campus, the young generations of Telangana activists and intellectuals promulgated a universal approach to the movement. A popular Telugu magazine, *Jambudweepam*,[22] was started by a resident of NRS, Vikram. Vikram is in his 40s and is completing his PhD in Telugu literature. He regularly visits villages to educate masses about Dalit ideology. Vikram shares his opinion about the movement:

> Telangana movement is a movement which made dozens of our students who think they are leaders but in reality, they are spoiling the other young students. They don't know even why they need a separate state. This movement has diverted the real issues of caste atrocities, caste humiliation. Now, nobody talks about Dalit issues. Either Telangana is formed as a separate state or not, would Dalit or *adivasis* of the region ever get any benefit?[23]

As Vikram speaks, his voice gradually gets louder, indicating his anger. He pauses for breath and continues, 'See, I don't want to waste my time about a waste movement; I would be happy to tell you about the caste problems in Telangana which is a much more serious issue than Telangana'. According to him, a separate Telangana will not solve social problems. Vikram is the most senior scholar in the NRS hostel. He is married with two children, lives in a rented flat near campus, and teaches at a college. Every evening, he visits the hostel after dinner and there is always somebody to meet him. Everyone knows his stand on Telangana. Student activists used to regularly invite him to their programmes, but his vocal criticism of the Telangana movement has made him a less popular speaker. Showing old issues of his magazine, he says, 'I want university students to write (in the magazine) and this is the need of the hour. We don't have any good scholars after Ambedkar. These present student leaders don't deserve to be students'. Activists like Vikram find student leadership corrupt as they misuse the name of Osmania to further their self-interests.

Among Leftist parties, there was also a contention over the question of private property accumulation, as historically, Dalits were denied the right to property in the Hindu social order. Hence, they have rightful claims over the resources. However, according to Dalit activists, a lot of speeches and debates took place, but they brought about little practical change. After serving in these radical group, Telangana student activists became disillusioned. 'We were struggling against issues like capitalism, imperialism, feudalism etc. and we worked against the state. But after decades we realised that Telangana has never become the primary agenda of all these radical groups. We again felt cheated,' Gogu Shyamala, a renowned poet, expresses. 'We were told not to accumulate private property. I gave up my house and everything I had to the party. After working for years with them, we found out that our leaders have flat in metro cities, their children are studying abroad. We were betrayed'. In fact, radical left intellectuals like Ilaiah (cited in Simhadri and Rao 1997: 25) mentioned that 'the real hegemony of *Andhratwam* (Andhraness) got established with the communist school of thought headed by Kammas and Reddys of Andhra, propagating formation of Vishalandhra but not a Telugu-centred linguistic state (Telugu)'. Disillusioned, many activists decided to return to their families, took up jobs, and started living a normal life. Nevertheless, the vision of a separate Telangana never wavered in the minds of the leading activists. Dr Chiranjeevi shares, 'I spend almost two decades running from police, hiding from the government and becoming so called radical but it was all illusion. When I hear first time in 1988, a slogan from BSP founder Kanshi Ram that "Ballet is more powerful than Bullet", it gave me hope that through democratic way, our dream of separate Telangana is possible'.

However, crucial to an understanding of Dalit mobilization and politicization is the organized attack launched against them by the Kammas of Karamchedu in Prakasham district in July 1985. Since 1980s, the advanced Green Revolution belt of coastal Andhra has witnessed intense caste-based polarization and mobilization on both sides of the social spectrum, that is, among landowning as well as labouring communities (Srinivasulu 2002: 29).

With the formation of hundreds of organizations publishing a saga of literature showing discrimination and humiliation, Telangana intellectuals started spreading cultural consciousness among masses.

In January 1986, a few activists from 1969 agitations decided to form 'Telangana Information Trust'. Their goal was to collect all the available literature on Telangana and spread it to the masses. Some of its members visited various parts of the world wherever Telangana diaspora resided. Various meeting and conferences were held nationally and internationally to chalk out the future strategy of how to get separate Telangana. Around 1991, Osmania students, with the help of 1969 activists, formed two organizations: Telangana Student Front (TSF) and Telangana Liberation Student Organisation (TLSO). In 1992, the Kakatiya unit of TSF was formed and organized various seminar on small states. Both the organizations agitated for 15 per cent supernumerary seats for Telangana students in OU. The cumulative effect of such small-scale activism kept the flame of the movement alive. After experiencing a lull since the 1970s, now the issue of separate Telangana started heating up again in political corridors. The reason behind this was that Congress, badly defeated by the Telugu Desam Party (TDP) in the state, wanted to regain its base. To gain sympathy of the masses, Congress demanded the creation of separate Telangana.

Many of the 1969 activists joined university services. They continued their exemplary activism through arts, literature, and politics. Similarly, there are many young university students who have penned their movement experiences and produced dozens of books. Most of these students read and are inspired by Dalit intellectuals and poets of Telangana.[24] According to Rahul, a campus activist, 'These intellectuals highlighted the local culture to oppose the exploitation of the Telangana people by the Andhra's dominant castes. Some of them were murdered during their public performances'.

During this phase, the movement worked silently as intellectuals of the movement (mainly those who were part of 1969 agitations) produced a saga of literature which gradually reached to the masses. During this period, a range of activists evolved who were influenced by senior activists. Those who sacrificed their lives in 1969 agitations, their family, friends, and relatives motivated subsequent generations to take up the issue of Telangana. These intellectuals collaborated with students of Arts College at OU. As a result, many university students became full-fledged activists who published magazines and books about Telangana.

An important Hyderabad convention was held on 1 December 1996 under the banner of 'Telangana Jana Sabha', which was followed by a series of public meetings and group meetings at Karimnagar, Siddipet, Janagaon, Nizamabad, Khammam, Nalgonda, Bhongir, and many other small towns in various districts. The Bhongir conference and public meeting was a major breakthrough in Telangana movement, where future strategy was discussed. It was addressed by Kaloji Narayan Rao, Professor Jayashankar, Professor Simhadri, Professsor P.L. Visweshwar Rao, Dr Srinivasulu, Sidda Reddy, and many others. These meetings laid the foundations for subsequent activism in the 1990s. In these meetings, intellectuals agreed that Telangana could be achieved only through democratic means. This example depicts how intellectuals of the university responded to the political scenario. French thinker Pierre Bourdieu (in Swartz 2013: 245) states, 'Political voices must come out of solid social scientific research'. A key role was played by the intellectuals of OU in shaping the Telangana movement. Apart from intellectuals, as Srikanth (2013: 39) suggests, 'the resurrection of the regional identity has been facilitated by the opportunism of political parties, the unjustifiable inaction of the left'. The movement was sustained and nurtured by a wide range of committed artists, singers, poets, writers, educated elite, intellectuals, democratic voices, and journalists (Haragopal 2010a: 58).

In 2000, the Indian government created three separate states[25]: Jharkhand, Chhattisgarh, and Uttarakhand. The aspiration to project their agendas at the national level was rekindled among Telangana supporters. Some senior activists and intellectuals from OU and Kakatiya University, under the leadership of Professor Jayashankar,[26] raised a demand of separate Telangana. Many of these intellectuals had experienced the 1969 movement, which had failed because of corrupt leadership. They also realized that without political motivation, this demand cannot reach the national level. They approached a local politician, Kalvakuntla Chandrashekhar Rao (popularly known as KCR), who was then deputy speaker of Legislative Assembly during the TDP rule, to form a new party. By not getting a ministerial post, KCR stepped out of the then ruling party TDP in 2000 and formed TRS in 2001. He was supported by all the Telangana movement organizations like Telangana Jana Sabha (TJS), Telangana Maha Sabha (TMS), and Telangana Aikya Vedika, and various research wings and individuals, Telangana movement could spread widely.[27]

Two influential organizations, TJS[28] and TMS, set out to focus on solving basic problems people faced. These organizations asserted that mere geographical formation of Telangana would not be sufficient, and demand for a Telangana that guarantees a promise of solving basic issues like distribution of land, construction of projects, providing water for drinking and irrigation, education, medical facilities, employment, welfare, ending caste discrimination, issues relating to women, protection of Dalit and tribal rights, and basic human rights of people. They worked with theoretical and practical perspectives to achieve liberty, equality, and self-rule in Telangana. During Chandrababu Naidu's regime, TJS became a target for brutal repression from state, and soon, beginning with Belli Lalita in 1999 till 2004, at least six activists of TJS and Telangana Kala Samiti (TKS) were murdered by the state or state-sponsored forces. The Telangana regional bourgeois class possesses rich experience in capitalizing Telangana cause for developing their own political identity. Thus, by 2000, there were enough associations, groups, and platforms at socio-economic, cultural, and political fronts.

Andhra Pradesh was ruled by TDP under the leadership of Chandrababu Naidu in 1990s. Maoism too was rampant in the state, and particularly in the Telangana region. Police, under the Naidu rule, made new strategies to counter Maoism. The *Jai Telangana Movement* was also labelled as 'Naxalite movement'. Many professors and students of OU were targeted as naxalites. According to a history professor at Osmania who actively participated in the 1969 movement, 'In those days government targeted many Osmania University students and labelled them as Maoist. This way it was easy for police to encounter them. There were cases where police personnel were taking bribe by putting fake cases on Osmania students.'

Many students use Telangana as a surname on their Facebook accounts. Twitter and YouTube Channels, Dalit Camera (an alternate media with more than 4,450 subscriptions), magazines, cassettes, CDs, calendars, key rings, and books also helped Osmania students and intellectuals spread their voice across India and the world. This changed the social and cultural life of Telangana. 'Jai Telangana' and revolutionary songs of Gaddar, Daruvu Tellanna, and Rasamayi Balakishen were ringtones on many activist' mobile phones. Even during 2009 movement, messages of pro-Telangana and pro-Naxalites filled social media. To counter this, many activists from abroad shared their status as 'I am from Telangana and I am not a Naxalite' (see E.S. Rao 2010: 118). The researcher had the opportunity to meet a group of activists in the United States of America with Telangana NRI Association (TeNA).[29] They formed *Telangana Cultural Society*[30] in Singapore and Canada as well, which celebrates social and cultural festivals such as *Bathukamma*. During the Telangana movement, they organized various seminars and conferences, published literature, and invited activists and intellectuals from Telangana as guest speakers.

The 1990–2000 period was crucial for intellectual activism. It was because of intellectuals' effort that Telangana issue was back in the limelight. A plethora of literature in the form of oral and written traditions—books, poetry, and folk songs—was produced by university professors. The Telangana debate was also reframed in the wake of Mandal agitation. The Andhra region had experienced heinous caste violence in Karamchedu (17 July 1985 in Prakasham district), Tsunduru (6 August 1991 in Tenali Mandal, Guntur district), and later in Vempentta (16 July 1998 in Kurnool district of Rayalaseem). Even for activists, the caste issue was taking a central focus among the Telangana activists. It led to a caste-based grouping among Telangana activists. Many caste groups emerged and Leftist groups started waning on campus. In 1991, OU alumnus and 'son of the soil', P.V. Narasimha Rao became the country's prime minister. Although the Telangana issue was not broached officially during his tenure, his contribution in introducing neo-liberal policies of globalization brought some structural changes to the state economy and strengthened the Telangana diaspora. It was during this time that networks between Telangana activists and diasporas were forged. Non-resident Indians (NRIs) helped academicians and activists financially in promoting Telangana folk, art, and activism for separate statehood.

Another example of successful portrayal of intellectuals' contribution was the preparation of the Statement of Agenda for People's Telangana. The organization that bought out this agenda was the People's Telangana Foundation. This document set the base for a concept which is known as 'Social Justice Telangana'. The same group formed 'Telangana Intellectual Forum', which became instrumental in devising strategies for mass mobilization for the movement. Another milestone intellectuals achieved was *Suryapet Declaration*[31] in 2012, which was to show the government the strength of people's movement. Along with Osmania intellectuals, Professor Kodandaram, Telangana's popular Singer, and artist Deshapathy Srinivas[32] were the heroes of *Samara Bheri* (Call to War) meeting.

Srinivas recounted how valiant leaders from Telangana like Arutla Rama Chandra Reddy and Arutla Kamala Devi fought on behalf of Telangana people. He asked the Telangana leaders whether they would stand on the side of Telangana martyr's mothers like Shankaramma (Srikantha Chary's mother) or on the side of Vijayamma, mother of a looter like Y.S. Jagan. This declaration not only strengthened the demand for separate statehood but also brought intellectuals and politicians together for future struggle.

Intellectuals often exist in a state of creative tension with the rules and restrictions imposed by the prevailing institutions on everyday life (Furedi 2004: 32). According to Lipset (1960: 311), intellectuals are 'all those who create, distribute, and apply culture, that is, the symbolic order of man, including art, science, and religion'. Historians who have studied youth movements have been concerned with the 'intellectual' and the 'political face of the student activism' (Wasserstrom and Xinyong 1989). Observing movements as knowledge producers underscores the role of movement intellectuals who articulate interests and cognitive praxis of the movement. Such activities, according to Buechler (2011: 182), create public intellectuals who take society as an object of analysis to develop new understanding of the object for reality. The demand for separate Telangana has been conceived, nurtured, directed, and articulated by such intellectuals.

Bourdieu (2003: 11) reminds us that intellectual efforts are crucial, but they 'cannot stand aside, neutral and indifferent, from the struggles in which the future of the world is at stake'. Intellectual's ideas do not remain limited to classrooms.[33]

According to P.L. Visweshwar Rao,

> During my tenure as Arts College Principal, I gave my students full freedom to organise meetings, rallies and whatever else they wanted to do during the 2009 agitation. But at the same time, I was expecting them to attend classes regularly. And I gave the highest number of PhDs, so that they can go back to the society and explore the history of their Telangana.[34]

TELANGANA MOBILIZATION AGAINST CULTURAL MARGINALIZATION

Like Amos, who had formed Telangana Non-Gazetted Officers' Association to mobilize Telangana masses and was one of the first Telanganaites to get job in Hyderabad in 1952, there were hundreds of other government employees who tolerated humiliations in their offices. But Amos could not take it after ten years and he decided to leave his job in 1962. He formed Telangana Non-Gazetted Officers' Association to mobilize Telangana masses against injustice and humiliation towards the people of Telangana. He was the general secretary of the association. This association was instrumental in mobilizing common public during a separate Telangana agitation in 1968, and raising the issue of utilization of surplus revenues of Telangana. An agitation took place at a meeting in Kakinada in November 1968 by students and Andhra people against the 'Telangana Safeguards'.[35] Employees collected various sets of data on the status of representation of Telangana people in jobs in comparison to the Andhras. This was the first generation of Telangana employees that gained government employment, and their entire family was dependent on them. As government employees, they also had a limitation that they could not agitate directly against the government. Therefore, they took these issues to youth and students. OU students, being in the capital city, closely observed the exploitation of Telangana employees during their visit to any office. Gradually, their campus politics also started centring on the issue of Telangana. In fact, the 1968 Osmania University Student Union (OUSU) was fought on the Telangana issue. However, two key posts went to opposing groups: the students who supported a separate Telangana won the presidency, while the secretary post went the group that supported the proper implementation of safeguards that were promised to Telangana as per the Gentlemen's Agreement. This election and the ensuing factional politics of students prepared the students for future agitations. Explaining the intensity of this victory, Mr Saiffuddin,[36] a law student in 1968 states:

> It was the victory of Mallikarjuna which gave students a hope that a separate Telangana is possible. The demand for safeguards implementation was supported by the government itself; therefore, the group was given

support by the administration as well. But the separate state demand caused trouble for the state and national governments. This factional politics was the beginning of the real movement for a separate Telangana.

Government employees from Telangana made several forums to make other people conscious about the issue of Telangana. Their main focus was university students. OU provided the platform to think and assert the indigenous identity. In 1969, student leaders realized that a separate Telangana was not possible without political power. Osmania students offered new avenues to activism into a political constituency by forming the *Telangana Praja Samithi* (TPS). The process of this formation is the evidence of their vision and attachment to their Telangana identity. They expanded the base of TPS and decided to mobilize masses for the next elections. As the movement spread across villages, it caught the attention of other political parties. TPS was an offshoot of the separate Telangana agitation. The TPS's precursor was the Telangana people's convention formed in February 1969 at a meeting attended by lawyers, doctors, journalists, peasants, businessmen, and others to press for granting of statehood for Telangana (Reddy and Sharma 1979: 57). The idea of TPS was given final shape after the successful *Telangana Bandh* on 3 March 1969 by the Telangana People's convention convenor Mr Madan Mohan. Other student leaders were Pratap Kishore, P.N. Swami, Raghuvira Rao, and Mallikarjuna. Sridhar Reddy made his own TPS.

Finding this a golden opportunity for a rebound into politics and a chance to regain popularity among masses, local leader Dr Marri Chenna Reddy[37] (MCR) managed to secure the post of TPS president.[38] Advocate Ramdass, a 1969 activist explains: 'MCR joined the movement almost five months after the movement started. Since he joined the movement, the division started taking place. All the Reddy students started supporting him as they found in him a political mentor'.

With MCR in place as the TPS president, students set up a delegation to meet important sources who could take their demand to parliament. According to the activists, 'We did all those things which MCR suggested us to do for the demand of Separate Telangana at the national level. Under his leadership, we got to know how to approach the national level politics. We met with political leaders. Within few months, we got busy like political leaders.'

The agitation became more intense as students pinned their high hopes on creation of a separate state of Telangana. The schedule of their activities demonstrates the intensity of their commitment to the movement:

- *May 23: Delegation met Chief Minister K. Brahmananda Reddy.*
- *June 4: Telegram sent to Prime Minister Indira Gandhi and union home minister for the immediate central intervention in view of the fast deteriorating conditions and the breakdown of law and order in Telangana region.*
- *June 8: Delegation of the convention met Union Home Minister Y.B. Chavan and impressed upon that the creation of separate Telangana can alone satisfy the aspirations of the people of Telangana.*
- *June 18: Delegation of the convention met minister for judicial and legislative department, government of West Bengal and a member of parliament.*
- *June 19: Delegation met a member of parliament from Bharatiya Kranti Dal, Mr Prakash Vir Shastry.*
- *June 20: Delegation of the convention met governor of Andhra Pradesh and apprised him of the research findings.*
- *June 25: Delegation met the revenue minister and governor of Andhra Pradesh.*
- *June 27: Meeting with Chairman, Region Committee Mr J. Chokka Rao to request him to take a lead to break the dead-lock.*

Showing this schedule, Reddy, now in his sixties, recalls: 'In those two months, we did not leave any stone unturned for our goal'. Agitations, protests, strikes, conferences, meetings, and negotiations with politicians were planned by student activists.

Beginning on 14 January 1969, their agitation lasted for almost nine months. This went down in history as the longest period for any student agitation in the world. To control the growing student agitations, police opted for violent means. The police's aggressive way of dealing with student agitation created more solidarity among activists. Jacob, an activist in 1969 who lost his best friend in police violence, emotionally recounts scenes from the agitation: 'As students protested, the police became aggressive with the agitators. This was one of the rare experiences in the history of agitations, that Andhra police, violating all the laws, shot directly in the head and chest of the peaceful student agitators. This action led to violent agitations.'

According to police rules, the use of tear gas is not allowed until the situation becomes critical. Moreover, the rule does not allow the police to shoot above the waist. However, 'the police not only used tear gas and lathi charge but also used real bullets instead of rubber ones', Stalin states. Dr Sanjeev, a medical student during the 1969 agitation, expressed his anger towards the media:

> Official data shows only 370 students were killed. Believe it or not, but according to our estimation more than 1000 students lost their lives. You can imagine a scene when I went to the Gandhi hospital to inquire about one of my friends who was killed in police firing and doctor took me to the room and it bodies were piled up on the top of each other as there was no space to keep bodies. They were kept in the rows and line by putting some wooden board to make lines. It was a genocide my dear. But Andhra politicians managed everything as it was their media and their government. But OU students know their realities.

An activist from 1969 agitations, Mr Suresh, a law student in those days and later joined radical communism reflects: 'Choosing May 1st as "Telangana Demand Day" also denotes that it was the demand to abolish the slavery which the people of Telangana were forced to do under the cruel regime of Andhra people. It was a message to tell Andhra people that we are fighting for our rights as labour, as human being.'

The pamphlets of the time described OU as a 'battlefield', 'battle-ground', 'war zone', and 'hotbed of politics' as used in the print media. According to the convener of OUSU in 1969, agitations were curbed by the state yet more repression was met with more intense agitations. Ramesh, who lost three of his close friends in police firing, states:

> In this yearlong agitation, we were arrested many times by the police, but our teachers were always helping by getting us bail. This served to strengthen the bond between students and teachers. After each student death, there were meetings and mourning, but every loss strengthened their spirit for the movement and encouraged students to fight the upcoming Parliamentary elections.

The agitations in 1969 shook the people's spirit for the separate Telangana. Student unity became a symbol of trust and masses lost trust in politicians. The empirical data shows example of their strong campus solidarity as one of the reasons that they could sustain their agitation for one year. Ramdas, a postgraduate student at the law college in 1969, expresses the solidarity among Osmania students:

> On January 24th, the firing occurred in Sadashivapeta in which 14 students were injured. A person name Shankar, 17 years old, was the first person who died in 1969 Telangana movement. Around 3000 people attended his funeral in Sadashivapeta. On the very Next day i.e. 25th January students were holding a meeting in front of Engineering College, during that meeting news reached that students who got injured in yesterday's firing admitted in Gandhi Hospital, need urgent blood for treatment. After listening that news, hundreds of students sitting in the meeting, started running towards Gandhi Hospital to donate their blood and saved lives of their fellow students. In those days, the students didn't have scooters and cycle motors. The spirit to go reach as soon as possible from University to Secunderabad Gandhi Hospital was a wonderful (apoorva) scence (drushyam or sunnivesham). Their sacrifice and deep concern for the life of their fellow activist was praised by many newspapers.[39]

This example is a depiction of what a community stands for.[40] It was the campus solidarity fermented over the years among its students. The importance of 'we' feeling builds a strong community. Strong communities produce strong networks. In these kinds of communities, social interaction occurs through cultural symbols and identities.[41] Since identities are created and shaped through social relations, networks play a crucial role. They build and reinforce identities of individuals and provide them with a political consciousness that allows them to get ideologically closer to a given political issue. Thus, a university campus constitutes a small, but a very strong community of activists. On virtual media, on social networking there are end number of groups which are also called online communities, online groups, and even the word family is used to show their unity. The terminology used in social media such as 'Campus Community' or 'Osmania Community' are used on social media, and it highlights Osmania as community of the activists. The real essence of the community lies in the fact that 'we' are one. We can derive that smaller the community is, the stronger the networks are.

During the 1969 movement, bound by the law, the police could not use real bullets. If the situation was tense, the police could use rubber bullets, but they were to be shot only below the waist. However, student activists are told that there was no law followed by the police. According to the activists, 'dealing with tear gas was a routine for activists. Police shot the real bullets openly at the students and hundreds of students lost their lives. It made us angry, if we had weapon we could also answer them back.' Recalling those days, one of the main activists of 1969, Dr Chianjeevi, explains the strategy their group planned to deal with tear gas shell:

> Collectively, we all top activists used to make strategies how to handle police attacks. We used to carry two handkerchiefs and two onions in our pocket. We were munching on our strong onion to stop the smell of the gas shell. The minute police used to throw the tear gas shell; it takes 15–20 second to burst. After 20 second, gas start coming out and make it boiling hot which is impossible to touch. Within those 20 second, we used to catch hold of one handkerchief to pick-up the shell and throw back on police. Then police used to run away. This way, we used to make use of our handkerchief.

The victory of the idea of separate Telangana in campus elections justified the demand for separate Telangana and strengthened the unity among students. This victory was followed by a series of protests, planned by the students. Janardhana (author of *Telangana Udyamamu, Prarambham-Vishtruti*),[42] a pre-university student, participated in the movement and witnessed the hunger strike of Sri Ravindranath Khammam. He noticed large-scale participation of the Social Welfare hostel students. Non-teaching Osmania staff also joined the protest in large numbers. This event was published in the newspapers titled, 'Non-domiciles in Telangana to Quit before February End'.[43] Thus, terminology such as non-domicile or non-mulki, as defined by the state, was used by activists to unite the people of Telangana against Andhra.

On 23 January, the then-education minister of the state of Andhra Pradesh, P.V. Narasimha Rao (who himself was from Telangana region) met with Osmania students and VC and appealed to suspend the agitation.[44] However, the negotiations did not lead to a positive result for the government. University students boycotted their classes. By June 1969, a mass satyagraha was organized in all districts of Telangana. 'For the entire academic year, students protested on the road denouncing police atrocities. Jails were overpopulated with students and schools in Telangana were used as detention centres. For 10 months, the government came to a standstill, with 'the only functioning department being the police', recalls Professor Keshav Rao Jadhav, one of the founding fathers of the movement. He claims that 'no policemen died or injured in these agitations', indicating that students were not armed but police told the media that students attacked them. Tadakamalla et al. (2009: 38) claim that 'the credit of raising mass consciousness about the movement and spreading awareness about the injustice goes to Osmania students'. Thus, the 1969 agitation cannot be imagined without the contribution of OU and its students.

A student of Arts College, Sriram[45] (president of an independent group which supported separate Telangana), who fought separately, explains his experience.

> During the agitation, I was arrested and jailed for nearly two and half months at Rajahmundry and Chanchalguda jails. There I met Mr Amos, and we used to discuss about Telangana. But once upon time, I was there for 15 days underground in a very severe atmosphere, where I had to live in a dark place without food. I was treated like a criminal.

Dr Sanjeev, a medical student in those days who actively led the agitation, repents:

> We made many mistakes in 1969. We were all young and protesting every day without thinking of any consequences. We lost our friends in police firings. We put tremendous effort to continue our protests for almost 9 months continuous. Our energy was drained, we were exhausted. Without proper planning, we wasted our energy.

Sriram, going against his family's will, left his studies after this experience and became a full time activist. He returned to the university to finish his PhD in 1978 and his thesis explains the 1969 student revolt that he had experienced. Like him, many students lost years of studies, but they continued their struggle to achieve an official identity of the separate statehood for Telangana.

Keeping their ideology aside, every political ideology from Left to Right responded to the agitations. Most of the organizations, though political in nature, focussed on culture in their mobilization strategies. They highlighted the cultural politics of Andhra and the gradual encroachment by the Andhra in the city of Hyderabad. They linked the issue of unemployment with the Andhras' rampant migration. Such comparisons were easily grasped by the people of Telangana as the basic survival issues such as jobs affected everyone. According to Mr Prashant, an Osmania activist, 'I have attended various meeting of these organisations. Each of these organisations highlighted the discrimination with Telangana employees on by making fun of their culture'. Everyday humiliation on cultural basis gradually built up anger against the Andhra employees so as with their region.

Students channelled their emotions in the form of votes in 1971 by-elections. Swimming against the currents entrenched in the Congress and the electoral Communists, OU students made their way through by winning 11 of 14 parliamentary seats from the Telangana region, under the banner of TPS. The student party, TPS, won 11 of 14 parliamentary seats they contested. The victory of TPS was preceded by the sympathy swayed due to the sacrifice of thousands of students and youth of Telangana during their year-long agitation throughout the region. This was the first time in the Indian political history that a new party, formed by students and employees, won the majority. This was a historic victory for any student movement turning into political party. This overwhelming victory in the region made students so confident that they prepared a grand celebration. This demonstrated how the masses shifted their trust from politicians to students. Student leaders were busy deciding the date of the separate statehood formation. They even had a meeting to decide their state cabinet ministries; they also prepared a flag with Telangana map on it.

However, before the political journey of TPS could take off, TPS chairman MCR was looking out for his next political move, or 'biding his time', as Suri (2016: 11) calls it. He played what some activists call 'opportunistic politics' and the politics of 'betrayal'. Reddy, after meeting with the then prime minister, Indira Gandhi,[46] decided to merge TPS with Congress party. As a result, Chief Minister Brahmananda Reddy (from Andhra region) resigned as the next tenure, according to Gentlemen's Agreement, was given to the Telangana Chief Minister. Thus, on 30 September 1971, P.V. Narasimha Rao was appointed the chief minister of Andhra Pradesh. The TPS was dissolved and its members re-joined the Congress.[47] MCR's decision was condemned by the entire student and intellectual community and he was declared as a 'traitor' by the students.

MCR's politicking and the eventual merger of TPS with the ruling Congress party led to a mixed reaction among students. A section of students hoped to get equal representation in jobs and resources. But there was a widespread frustration among student activists, who lost their close friends in this struggle and felt betrayed by the politicians. They lost trust in the state and in electoral democracy. Many of them joined numerous radical movements and opted for the anti-state positions which continued for almost few decades. This was the rare historical moment which offers many explanations about politics behind the movement and how politics corrupt the movement. OU student activism witnessed such historic moment of democratic and political upheaval. For their electoral gain, it was easy for politicians like Chenna Reddy to change their positions. 'We shouted for days that *Chenna Reddy chor hai* (Chenna Reddy is a thief) but nobody bother to hear us anymore', Dr Chiranjeevi recalls those days. Commenting on the failure of the student struggle, the president of 1969 movement Founders' Forum, Mr Basant,[48] states:

> It was not the defeat of Indian democracy. It was the political culture of Andhra lobby not to accept others' opinion. We received a democratic mandate through elections. But they (Andhra political lobby) bought our leader with the help of Congress. Now, in the history of Telangana, Chenna Reddy is the biggest enemy but if you see who created Chenna Reddy and who destroyed Chenna Reddy—it was the Andhra politicians who didn't believe in democracy.

Meanwhile, the Andhra Pradesh High Court, in a judgement on 17 February 1973, stated that the status of mulki applies to those who live in Hyderabad and not the ones who were born here. This caused a huge disappointment; resentment ran deep among Telangana activists, which led to more agitations against the state government. To avoid any further agitations, government made an arrangement known as Six-Point formula, which was endorsed by the leaders of both the regions. Except from jobs, resources, and backward caste classics, there was one point that emphasized was the establishing a central university in Hyderabad (see Benichou 2000: 282).

The socio-political situation of Telangana and Andhra grew intense as the ruling class of Andhra was starkly challenged by the regional Telangana politics and the growing consciousness of Telangana masses. Between 1969 and 1971, in the turbulent period of Telangana sub-nationalism, only two major parties, TPS and Congress, were trying to influence the mass political behaviour, according to Reddy and Sharma (1979: 244). People identified themselves with the TPS on emotional grounds and justified their association with a regional party that was devoid of any national directives and commitments (1979: 245–6). Regionalism was a powerful factor in state politics, causing tension and 'affecting the political process in the form of defections among legislators and party leaders, switchover and the dropouts among voters' (1979: 312).

Telangana activists realized that their weakness lies only in their alliance with corrupt political leadership. From 1973 to 2000, the issue of Telangana remained silent in political sphere. No major rally or mobilization took place during this period on campus. From 1972 onwards, many Telangana activists who participated in 1969 agitation, felt betrayed by the politicians. It was an emotional set back to the student movement. They developed anger against the state. They were looking for an alternative. As sympathies swayed towards the extreme Left,[49] many student leaders joined the Naxal movement[50] and People's War Group (PWG). Many student leaders like Kolluri Chiranjeevi, Ram Das, Srinivasulu, and many of their batch mates joined such groups in the forests and left their student life. The 'people think that because of the growth of Naxalism, government did not form separate Telangana. But actually, Naxalism grew because government ignored Telangana problems'.[51] For a long time after 1972, the Osmania campus remained silent on the issue of separate statehood. However, these radical groups (Radical Student Union and PDSU) were in constant touch with university students and formed their unions on campuses.

Though the 1969 agitation did not achieve its goal of separate statehood, it ignited the spirit of separation and motivated campus activism politically. It turned the student politics into radical activism. Student realized the weakness of democratic institutions. Many of them lost their faith in democratic politics. Right after the political 'betrayal' of student's efforts, they channelized their energy into radical ideologies such as Marxism, Leninism, and Maoism and embraced violent activism to ensure justice to peasants, landless, and poor. Due to students' shift to Naxalism and the Maoist movement, PWG, campus activism suffered from 1972 to 1980. The year 1973 brought an end to the campus activities for Telangana for a decade. Gradually, the demand of Telangana faded from popular debate and discussion. Left activists found other reasons to keep the ideological class struggle alive on campus. One such Left ideologue was Mr George Reddy, an OU student who served as one of the founders of RSU on campus. On 14 April 1972, he was killed by his ideological opponents on the campus. George Reddy's death came as a shock and loss for the academic community, as he was a brilliant scholar and left ideologue. When no police action was taken against the culprit, anger swelled against the Andhra police and administration. This factor also contributed to the growth of radical movements across the state. The APRSU and RSU were formed in 1974. Remembering those days, Dr Sanjeev shares his experience: 'I joined People's War Group. Mr Pattabhi Sitaramaiyya was captain number one of our union and I was number two. From 1972–77, I was underground. After 17 years, I realised that the Naxalite movement has diverted the agenda of separate Telangana'.

Like him, many other activists, after a decade or more, realized that Telangana had never been the primary agenda of the Naxal parties. They became hopeless, and many returned to their families to lead a normal life. They realized that without proper political interference, their dream of a separate state was not possible.

Mr Ajit,[52] who spent almost 17 years in the Maoist movement, reveals:

> Our government spread the wrong message that the demand of separate Telangana came into existence because of Naxalism. But actually, Naxalism grew because government kept ignoring the people's demand of separate Telangana. We tried all the possible democratic method, agitation, formed political party, fought and won elections but even then, we did not get our Telangana.[53] Government forced us to adapt violent means.

The state targeted the radical students and among the common masses, the image of such students is made to look like anti-national, criminal. Being a Maoist is not taboo at Osmania. Many professors proudly declare, 'Many of our top students are Naxalite and Maoist'. Such pedagogy tends to be opposed by the state as it goes against the establishment. As Sridhar Reddy remarks, 'I am also a Naxalite but without gun. How does Naxalism develop? It comes from dissatisfaction and discrimination done to Telangana people by the Andhra governments. I have given a big philosophy on Naxalism. Naxalism does not come from forest but it comes from disparity and discrimination.'

After 1972 political betrayal, Hamza Alavi terms the Telangana movement 'the most revolutionary movement that has yet arisen in India' (Alavi 1973: 325). In Haragopal's (2010a: 54) words, 'the birth of the Naxalite movement took up the agenda of radical agrarian changes. This movement was partly to complete the unfinished agenda of the Telangana armed struggle in 1940s'. In other words, due to such radical groups, the question of land and land reforms became the political agenda. The activities of Naxalite movement started affecting the political class of Andhra as well as Telangana elite. And no doubt, with this contention over land issues, the Andhra had dominated the Telangana elites. This was the beginning of regional politics and decline of national politics of Congress. The debate on campus was again changing. There were left wing and right wing but there was no debate on Telangana until late 1980s. Radical groups in the forest had their student's wings at Osmania such as PDSU, RSU, and SFI. The popular face of Osmania in 1970s, George Reddy used to run a study group called The Progressive Democratic Students. Jampala Chandra Shekhar Prasad changed it into PDSU. During the 1980s and 1990s, under the regime of Chandrababu Naidu, hundreds of students were killed by the police in the name of Maoism or Naxalism. Waseem, a member of RSU in early 1990s, shared his concern: 'In those days, if any Osmania student was found involved in Separate Telangana activities, he was arrested and labelled as Maoist. I have seen in those days, Gaddar was the only hope for students who managed to get them released on bail through all his political connection and because of his popularity in Telangana'.

According to Waseem,[54] who was running a campus magazine in late 1999, there were many organizations formed during the early 1990s but many of them worked underground for fear of the government retaliation. OU was the dual target of police and politics. Alumni maintained their networks nationally and internationally, contributing to a vibrant political scene. The Telangana Information Trust and Telangana Resource Centre were established by retired university professors, engineers, doctors, and journalists were part of this trust, which published extensive material on Telangana and created a database of Telangana literature. They met with the Telangana diaspora to garner financial support. Telangana Development Forum (TDF) was formed by the Telangana NRI settled in the other countries like the

United States of America, New Zealand, Australia, and UK. Telangana activists like Er Vidya Sagar Rao, Dr Gopal Reddy Gade, and Professor Harinath Polasa were the main speakers of these programmes organized by TDF abroad. Popular cultural artist, Rasmai Balkishan, was invited to mobilize the NRIs abroad.[55] Thus, OU intellectuals played a key role in creating consciousness about regional pride and identity. Since 1960s, campus has been producing generations of intellectuals. They have not only served as the guiding force for young generations but also contributed to the state and national politics and academia. Srinivasulu (2017: 20) describes the contribution of Osmania:

> The role of the university and its teaching and student community in the Telangana state agitation in the late-1960s, in the struggle against the internal Emergency in the mid-1970s, in the expanding democratic and civil rights movement against the repressive policies of regimes since the 1980s, and in autonomous student mobilisation demanding a separate state of Telangana, from the 1990s until its realization in 2014, demonstrates the university's vibrancy to larger societal and political issues.

In short, OU's contribution to the several social movements proves how a university contributed to the larger society by cultivating academicians into public intellectuals and raising issues of awareness and resisting which is against the common welfare of the society. Although the medium of instruction and official work is English, OU allows the students to write their exams in Telugu. Thus, it gives hope to those new entrants from the subaltern section, especially who are first generation learner in their families and making it to higher education. This is a liberal aspect of OU and its contribution to the inclusion of students from rural background.

* * *

The history and legacy of OU reflects a culture of resistance. OU students and intellectuals ignited the movement by raising debates, organizing seminars, rallies, making protests strategies for the movement. Their first major agitation of 1969 effectively created consciousness among common masses. Due to the failure of its leadership, it could not yield any result. Telangana students' participation in the radical movement was the offshoot of this 'political failure' or what activists call 'political betrayal' in 1972. From 1973 to later early 1990s, Osmania intellectuals kept the Telangana spirit alive through their off-campus activism in the form of civil society activism and gradually making national and global networks. Students did not let the issue of Telangana die. In 2001, with the formation of TRS, the aspirations for Telangana were rekindled and young generation of students gained a moral and political support to fight for separate Telangana. By framing new ideologies, devising new strategies, and mobilizing masses by promoting Telangana folk culture and music, Osmania intellectual led the movement to its successful path.

NOTES

1. Available at http://www.osmania.ac.in/aboutus-originandhistory.php, accessed 8 August 2015.
2. Interviewed at his residence in Vidya Nagar on 17 September 2013.
3. Interview at his residence in Secundarabad, 22 September 2013. He was the first to publish an edited volume on Telangana issues in English in 1997, and was a popular principal at Arts College.
4. It was written by Bankim Chandra Chatterjee in his novel *Anand Math*. It became the inspiration for Swadeshi Andolan in 1905.
5. Golkonda Patrika. 1938. 'Vande Mataram Movement', 1 December, 2.
6. B.C. Mahabaleshwrappa. 1997. *Hyderabad Karnatakadali Rajkiya Chluvaligalu 1946–56*. Gulbarga: Gulbarga University Prasaranga.
7. Translated from Urdu:

   May God Preserve unto eternity thy kingdom,
   And thee, Osman, in thy splendour;
   May he make thy religion glorious
   As he has made thee superb among kings.

   Available at http://www.thehindu.com/news/cities/Hyderabad/when-vande-mataram-landed-students-in-trouble/article18064764.ece.
8. Interviewed on 2 June 2013 at his residence.
9. The education system fulfils a culturally legitimizing function by reproducing, via the delimitation of what deserves to be conserved, transmitted, and acquired, the distinction between the legitimate and the illegitimate way of dealing with legitimate works (Bourdieu 1985: 23).
10. Interviewed at his residence.
11. Interviewed at his residence.
12. Available at http://www.csds.in/events/rajni-kothari-1928-2015.

13. Talk on 'Dalit-Bahujan English Education Day' held at Arts College on 5 October 2013.
14. In Thota (1969).
15. Interview in Hyderabad, September 2013.
16. Interview in Hyderabad, September 2013.
17. During the 1969 agitation, Sri Sri's poetry influenced the youth and students. In 2009, the same role was played by balladeers Gaddar and Balkishan. And during the Million March in 2011, dozens of statues, including Andhra Pradesh's people's poet Sri Sri, was also dismantled. After the demolition, OU students stated in a press conferences: 'we made it very clear that Andhra icons are not welcomed here in Telangana'.
18. The association was functional even during 2009 movement and popular artists like Vimalaka, Rasmai Balkishan, Daruvu Yellana, and Warangal Ravi became part of it.
19. Interviewed on 1 September 2013 at his residence.
20. Gummadi Vittal Rao is known as Gaddar. He adopted this name as a tribute to the pre-independence Gaddar Party, which opposed British Colonial rule in Punjab during the 1910s.
21. Interview at his residence in Hyderabad, on 12 October 2013.
22. An ideal-type or an imaginary island of an egalitarian society.
23. Interview in NRS hostel, 25 September 2013.
24. Poets such as Kalekuri Prasad, Madduri Nagesh Babu, Master Jee, Bojja Tarakam, Katti Padmarao, Endluri Sudhakar, Shikamani, Boya Jangaiah di Theresh Babu, Nagappagori Sunder Raju, and Dalit feminist writers like Boyi Vijaya Barathi, Challapalli Swaroopa Rani, Madduri Vijaya Rani, Darisi Sasinirmala, G. Vijayalakshmi Rani, Karri Vijakumari, Seetha Mahalakshmi, Nakka Vijaya Bharathi, Jajula Gouri, Gogu Syamala, Jupaka Subhadra, M. Gouri were well-known faces of Telangana. Revolutionary singer Belli Lalita was the convener of *Telangana Kala Samiti*, an organization affiliated to *Telangana Jana Sabha*. Through her folk and cultural performances, she propagated the demand for separate Telangana since the 1990s. She was also a leader of *Dol-Debba* (an association of Yadavas).
25. Compared to that of Telangana, the demand for these states was not serious or urgent.
26. Professor Kothapalli Jayashankar was a student activist in 1952 agitation and a teacher-activist in the Jai Telangana Movement in 1969. He was against the formation of Vishalandhra.
27. According to Nag (2011: 123–4), KCR was not the only man to tap the opportunity that presented itself. Ale Narendra, known as 'Tiger', a three-term BJP MLA and two-term MP had been weighing his position after breaking away from BJP. He floated his own outfit, Telangana Sadhna Samithi (TSS).

In August 2002, Narendra merged TSS with TRS, pledging to work jointly for the cause of a new state.

28. *Telangana Jana Sabha* was formed in 1998 by Akula Bhoomiaha. TJS, along with its sister organizations, Telangana Students Front and *Telangana Kala Samiti*, made a great impact on the movement during the late 1990s and early 2000s.

29. TeNA started a magazine called *Tengedu*, which covers news and articles on Telangana political and social developments. Some Osmania professors and activists write articles for this magazines.

30. After the formation of Telangana state, TeNA has been organizing parades and showcasing Telangana identity and culture by displaying Telangana symbols such as Bathukamma, Bonalu, Pochampally sarees, Pembarthy metal works, Warangal Fort Thoranam, Charminar, and displaying Kakatheeya Thonranam, bathukammalu, bonalu, peerlu, and pictures of Telangana legends and icons.

31. Available at http://missiontelangana.com/suryapet-shows-the-power-of-telangana-movement/

32. He was a school teacher but his passion for Telangana movement made him a popular singer. He is considered the personal advisor of KCR.

33. Paolo Freire, in his *Pedagogy of the Oppressed* (1970), observes the potential of education to challenge the oppressive myths and ideologies dominant in postcolonial life and encourage the possibility of freedom through critical thinking and transformation of the self. His approach to the classroom emphasized praxis, where ideas are put into thoughtful, reflective practice to achieve social change.

34. Interview at his residence in Hyderabad, on 1 September 2013.

35. 10 July 1968 was observed as 'Telangana Safeguards Day' by Telangana people in response to the injustice done to them.

36. Interviewed on 30 August 2013.

37. Before May 1969, MCR was a minister in the central government and prior to that he was a minister in Andhra Pradesh under Brahmananda Reddy. Gandhi made him a central minister and therefore, he had to resign from his MLA seat. When he was contesting, his opponent, Mr Vandemataram Ramchandra Rao (famous ideologue of the Vande Mataram movement in the 1940s), filed a nomination against him. MCR won but V. Ramchandra Rao filed a case against him in Supreme Court, and ultimately, his ministership was nullified by the court and he was barred for six years from elections. He was compelled to resign as a minister. He became politically unemployed. He found the opportunity to join the Telangana movement, not as a politician. There was a Reddy domination in Telangana region. He made the Telangana movement his full time job, and headed the *Telangana Praja Samiti*, formed by OU students.

38. MCR was acquainted with Gopal Krishna, the elder brother of TPS president, Madan Mohan. He expressed his desire to become president of TPS. Soon, Madan Mohan handed over the chairmanship of TPS to MCR.

39. Taken and translated from Lokeshwar, P. 2007. *Pratyeka Telangana Udyamala Charithra* (Third Reprint), p. 62. Hyderabad: Gandhi Publication.

40. This incident and such severe nature of the movement has been recorded by a local reporter and later published in many books.

41. Identity is a group action that occurs again and again over time by way of action, decisions, processes, and structures (Clark and Hoffmann-Martinot 1998: 214).

42. Special Issue dated 5 June 1969, republished in 1969 *Udyammamu-Charitraka Patralu* 2 (eds) by Tadikamalla Vivek, et al., Telangana History Society, Hyderabad 2009.

43. *The Hindu*, 23 January 1970. During these student agitations, residents of Hyderabad who were basically from the Andhra region were scared because there were some students who spread rumours about the evacuation 'Andhra settlers'. However, yet there was no such incident.

44. 'Bid to End Telangana Agitation', *The Hindu*, 24 January 1969.

45. Interviewed on 3 September 2013.

46. Prime Minister Indira Gandhi was against the bifurcation: 'I stand firmly for an integrated state ... There is an overall rationality in the foundation of our states and we should be very careful not to break the foundation of rationality in momentary passion' (Gray 1974: 183).

47. In 1972, when the Supreme Court upheld the Mulki rules, the Jai Andhra Movement was started in Coastal Andhra and Rayalaseema regions with the aim of reforming a separate state of Andhra. The movement lasted for 110 days. The Supreme Court upheld the implementation of Mulki rules. The people from the Andhra region viewed the Mulki rules as 'treating them like aliens in their own land', according to Sunil, an OU activist.

48. Interviewed on 22 June 2013.

49. Since the establishment of *Vrasam* (Revolutionary Writers Association) in 1970 and *Jana Natya Mandali* in 1972, educational institutions became the centre for spreading the revolutionary culture and ideology, inspired from the Naxalbari movement. In October 1974, Andhra Pradesh Radical Student Union (APRSU) was formed based on the radical ideology of Marx, Lenin, and Mao.

50. The Naxalite youth upsurge is perhaps the best remembered because of the participation of several *brilliant* students from elite institutions, the most famous among which was Presidency College in Kolkata. Many of these students joined the movement out of a sense of disillusionment with the existing educational system and with the socio-economic condition prevailing in

the urban areas. The Naxalbari uprising provided these students with a sense of purpose and oriented them further towards armed (Dasgupta 2006).

51. From the focus group discussion on 26 September 2013.

52. Interviewed on 18 September 2013.

53. Students supported MCR by making him the leader of their political party but he abandoned them by merging TPS with the Congress party.

54. Interviewed on 25 June 2013 in his hostel.

55. Available at http://www.deccanabroad.com/telangana-dhoom-dhaam-atlanta-rasamai-balkishan-show-saturday-july-23rd/, accessed 28 August 2016.

3 Campus Networks and Agitations

The Making of a Student Activist

Examining everyday practices extends our understanding of how the processes work in any protest or movement.

Alberto Melucci (1996)

This chapter attempts to present the 'lifeworld' that activists inhabited at Osmania University (OU). It examines various networks student activists formed and explores the inner mechanisms of their activism. What motivates a student to choose a path of activism? How can we understand the campus culture in relation to activists' backgrounds and their understanding of the movement? Ethnographic observations, interviews with old and new leaders, insights from informal and formal chats and discussions, as well as popular slogans from a year of fieldwork from December 2012 to December 2013 are presented. What elements of daily campus life and culture helped in the production and functioning of various networks? How did students change the tide to make it a mass movement for Telangana? To understand this, the ethnographer investigated the spatial practices of activists and became a keen participant observer. The chapter discusses how students are inducted to a 'network culture', trained and made part of the movement on campus and shows how networks are rooted in Telangana cultural ethos.

ORGANIC LINKAGES BETWEEN ACTIVISTS AND CAMPUS

Sunil parks his bike in front of his college. He gets off slowly as his concentration is fixed on the building's wall which is flooded with coloured posters and pamphlets of different student organizations, both in Telugu and English. Pictures of student leaders overpower the text. He closely examines them and finds his own picture in his organization's poster. This gives him deep satisfaction, and with confident look on his face he walks up the stairs and bows his head in front of the building. As he walks into the corridors, the guard and peon of the building greet him with '*Namastey Anna*' [Hello, brother], and he reciprocates the greeting. His doctoral supervisor approaches him from the opposite direction and he nods his head to greet. His guide shakes hands with him. Sunil replies, '*Nenu bagunnanu*' [I am fine]. They spend a few minutes chatting over a cup of tea. Sunil invites his guide for a post-lunch protest organized by his student union. He comes out of the college building and rings some of his friends asking them to bring the banner for the protest. Within half an hour, there is a small tent set up in front of the building. In no time, almost 50 activists gather together shouting *Jai Telangana* and give speeches to the standing audience. The principal of the college also delivers a 10-minute speech. Non-teaching employees of the university congregate in a corner, sipping tea and chatting, glancing at the numerous posters on the wall. Meanwhile, students on bikes continue to arrive. In the next 10 minutes, media vans are seen buzzing around. Sunil and three other leaders speak to the Telugu media and warn the government that if they do not form a separate statehood, students will sacrifice their lives for Telangana. When the media leaves, Sunil mounts his bike and with two other activists, both on their phones, sets out to mobilize more students in the hostels for an upcoming protest march organized by the students' Joint Action Committee.

The scene described above is typical of Arts College, the most popular and prestigious college among 400 other affiliated colleges of OU. This college served as a popular landmark for activists' meetings and the epicentre of Telangana activism. The majestic building of Arts College is made of pink granite and a grand archway at the centre is flanked by huge doorways. In front of this is a long, ornamental fountain. Most of the activist meetings are held inside this building. Strikes, public gatherings, sit-ins, rallies, and processions are held in front of the building, known for its awe-inspiring facade.

Arts College is surrounded by small parks which are maintained by the college administration. During the evening, students gather here to have tea at one of the nearby food stalls. The park is a common site for students—whether activists or not—to meet informally. This space is of historic and symbolic significance to the spirit of the movement. In many ways, the park served as the interface between the student movement and the general public. Every evening, families and friends from the nearby areas come to pass their leisure time. As a result, they have become spectators to the frequent protests at the Arts College. The area is large enough to hold rallies and state level protests. As it is located on the OU main road, it gathers crowds from the passing traffic, pedestrians, and local tourists. From this road, passers-by are able to view the college and park. People sitting in the park view the posters, banners, and flags set up by the students on daily basis as programmes are frequently organized by various student unions, even after the state's formation. OU alumni who visit fondly recount their time at Arts College and remember the martyrs of the 1969 agitation. Thus, for nearby residents, the Arts College main building is the symbol of struggle, dedication, and activism.

During the 2009 agitation, students held a rally called *Vidyarthi Mahagarjana*. Newspapers estimated that around two to three hundred thousand people participated. Students did not vacate the park for nearly a month. They played revolutionary songs, dramas, and gave speeches alongside social activists. During field research in 2013, the OU Madiga Students' Front organized a massive meeting, which was addressed by the popular Madiga leader, Mr M. Krishna Madiga. During this rally, more than 50 news cameras covered the event. Media vehicles packed the road. Students from Kakatiya and other state universities joined the rally and called their relatives and families to join, making it a family affair.

Although the park is a public space, it serves as an 'identity affirming space' (Carter 2007). This kind of space is qualitatively different than other public spaces as it is an expression of society. Castells (1983) aptly states, 'Space is not a reflection of society; it is society'. This society, rooted in local culture, has its linkages with the Telangana movement. It is the extension of the Arts College. Sunder, a vendor who sell snacks in the park every day from 11 am to 9 pm shares his viewpoint with a shy expression: 'I wish there is agitation everyday ... it will bring more business. Without these rallies or protests, this park and my business both seem lifeless'.[1]

Aside from rallies, protests, or meetings, wedding receptions are another occasion where student activists network and display their stature within in the community. What is interesting about this site is that it is one rare occasion where student activists across party lines come together. Student leaders bring along their supporters, and the number of supporter shows his strength or power. Often times, popular political figures of the movement (such as Kalvakuntala Chandrashekhar Rao (henceforth KCR), President of Telangana Rashtra Samiti (TRS); Professor Kodandaram; and Gaddar) attend these receptions. It is important to note that these wedding functions are an open invitation to all Telangana activists. Other activists, journalists, professors, and local and national politicians concerned with Telangana issues are also invited. In this way, every kind of social gathering—marriage ceremonies included—serve as a medium of networking among Telangana activists.

For the masses, being a Telangana activist is considered very honourable. Those who have arranged marriages customarily receive a sizable dowry. Their activism adds as a plus point to their profile and in negotiations for a larger dowry. To make an impression on a prospective bride's family, activists show files of news coverage with pictures showing them addressing or leading a rally. These pictures are also uploaded on social media, typically Facebook. Other activists have their picture taken with a famous personality or politician, and this photo is used in their marriage profile (bio-data). Similar to pamphlets and posters, wedding invitations also have the slogan, '*Jai Telangana, Jai Jai Telangana*' printed on the card.

The researcher had the opportunity to attend two student wedding receptions, both of which were held on campus and were open to the entire university. To be sure, these were ideal opportunities to witness a unique tradition among activists as well as meet new activists. Everyone proudly introduced themselves and their association with the Telangana movement and exchanged their visiting cards. Most of the cards labelled their role as state president or chairman, Osmania University-Joint Action Committee (OU-JAC) or TS-JAC, and at the same time, as office bearer of Madiga Student Federation (MSF) or Telangana Student Front (TSF), and so on. Nearly all visiting cards are printed in English. This indicates a political aspiration to connect with all political leadership, especially to the ruling party ruling at the centre. The cards also show their pride in declaring themselves part of the Telangana movement. Ever-present is the OU logo and the slogan *Jai Telangana* (Long Live Telangana). When asked 'why only *Jai Telangana*, why not *Jai Osmania?*', an activist replied, 'See brother, everyone knows that we [students] all are from Osmania. But our visiting cards are temporary. We are fighting for our Telangana identity which is our permanent affiliation. We have printed our dream and our goal on these cards, *Jai Telangana!*'

Such a prompt reply makes one think how seasoned these activists have become in delivering memorable sound bites, easily quotable, and digestible by the media.

Interestingly, out of the 47 student activists from the 2009 agitations who were surveyed, 40 were married with children. Three got married as fieldwork was conducted and four were bachelors, including one who has taken an oath that he 'will never marry, but will serve the people of Telangana as a political leader'. Such is the dedication to the movement, but more importantly, it points to how the movement affected all aspects of life. Marriage, personal appearance and dress, vocation and lifestyle were all confronted with the mission of Telangana independence.

Among left-wing students, there is also a trend to oppose traditional forms of rituals and celebrations. There were occasions when the Left students were married after a public talk or seminar organized by their party. With little preparation or arrangements, they exchange garlands in front of a small gathering, as a token of marriage. Left parties and Dalit students of Osmania campuses have set such examples to oppose the traditional ritualistic way of marrying, with dowry and pomp and show. A Progressive Democratic Student Union (PDSU) activist describes his marriage experience, 'I had such a simple marriage, in a seminar. After all the speeches by our teachers, we exchanged our garland and everyone clapped and greeted us. My parents were at the stage. My wife is from Andhra region … we faced lots of difficulties but then after we had our baby, things started getting better.'

Such programmes on campus hailed a new culture among activists that that made a social statement. This was one of many cultural contributions credited to the Telangana movement. An activist, Murali, whose brother committed suicide in 2010 due to poverty, shared a philosophy behind the trend of simple celebrations:

> Peasants and common masses are committing suicide in Telangana due to poverty and it is ironic to see that people are spending lavishly in their wedding functions. What is the use of this education if we cannot think about the situation of our fellow human beings? I am happy at least our Osmania students are trying to bring cultural change by introducing new rituals.[2]

This new cultural pattern is unique among students of Osmania and is partially resulted out of consciousness provided by the movements. It is also interesting to note how all aspects of their lives, including the act of marriage, take place within campus space, with the university community serving as a surrogate family. Such celebrations inspire other students to emulate these practices and join the cause. They also influence and change thinking around dowry and inter-caste marriages, beyond the walls of campus.

IDENTITY NETWORKS AND ACTIVISM ON CAMPUS

Networks played an essential role in the mass movement for Telangana statehood. Students were mobilized on their cultural identity of belonging to Telangana as well as their caste background, since the vast majority of students at OU belong to other backward classes (OBC), scheduled caste (SC), and scheduled tribe (ST) communities. Melucci (1985, 1986) places great emphasis on the role of everyday processes of networking, learning, and construction of meaning in a social movement. Networks are consciously organized to protest and demonstrate. Everyday practices can 'develop and establish relationship of cooperation, learning a culture of experimentation with political idea about everyday life'[3] (Yates 2015: 238). The everyday life of an activist in a university campus influences students and shapes their aspirations for Telangana state. What follows is an account of one activist the researcher observed. It demonstrates the web of networks an activist creates around himself, in order to 'get the work of the movement done', as they say.

> The day is 14th April, the birth anniversary of Dr B.R. Ambedkar, the father of the Indian Constitution. It is a busy day for Manish as he

is invited to speak at six different programmes. He wakes up around 8:30 a.m. with the sound of flipping of newspaper pages, as his three roommates are reading the news coverage of the previous day's function which they all attended. As his phone rings, Manish leaves his room, his toothbrush sticking out of his mouth as he greets his hostel mates. Manish is the general-secretary of the Telangana Student Union and a leader of the OU-JAC. As a Dalit leader, he has been invited in his village to participate in another programme organized by the district committee of the Telangana Rashtra Samiti. There are three parallel programmes running in Arts College entitled 'Ambedkar's Idea on Separate State', 'Ambedkar and Social Justice', and 'Ambedkar's Ideas on Nation'. Manish has not prepared any speech yet, but he is not too worried. He gives up searching for material on Google, as it is all in English, which he struggles with. He finds online speeches on Ambedkar by activist Professors Kancha Ilaiah and Kodandaram and begins taking notes in Telugu. Meanwhile, he receives call after call from the various programme organizers, reminding him of the programmes. He reassures them he will come. The first programme is scheduled for 10 a.m. but he doesn't plan to arrive before 12:30 p.m. First, he needs to visit his party's office to show his face—one doesn't get far in politics if one does not network with the big leaders. To display his status, he brings ten students with him. One of them arranges for a big car. They arrive at 11:30 a.m. There are around 100 people waiting for their leader to come. In the mean-time, Manish introduces himself to many other student leaders and popular main-stream leaders with his visiting cards. He constantly receives phone calls and continues to reassure them that he is on his way. Finally, the party leader comes around 1:30 p.m. and has lunch with party workers. After lunch, the party leader distributes T-shirts printed with Ambedkar's image. Around 3 p.m., he returns to Arts College to attend the programme organized by the Girijana student association which was supposed to start at 10 a.m. and end at 1 p.m. The organisers make way for him through the audience up to the dais. He spends one hour listening to other speakers before he gives a 10-minute speech. He immediately leaves for another programme at Nizam College. At 5 p.m., he gives a press statement with seven other student leaders at Arts College regarding separate Telangana. This lasts about an hour. There is yet another programme organized by the Gulla Kulam Student Front, but Manish is not able to attend. At 10 p.m., after having dinner with students from the Madiga Student Forum, he returns to his room. He is greeted by three guests—none of whom he has met before—but who were sent by one of his close activist friends. He goes to another friend's

> room to sleep. He is welcomed warmly and they go for tea with six junior students from another hostel. They chat and smoke for two hours. The discussion centres on the activists' struggle to approach and curry favour with politicians. Around 2 a.m., he goes to his bed while checking Facebook for comments and likes to his recent posts.

Student leaders do not attend any programme alone—there is always a group of students who forms an entourage. They assist with receiving phone calls for him and arranging his schedule. They never say no to any request; 'Yes, anna. Sure, anna' is their answer to every call. Manish explains why this is so: 'Anna, this is all about maintaining good relations and meeting new people. We work in different organisations but are connected. We all are the same. We all struggle for the separate statehood for Telangana'. As a student leader, Manish is well aware that he needs to devote substantial time networking. Networking is an important aspect of student politics, especially in movements. Manish dresses every morning in the same clothing: blue jeans and a white shirt with a pocket, where he keeps his smartphone. He belongs to a poor family from a rural area of Nalagonda district in Telangana. The happiest moment of his life was gaining admission in OU as an MA student. It took him two years to prepare for the entrance exam. He explains:

> I came to Hyderabad with only one aim: to study in Arts College. I stayed with one of my friends for a few months. It was expensive living in the city. I used to come here to Osmania to learn from students how to crack the entrance exam. I also started preparing for competitive exams. When I got admission in Telugu literature, that day I was so happy when I told this news to my family, they distributed sweets in my village. Living in the capital and having your own room is the most important thing in one's life. Slowly, I began mixing with all kinds of students and parties and now I know people in politics, media, bureaucracy, police and academia. Recently in my brother's wedding, I invited all the big names in Telangana and they all came to attend the reception.

For the majority of OU activists, their first visit to Hyderabad is once they have gained admission to Osmania. As many come from villages and towns across Telangana, the shift is significant. It is matter of pride for their families and relatives to be part of the capital city. Settling in Hyderabad is equated with making valuable connections and being part of a cosmopolitan network. However, after students arrive in the city, they quickly become aware of the level of competition they face in exams, jobs, and housing and the marriage market.

NETWORKING AT WORK

OU is considered the most popular and prestigious university in the region. Almost 85 per cent of students come from the Telangana region and the rest are from Hyderabad.[4] Most students who join OU are products of the Andhra Pradesh Residential School system, which has branches across the state. Students who earn the state scholarship receive free education and lodging in these schools. A large section of these students who come to Osmania belong to economically lower-class families, and are the first in their family to attend a university. At OU, they become members of the Andhra Pradesh Residential School Alumnus Association on campus. There is a feeling of solidarity and friendship among this group, especially as most of them are SCs or STs. Explaining the reason behind this, Amar,[5] an activist from a radical student group recounts:

> During our school days, some Leftist groups used to come and distribute their pamphlets on various social problems. The content in the pamphlets was so radical and anti-government but was very appealing to us. These pamphlets enhanced our understanding about activism and Telangana problems. In their speeches they used to mention Osmania University and its history of producing radical activists. The first time I got to know about George Reddy who was a brilliant scholar and Left ideologue in 1970s; but he was shot dead by the Right-wing in his hostel. That scene was just imprinted in my mind. I was so excited to read about such leaders. My group of friends started dreaming of studying in Osmania.

Because of their exposure to these ideologues, students who graduate from these schools have a heightened awareness of Telangana issues and are sympathetic to the cause for statehood. That, combined with the solidarity they experience when arriving at OU and the intense activism on campus, serves to crystallize their involvement in the movement.

For every movement to survive, enlisting new members to sustain the activism is crucial. Predictably, thousands of new students arriving on campus every July become the target of activists' recruitment efforts. Building trust is of prime importance, and various student groups compete for this trust. Social networks are important channels for the recruitment of new students. Diani and McAdam (2003: 33) explain the structural function of networks as it operates in two organizations studied. They hypothesized that the individuals who have social ties with people already involved in a movement organization are more likely to become involved in that organization. But for newcomers who are not 'connected', trust becomes an important aspect before joining an organization.[6] Trust keeps the movement spirit going, despite the 'ebbs and flows of social interactions' (Diani and McAdam 2003: 36).

Activists from different parties on campus compete to win the trust of 'new comer' students. Deepak, an ST student who comes from a lower middle-class family, states:

> Telangana issue is very genuine and we are so concerned about having a separate state. But I had never thought that I will be so actively involved in the movement and sacrifice my academic career. Sometimes I feel that I was not meant for leadership but it was due to the police and government attitude towards us which makes us activists. I remember during 2009–2010 agitations, police registered some cases against us. My name also came in the list as protesters. When I saw my name, I was shocked to see that every possible criminal charge was made against us. I had sleepless nights. My dream of joining into academics was shattering. I had no other option except stick with the activists and running after court and politicians to remove my charges. We had only one hope that if Telangana comes, we will get rid of these charges.

When new students take admission at Arts College (as well as other colleges), activists greet students at the time of admission and offer assistance. They provide them with free university admission booklets which feature various student parties. For a new student, it is the first exposure to campus politics.

All student organizations 'publish' their own information booklets. Though they all contain the same information—the university syllabus and fee structure—the cover page is added by student unions who wish to advertise their party. Interestingly, for this rather costly coloured printing, student unions find sponsors, which are generally the owners of private engineering or medical colleges. This helps student unions cover the cost of these publications. These booklets attract new students who come from rural areas, as they think it is the official university booklet and that the student union is an official university entity. Interestingly, OU does not have any official unions; since 1988, student union elections have been banned. Yet, even without any formal student unions, activism remained alive and flourished due to students' unwavering commitment to the Telangana cause. Moreover, the university itself proved to be a safe and nurturing haven for the 'business' of movement activism.

For activists, 'new students' are not only those who are enrolled in the university but also those who prepare to enter the following year and who currently stay in the OU hostels illegally as 'non-boarders'. Non-boarders are usually enrolled in a coaching centre to prepare for a range of competitive exams. These coaching centres charge a sizable tuition fee—unaffordable for poor, rural students. OU student activists help these students gain admission in coaching centres. They bargain with the coaching centres' director or manager to lower the fee by almost half. In some cases, they are able to get a full fee waiver. This is the strategy to win the trust of newcomers and gain their support. Activists invest their time in helping them, banking on the fact that they will inevitably wind up at the university. Many youths who try to survive in expensive city like Hyderabad will sooner or later aspire to become a university student to get subsidized accommodation. Once they join OU, activists can count on their participation and backing whenever there is a call for any rally or agitation. In fact, some student leaders have used their unions' power to establish a nexus between coaching centres and student unions. Campus walls are flooded with advertisements for coaching institutes.

Geographic location has also been an important aspect for any kind of networking. Crossley (2012) states that urbanization had this effect because it drew large groups of individuals with similar interests together, allowing them to form networks and thereby to influence one another, organize and mount collective actions. He suggests that university campuses have a similar effect. Thousands of Osmania students reside beyond the hostel area in three areas called Taranaka, Uppal, and Basti. They are a stone's throw from campus, and are home to many students after they get married. Even then, they continue making use of their allotted room on campus until the submission of their doctoral thesis. As per the flexible university rules, there is no fixed deadline for PhD thesis submission. 'Career' student activists are by-products of this policy, which contributes to the way in which the university serves as a fertile site of resistance.

Types of Networks

Like other campuses, national and regional political parties have established student wings in OU, all of which support the movement for separate Telangana. In 2013, there were more than twenty major parties on campus. Activism from the National Congress Party's student wing, National Student Union of India (NSUI),[7] spiked in 2009, when the Indian government indicated Telangana state formation was imminent. The Bahujan Student Front (BSF), the unofficial student wing[8] of the Bahujan Samaj Party (BSP), failed to gain traction despite the dominance of SC/ST/OBC students on campus. This may be due to the party's limited vote bank in the state. Due to their ambiguous stand on Telangana, the Bhartiya Janata Party (BJP) and Telugu Desam Party (TDP) were comparatively late in the game in establishing their student unions on campus; they changed their stance several times before eventually supporting the movement.[9]

However, many left-wing student parties had the similar ambiguities, causing disillusion among students. According to activists, it was because of 'ideological differences'. However, analysing the number of divisions and groups, it appears to be personal differences within leadership rather than ideological. Therefore, some activists, after working in several left groups, began to work independently in search of a political mentor. Gaddar, a 1972 alumnus and dedicated leader, gained popularity as a revolutionary face of the movement. Masses regard his contribution to the movement. Similarly, Rasmai Balkrishnan (the founder of a cultural group called Dhoom-Dhaam), and Akala Bhumaiah also had a huge fan following on campus. Each activist maintains his own personal network that extends beyond the campus.

The oldest student wing working on campus is PDSU.[10] It gained popularity on campus because of its committed leadership and visionary approach post-Telangana politics. It questions that post-separate statehood, how would the government solve the problems of unemployment, farmers' suicide, land issues, and so on. It helped the students to understand and be aware of the Telangana politicians who are upper caste feudal lords. PDSU's approach has been to make students understand and highlight the likelihood of a Telangana state which would be 'as gloomy as it is now because it would be a power transfer from Andhra capitalists to Telangana feudal lords', according to Rajesh, one of the OU-JAC leaders. To some extent, the ideological networking does try to answer the larger questions but there is no mobilization on this basis. The divide between the Left and the Right also seems blurred. In every existing ideology, the membership and leadership is largely of lower-caste students who also represent the separate Telangana movement and other significant issues such as reservation, caste atrocities, and caste injustice.

Where student parties failed, JACs flourished. JACs are the best example of mobilization process of the movement and one of the most organic. JAC has been an ideal framework for the movement to reach out to the masses. This trend can also be looked as a democratization process within movement institution. This democratic representation among the students reflected in their mobilization and unionization. Therefore, by the end of 2012, there were voices from every caste, religion, and cultural front. Such collectivities have identity-sets, according to Oommen (2010: 38). They have multiple identities. JAC represented those whom Oommen would define as 'the dominated and stigmatised are in search of dignity which democracy promises but does not always deliver' (Oommen 2010: 42). A democracy cannot function if the institutional logic of the system is made subservient to the personal ambition or the ideological predilections of political leaders (Varshney 1998: 44). JAC served as an ideal equalizer between personal ambition of student leaders and their commitment to the demand of separate Telangana.

Caste-Based Networks

A new student's initial network tends to form easily on the basis of one's affiliation to their hometown or village, caste, or alma mater. Each caste organization on campus organizes welcome parties—'Freshers' Welcome'—for new students. Gradually, new Osmanians become well informed on Telangana's problems and politics and join the cause. Whenever there is a call for strike, rally, or protest, these networks make the mobilization easier for activists.

Gradually, caste issues and interests started taking precedence in Telangana student politics. Melucci (cited in Diani and McAdam 2003:

306–7) argues that '"who identifies whom and is identified by whom as part of a movement" is an interesting question …' However, caste controls their known circle and limits their personal networks. But to make close connections, a student leader connects with new students in different ways:

1. Arranging admissions for new students in the schools and colleges and especially coaching centre. Activists help the concerned students who are unable to pay high fees of private colleges or coaching centres for civil services. The student leaders talk to the director of the college and try to settle down fees and other expenses. Sometimes he is able to get these students full fee concession. As the majority of students prepare for group I and group II services, they study by themselves and avoid taking coaching. But arranging for coaching classes at affordable rates is the best medium for an activist to win favour from new students.
2. With their political connection, student activists help the common students to get an ad-hoc job in the degree college as a lecturer. This is another way to attract the common students and win their trust. There is a huge number of such jobs. Colleges in Hyderabad have more than 50 per cent ad-hoc staff.

As stated earlier, the vast majority of students on campus belong to lower castes (STs, SCs, and OBCs). By 2013, there were more than 50 subcastes represented on campus. As a result, more than 15 major caste organizations were formed. Caste solidarity works at a much deeper level than any other form of identity or ideology. In Telangana, the largest population among SCs are the Madigas. Because of the organization, *Madiga Reservation Porata Samiti* (MRPS), which later became a movement, their platform is wholly tied to caste. The MRPS emerged against the dominance of Malas in government jobs and therefore their demand centred on creating a subcategorization of reservation. As the largest beneficiaries of reservation policy, Malas have the highest cultural capital among SCs. Many of them are journalists, writers, academicians, and politicians.

The MRPS movement originated in 1994 with a demand of reservation on the basis of subcategorization. Thereafter, sub-caste leadership began to emerge and by 2010 it was much more prevalent in politics.[11] MRPS formed its student wing, the MSF, on campus.

Student leader Vengapalli Srinivas was instrumental in its formation. Many villages where Madiga students came from hoisted a flag of MRPS to counter the TRS flag. After MSF, there were other popular caste groups such as BC Sankshema Sangam (founded by Ramarao), Telangana Girijana Vidyarthi Sangam (TGVS; founded by Nehru Naik), Bahujan Student Union, Telangana Praja Front, and Telangana Bahujan Vidyarthi Vedika.

Ajay, a history student spoke about his experience:

> When I came to this hostel, I did not know anybody. I had no friends. Then I got to know that if I have to get an ad-hoc job, I had to make friends with the student leaders. I attended dozens of their program to just be in their eyes. Many times, I had to mobilise students for their programs. It took me few months to get to know everybody and then I started approaching them for this job. Finally, I got it through their approach. Now, for the past three years, I have been teaching ad-hoc. But still I have shown loyalty towards them. If they ask for any help or money, I give them. I have to be part of the movement as they assure us that if our own state Telangana is formed, we will be getting permanent jobs.

This is an effective network to connect not only with new students but also with those who are aspirants of joining the university. Senior activists try to bring new students from their own villages and their relatives to prepare them for activism. Thus, Osmania activists have approached students from different venues. After all, the formations on campus are not solely for the mobilization for Telangana; there were other issues which were contributing to this activism.

Campus Political Networks

Osmania activists have established their network nationally and globally. They try to connect with every possible state and country where Telangana people reside and encourage them to form their JAC. Student groups who are affiliated by the mainstream political parties get some amount of funding from their parent party. For example, TRS, TDP, and NSUI invest some money in such organization. These student leaders have to keep meeting the local head or their parent party. Every leader has a bike and has to run around. There is no rest for a leader. If there is any call from the party regarding protest, they have to mobilize students and organize protests on own his own. 'We collect money from professors and also from students to organise these protests', says Mohit, a leader from NSUI. 'I am emotionally attached with the movement, I sacrificed everything for this movement with this hope that we will work only when we will get our own separate state'.

Himesh,[12] a Telugu literature student who writes all the pamphlets for his OBC organization explain the ideology of the movement:

> Now, the movement is not limited to Telangana only. It has brought a cultural revolution. We are opposing the celebration of Ganesh Chaturthi on campus. We are celebrating Mahisaur, Ravana, Hidimba etc. We projected our Telangana icon Komaram Bheem along with Phule, Ambedkar and Periyar. We want Dalit-Bhaujan Telangana where power should be in our hand. On the other hand, TRS wants power, they don't care about Telangana.

However, Jitendra, a Telangana Rashtra Samiti Vidyarthi Vibhagam (TRSV) ideologue, says, 'people give different argument saying that irrespective of politics, we have to first get our Telangana. But these communist and other ideologies are delaying this process. They don't understand what we are saying that let Telangana come into existence and then you can fight for whatever you want'.

Apart from the political differences, TRSV actively participated in all the rallies and marches organized by the JAC such as *Chalo Assembly; Chalo Parliament; Chalo Delhi; Chalo Hyderabad*; Million March; *Vidyarthi Garjana, Vidyathi Mahagarjana*, and so on. Beyond their caste, class, and ideological difference, students and common masses actively participate in all of these protests. The common goal of achieving their statehood evoked regional sentiments. The intensity of these protests can be better understood when we compare it with the Jai Andhra movement that emerged only to counter Telangana movement.

K. Srinivasulu, who is now a retired engineer but was actively involved in the 1969 activism, claims:

> What makes an activist is his ideological commitment to the issue. Ideology can be anything but one has to be committed honestly which requires lots of sacrifice. In case of Andhra, we don't see a single leader, professor, Chancellor or anybody from the any district coming out and devote their life for united Andhra. They give press statement and then disappear. They are all over the media because it is their media,

> with their small protests in Hyderabad. We lost thousands of people but they call our demand political. Isn't this ironic, that we are nowhere in mainstream politics, but we are 'political' for them who have ruined our movement and our politics.

Expressing similar anger, the former principal of Arts College, remembers a time during 2009–10 agitation:

> I was getting calls from the politicians, from police, from media about how to tackle the student agitation in front of Arts College. I had to save students' life and also control their anger. I tried my best to provide them what I could as the issues they were fighting were larger but nobody could imagine their vision. I had complete trust on students.

Media also played an important part in making the claim of Telangana movement at the national and global level. However, the ownership of media was another question which was raised by the movement leaders. When the question of Andhra ownership came into existence, the question of caste also emerged at the same time. An activist highlights the lack of equity: 'Isn't it ironic that each time we have to go to Andhra businessmen to publish our pamphlet and poster for our anti-Andhra protest, because they have big printing establishment. This is a question to ask why we [from Telangana] were not given equal representation in business by the government. Are we lazy or are they afraid of us?'

Table 3.1 provides a picture of the Andhra upper-caste dominance in media. All the 15 major media houses in Andhra Pradesh are controlled by the upper-caste Andhra businessmen.

Such data was mentioned by speakers in public talks on Telangana held at Arts College. Student activists collected data on caste and discussed it in their meetings. The movement eventually entangled with the caste–class issue. The cultural difference and regional imbalances are further accentuated by the alliances among the upper castes[13] (Bheenaveni 2013). With the consciousness of Andhra ownership, a large section of students started boycotting Andhra films. Amit, a PhD student of economics and a left-wing activist, starts his day by reading a minimum three newspapers. He spoke of the effect of the boycott on news coverage in the region: 'Since we decided to boycott Andhra films, Andhra media got scared and they started covering news on Telangana. Since our Telangana businessmen started one newspaper called *Namastey Telangana*, it posed a challenge for the Andhra newspapers.

TABLE 3.1 Andhra Upper-Caste Dominance in Media

	Media House	Ownership
1	Enadu	Kamma
2	Vaartha	Vaishya
3	Saakshi	Reddy
4	Andhra Jyoti	Vaishya
5	Andhra Prabha	Vaishya
6	Andhra Bhoomi	Reddy
7	Prajashakti	Reddy
8	Vishalandhra	Reddy
9	Deccan Chronicle	Reddy
10	ETV	Kamma
11	TV9	Kamma/Raju/Reddy
12	TV 5	Kamma
13	Gemini	Kamma
14	NTV	Kamma
15	Maa TV	Raju, Kapu/Kamma

Source: Various pamphlets published by the student organizations.

This is their business strategy. For businessmen, people's emotions are business and nothing else.'

The movement's dynamics manifested as 'us' *vs.* 'them'. The region, as a source of inspiration, evoked activists' aspirations. There were many activists who took oaths, pledging allegiance to an independent Telangana by not cutting their beard until Telangana is formed,[14] 'not joining any government job until Telangana gets its own government', and 'not celebrating any Andhra festivals'. As Reddy (2009: 165) puts it, 'A feeling of the time has come when people should belong first to Telangana and then to their parents'.

Over the past four decades, social movement studies have explored the linkage between the context of social movement and political opportunity. The concept of political opportunity structure is 'in danger of becoming a sponge that soaks up every aspect of the social movement environment' (Gamson and Meyer 1996: 275). Scholars (Meyer and Corrigall-Brown 2005; Tarrow 1998; Tilly 1978) suggest studying social movement coalition politics and the role of political context on shaping such coalition. JAC as a social movement organization is akin to the process whereby individuals join social movements, involving an assessment of cost, benefits, and identity. As the political context changes, the cost and benefits are assessed differently, and for this reason, actively engaged coalitions are difficult to sustain over a long period as circumstances change.

Student leaders tend to have a few student helpers with them at all times. Functioning as personal assistants, these students serve as the 'right hand' to the leaders by maintaining their daily schedules, Facebook accounts, looking after guests, and planning for events. Those who are fluent enough in English are tasked with replying to official correspondence. These helpers play an important role in enabling the movement by empowering leading activists to multitask and broaden their network. They also serve as gatekeepers to the activists they serve. Like a well-oiled machine, students at OU plan, strategize, and execute their plans with a thoroughness of mainstream politicians. Rakesh, a Leftist activist, comments in a lighter note: 'These student helpers volunteer their time and energy with the hope of benefitting from it later. In fact, they also write their leader's doctoral thesis.' A political science professor agrees to this saying:

> Many times students who are into working in jobs in the city or outside the city, don't get time to work for their thesis. Such students generally pay money to some needy student who writes thesis for them. We know all this is happening but we remain silent because there is issue of survival for majority of students. Not everyone gets fellowship.

The researcher befriended a student named Srinivas, who later introduced him to one of the main student (JAC) leaders, Rajiv. After dinner in the mess hall, he took the researcher to meet Rajiv in his room. The scene was as follows:

There were five men in the room and only two of them were OU students. Rajiv was on the phone, talking loud in Telugu. Ramu, lanky and long haired, was uploading pictures to update Rajiv's Facebook. Another was a student leader around 38 years of age, while the others were in their late 40s. In the small single room, there were two beds. Three men were sleeping on the floor, one of whom was a mess worker who provides food to Rajiv and his friends. One wall was dominated by a big framed picture showing Rajiv addressing a student rally during the main agitation of 2010 at Arts College. There were also pictures of Ambedkar, Kanshi Ram, and Mayawati adorning the other walls. Ramu, started showing all the newspaper cuttings and pictures of agitations where Rajiv's name was mentioned. It was a thick file of more than 100 pages and each page contained a minimum of 3 news clippings.

Pointing to his picture, Rajiv explains in broken Hindi:

> This was the most important part of the student movement. When we started *Padayatra* and reached the villages, women greeted us by washing our feet with milk. This news was widely circulated in the media. It was the best moment of our life; when we felt that the common masses trusted us more than politicians.

Ramu, fixing his hair with his right hand, interrupts in his broken English and says, 'I was also there and experiencing all of this and realised the importance of a mass movement. I became a full-fledged activist and started working with anna (Rajiv). Anna is the most dedicated leader and we want to see him get into politics'.

Rajiv is also known for his commitment to the movement and decided not to get married. He declared that he will sacrifice his life for the public. He comes from an economically poor family and is a first-generation learner. In 2009, he became an important voice of the movement and has been a part of various Dalit ideological streams and a member of the SC/ST student union and the Bahujan Student Forum. He is influenced by Ambedkar, Kanshi Ram, and Mayawati, and dreams of meeting the latter. 'My student supporters want me to fight [politically]. I am getting some offers [from political parties]. My intention is not to get fame; rather I want to just represent my people so the real issues can come in the forefront. I want to live and die for Telangana'.

There are student activists who follow Rajiv's ideas on Telangana as they think he is a 'down to earth' person and will listen to everyone. He helps poor students gain admission in colleges and coaching centres. The support from students motivates him and nurtures his political aspirations.

Similarly, there are other student leaders who also consider themselves equal to Rajiv but their fan following is not as strong as his. Dr Surya, a professor at Osmania, shares his opinion about Rajiv: 'Rajiv as a student leader is popular for his simplicity and humbleness among common students. Poor students see him as one of them'. In a university campus, a student leader's image primarily depends on rapport building, within the dormitory space she or he lives in; and secondly her or his affiliation with a particular political party.

HOSTEL AS AN ABODE FOR CAREER ACTIVISTS

During their campus stay, students spend a considerable time in the hostel. Osmania campus has 24 hostels, and most of them are named after Indian rivers: Godavari (A), Krishnaveni (B), Kaveri (C), Thungbhadra (D), Gowthami (E), Bhagirathi (Old PG), Narmada Research Scholar Hostel (NRSH), Yamuna (New PG), Maneru Hostel, Pinakini, Manjeera, Kinnera, Ganga, Swarnamuk, Sabari, Sutlej, Gomathi, Saraswathi, Pranahita, Triveni, BEd Hostel, Hi-Tech Hostel, Technology Hostel, and the Ladies Hostel.

A hostel named E-1 (Gouthami hostel) is located in front of Law College on the busiest road of the campus. This hostel is located just 20 paces away from the main road. The area between hostel and the main road is bordered by low bushes and small trees. In this semi-private area, some students bathe in the open in front of the hostel. This is the everyday scene of life in hostels, though it may look like a village scene.

There are separate hostels for research scholars and postgraduate students. One of the important aspects of hostel life is that there are more 'outsiders' in the hostels than 'insiders' or enrolled students. Outsiders are also referred to as 'non-boarders' while hostel students are called 'boarders'. There is no strict rule on campus so almost each and every room, which is allotted to one person officially, has two or three people. In some of the older hostels, rooms are comparatively large and allotted to three students, but oftentimes more than five people live there. During fieldwork, the researcher found that nearly every room hosted at least one non-boarder, and if the room belonged to a student leader, they often accommodated as many as four guests. This is what makes this hostel life a community. Since the hostel mess hall only serves food to boarders, many students and their guests cook together in their rooms. They have cooking utensils and a small gas stove to prepare food in the room. An electric rice cooker is present in nearly every room. During a focus group discussion, a senior activist stated that 'until 2005, when there used to be lots of Andhra students, hostels were providing Andhra meals, but gradually we started boycotted their food item'. Plain rice, daal or sambhar, and home-made pickle make up their staple diet, which they generally consume together sitting on the floor. On some special occasions, they cook meat. Normally, there is a trend to take a 'power nap' after lunch. Around 5 pm, students start going out of the hostels to meet and socialize. The presence of the non-boarders helps in creating a 'collective consciousness' as they have ample time to spend among students and become part of the campus community. Consuming alcohol is not common among students, and for many, it is an expensive habit. However, non-activist students believe that student leaders have their dinner in big hotels, enjoying 'biryani and whisky'.

Due to widespread friendships and a deep sense of community, some non-boarders keep their belongings in one friend's room, may dine in another friend's room, and sleep in yet another's room. These non-boarders generally range in age from 25 to 35 years. Despite being employed in the city, their main goal is to gain admission to OU. During their stay, they inevitably become involved in the protests and rallies being held, and this deepens their interest in officially becoming a part of the university. Thus, the hostel serves as an ideal residence for outsiders where they come to know and bond student activists who may eventually help them securing a better future.

Student activists generally spend their mornings reading the Telugu newspapers to understand the political dynamics. Accordingly, they plan their protests and strategize. For example, if any political party leader gives any anti-Telangana statement, student leaders of different parties will gather and burn the effigy of that person. They arrange press conferences in front of Arts College and try to highlight the issue to mobilize student population.

During the day, non-boarders who are not employed prepare for the civil service and other competitive exams in their room or in the library. Some of them take coaching classes nearby. This is done concurrently with preparing for the OU entrance test for Arts College to get a hostel room. During their stay, they read more about Telangana movement and its history. Their stay in hostels makes them more aware about the Telangana movement. They actively participate in the agitations and rallies. There are many activists who are non-boarders but people know them as a student leader. While interviewing some student leaders, the researcher also found out such cases.

In front of boys' hostels, specifically Narmada Research Scholars (NRS), a barber sets himself under a tree with his tools: an old style wooden chair, a mirror, shaving cream and a knife, some branded shave lotions, and cream. He charges Rs 10 for a haircut, much cheaper than the market rates. On the other side of hostel, there is a tea shop or dhaba. From morning to evening, different vendors come to sell fresh vegetables and different snacks door to door. The scene conjures a feeling of a village community where interpersonal communication and interdependency is very strong. People know each other's private and public lives. At OU, hostel life is akin to living at home, embedded in local practices and customs.

Food vendors come right in front of NRS hostel. There is a long queue of vendors on their cycles and mopeds in the morning between 8 and 10 am. They sell south Indian food items such as idli, vada, *dosa*, and puri for breakfast. Interestingly, none of these vendors come from the Telangana region; they are originally from the Andhra region. During the 2009 movement for separate Telangana, when the university closed the hostels[15] and the mess hall to curb the movement and closed down the roads, these vendors managed to hide from the police and reach the hostels on their small bikes and supply food to the students. Though they were caught many times by the police; they paid bribes and continued coming to the campus.

In the 2009 agitations, some hostels received lot of fame as they were featured in the news. Osmania hostels turned into war rooms. Students organized themselves into groups, brainstormed over protest programmes, and resolved not to let the fight fizzle out, as was the media's running headlines during the agitation. The most popular hostel is NRS, which is also known as Dr B.R. Ambedkar Hostel. It has been the hallowed abode of all Telangana activists and student leaders, as every other room in NRS has a different student union or members of different JACs. It is difficult to make out exactly how many groups exist as every individual has a membership of multiple unions.

Generally, university space is known for its academic activities. In the case of OU, it is known for its leading role and active participation in the movement. Every site of the campus offers some kind of history and students proudly relate themselves with campus site. 'I belong to the hostel where George Reddy used to stay' or 'the main leader of the movement is my neighbour in the hostel' is how activists explain where they live, when speaking with an outsider.

As per the university rules, if a student gets government or permanent employment, he must vacate the hostel. Yet, since so many students do not gain employment or only temporary or contract based, many linger beyond their degree or take years to complete their studies. Their Telangana identity and their affiliation with the movement also delays their departure from student life and entry to the workforce. In this sense, having free shelter and subsidized food can make this struggle more manageable. Many professors acknowledge the trend on public university campuses in India of students not leaving the campus until they have government jobs. Some even stay on after getting into job, residing illegally/unofficially in the hostel. Therefore, the hostel serves as a space not merely for accommodation but as a survival space for unemployed youth—boarders and non-boarders alike. In other words, the institutional space shared by non-institutional people also makes it a more open and 'public' space.

In OU, students join any course (irrespective of their interest) to get into Arts College. During interactions with non-activist students, the researcher found[16] that there is a term affectionately called a 'food course' (a medium used to stay in hostel and get hostel food). Once they get in the university, they continue to prepare for another subject for another MA, to remain a student. There are cases where students have enrolled in a master's degree *after* completing their PhD for the sole purpose of remaining in the hostels. As a result, the dean of students of the Arts College recently added to the hostel rules a provision that those who are undertaking the same degree for a second time will be given the last preference for the hostel. Thus, the academic space is a pull factor for use of and access to the non-academic benefits (food and lodging). Comparing it with his time, former Arts College principal, Professor P.L.V. Rao,[17] states:

> If government does not create jobs, there will be no food to eat, no food for thought. Not only Masters, but PhD is used as a food course in Arts College. In our time, master degree was enough to get you a decent job, but now I see doctoral students are applying for fourth class jobs. This is the state of affair of our university education. There is no research or innovation.

The majority of students in the social sciences have access to free hostels, which provide water, electricity, wireless internet connection, and subsidized food. Their degree takes a backseat to preparation for state-wide competitive exams for administrative jobs. To tackle this situation, the university eliminated the two-year MPhil course and offers only a direct PhD after MA. However, the problem of overstaying in the hostels was not resolved chiefly due to the extremely low ratio of PhD submissions, aided by the university's policy (or lack therefore) of a deadline to submit theses. According to the records of the political science department at Arts College, from 2003–12, there has been an extremely low ratio of doctoral submissions. Students have taken admission and they tend to stay enrolled until they get a government job. This is affecting the new students as they do not get rooms in the hostel because the earlier occupant is not ready to finish his/her studies and leave their room. The problem is more serious among PhD students who are not allotted a hostel. It is very difficult to get a room in a hostel like NRS which is a single-seater hostel. Interestingly, all of the residents belong to SC or OBC. There are very few upper-caste students in the social sciences. To get a room, one needs to have a good network, and usually these are along caste lines. According to Sunil, one of the respondents from NRS hostel, 'the student who was previously living in this room was an OBC. Before giving his room to me, he made sure that I also belong to the OBC community and this is an unwritten law one has to follow.' Even after knowing this fact, students want to live and enjoy the rich political culture of this hostel. NRS hostel, built in 1979, is called the 'headquarters' of different student parties.

The hostel space also became instrumental in students' expression of their feeling as Telangana *Prajalu*. During the 2009 movement, hundreds of students wrote about their experiences, their emotional attachment with the movement. There are many students who have written more than 10 books during their stay in the hostel. One student has written 40 books, describing his feelings about Telangana. The hostel provides a sense of community. Popular singers, musicians, writers, composers, artists, and painters have called these hostels their home. There are groups working within hostels which organize monthly meetings to discuss suffering and humiliation faced by the people of Telangana in different regions.

Similarly, the hostel serves as a space for consumption of global technology. Students use YouTube, Facebook, and other sites to get news on Telangana. Living in the hostels where previous generations of activists lived inspires them to read novels, poetry, and writings of said activists. As in recent past, some TV channels like TV6 covered Telangana movement stories attracted students. They frequent the nearby shopping malls and purchase clothing, mobile phones, and watch the latest films. Some have also purchased bikes and financed weddings in their family. Student consumption patterns have changed drastically in recent years due to the rise of market forces coupled with the institution of generous academic scholarships.

Students who receive fellowships often manage to save enough to purchase a motorcycle. It is especially useful for a student leader as it is easier to go around campus and within the city by bike. On an average, there are dozens of bikes parked in front of every hostel.

Interestingly, when we talk about the public university, we think about a life 'subsidized' in terms of its minimum living cost compared to the outside campus space. However, university education opens many career opportunities for the students, especially in the capital. Nevertheless, securing a government job becomes an endless struggle for Osmania students. Private jobs are also hard to get for Osmania students. Harish, a student who works for a Telangana channel which is owned by TRS party shares his experiences: 'When we apply for any private job and face an interview. The minute these [Andhra] people know that we are from Osmania, they won't hire us. For them Osmania campus means only movement'. Such experiences build up anger against the Andhras and create strong solidarity among Telangana activists. 'Our enemy [the Andhra elite] is strong. He has money, he has power. All we have is our commitment for Telangana, our vote for Telangana and the future of Telangana' (Manne 2013: 92).

Dhabas as 'Strategy Forums' of the Movement

University campuses usually have some places for students to socialize, such as tea shops and canteens. In the present time of globalization, one can notice in every university campus a particular kind of modern structure of tea shop, with a cash counter and service window. Contrary to this, Osmania campus has old style tea shops (called '*dhabbas*' or 'dhabas') that are usually temporary kinds of structures—there are no tables and students sit on large stones. Dhabas, especially those within the city, have a culture where people discuss everyday socio-political situations.

Newspaper is also an important part of dhabas. In understanding a university, one can glean as much useful information about academic departments and offerings as one can about the social spaces where students engage in non-academic activities. Tea shops and eateries are some key spaces where student life revolves around on the OU campus. In the evening, students come outside to have tea at dhabas. Mostly, tea shops are called canteens, which have a proper concrete structure.

Tea acts as the social glue among activists. Activists spent a great deal of time socializing at tea shops or dhabas as this helps in building a collective consciousness. In front of every hostel there is a dhaba where students congregate in the evening over a cup of tea and snacks, which is conducive to extended discussions.[18] Most of these discussions centre on the latest news headlines or some personal/family issues where job and marriage are highly debated topics. For students, it is about discussing personal stuff, but for student activists, it is an 'activists' laboratory', where they test the mood of the campus. Even officials from government intelligence department in civil uniform spent hours at the dhabas during strikes and agitations to understand the strategies of the activists. OU Alumni, who are working near the campus area, often come to have tea at these dhabas. Thus, these dhabas serve as 'strategy forums' for student leaders and activists. Discussions at these dhabas sometimes turn so political that in the late evening, many political leaders come to understand the mood of the students. The crowd and intensity of the discussions at these dhabas makes an impression on student leaders and set the tone for their upcoming rally or protest.

Another attractive feature of these dhabas is that student unions hang their posters at these dhabas. On an average two–three new posters appear on these walls every day. Each poster contains the slogan '*Jai Telangana*' on the left side and '*Jai Jai Telangana*' on the other. This gives students something to talk about. Some of these dhabas have the local Telugu newspapers, which provide starting points for students to initiate discussions. The daily news coverage of university student leaders was the most common phenomenon during 2009–13. Strategies for protest marches, rallies, and press statements are discussed primarily at these dhabas. From 5 pm to 8 pm, the dhabas fill up with students and activists. Senior activists bring new students to introduce them to other student leaders. As everyone is from Telangana, it is very easy for student leaders to initiate discussion. New students are impressed to meet student leaders they have heard about in the media. These dhabas serve as a platform for meetings between these new students and long-standing student leaders of the university. Although these student leaders live in hostels, they are often so busy that one must approach them through mutual friends. Their schedules are often long and demanding. They have to update themselves with Telangana issues and be ready with their press statements. Bharat, one of the activists, describes:

> Few years ago, before I joined OU, I came here to see one friend. We met at a dhaba for tea. Suddenly, I saw a senior student leader from my home town that I regard so much, was having tea there. I went to meet him and introduce myself. He was happy to know that I was from his town. He called somebody and introduced me and within half an hour, I met so many students from my hometown. They told me how to crack the exam and get in Osmania. It was only because of that meeting at dhaba that now I am not only an Osmania student but also an activist.

According to Rajiv, the Bahujan Student Union activist, '… [from] 5 p.m. to 8 p.m., I generally spent at dhabas. I come here because everyone wants to meet me. As a senior activist, it does not look good for me to go to every single room and meet new students. But dhaba is the best place to interact with them about our politics on Telangana.'

Monu, another activist from MSF, frequents the dhabas not for refreshment but for the social component. He says, 'Although I don't drink tea but I meet all my friends at dhaba. The beauty of these dhabas is that you meet unexpected faces people every day. I met many students on these dhabas who later became my best friends.'

Sachin, a popular activist who has a huge fan following on campus, explains his experience, 'What I learnt from my experience as an activist is that a leader has to be with masses fully. He has to drink tea with them even if he is in not in mood of having tea. Every action of an activist shapes his image among common students.'

Recruitment to the movement is often achieved by means of pre-existing networks (Snow, Zurcher, and Ekland-Olson 1980), such as friends. Moreover, they are more likely to follow through on expressed interest in political projects where they have friends who do likewise (McAdam 1986). Connections to activists shapes the way in which individuals perceive activism, encouraging assimilation of a positive activist identity (Passy 2001). This connection can occur through many ways. One way is having a friendship with the student leader or activist. In some cases, and despite the low ratio of female activists, love affairs among activists is an important way to stay with the movement.[19] However, the male–female friendship does not happen on the dhabas, as generally, it is male students or activists who meet at these dhabas and smoke cigarettes. A Leftist student, who had been a leading figure in 2009 agitation and was arrested and jailed for few months, explains the significance of dhabas: 'The discussion on these dhabas involve those petty issues that you won't even think in your everyday life but it affects your life. Chai, cigarette, and chatting is what makes an activist'.

Talking about another popular feature of the dhaba culture on Indian campuses, Pathania (2011) writes, 'the combination of tea and cigarettes makes the discussion spirit high, healthy and argumentative'. Besides tea, cigarettes, and snacks, dhabas often have newspapers[20] which frequently fuel discussions on the headlines. It is an informative source of daily action and reaction between the protestors and government. Habermas, while defining space (in the European context), describes the 'cafe as the sphere of private people comes together as public' (Haine 2013: 13). The private issues sometime take over the political ones. Similarly, most of the activists are questioned on what is happening over Telangana. For example, at the end of 2013, the Telangana bill was tabled in parliament and people were assured of a separate Telangana. After July 2013, the discussion shifted to 'who will get the MLA ticket' among student activists. Activists started changing parties. Dhaba discussions were centred on this political upheaval. Generally with chai, chatting begins on a personal note. At times, one's personal life intersects with political situations. In one of the discussion, a student shares:

> I have to arrange my sister's wedding. I am looking for a guy for her. But now I am thinking to postpone it for some time because I want to try for MLA ticket, Therefore, I will keep her wedding on hold. I have to mobilise more students and meet political leaders for ticket. Running after these politicians also costs lots of money.

In many ways, the dhaba as social space connects activists in a very informal manner and serves as a site where various unexpected networks are also formed. Generally, when a newcomer participates in discussions at the dhaba, it creates friendship between the newcomer and the people who frequent the dhaba. Being a small campus community, students share interpersonal relationships.

Until early 1980s, there used to be some discussion group gatherings at these dhabas. A popular group called 'Banda-canteen Broadcast' used to discuss all national and international issues. One of the alumni explained:

> There was a discussion on Vietnam War between George Reddy and Kulkarni. There were many new students sitting and curiously listening to the debate but had no idea about the terminology used by the debaters. Then George Reddy advised everyone to read 'At War With Asia' by Noam Chomsky, Gradually, after the murder of George Reddy by some Right wing ideologue, the discussion and debate sessions at dhabas disappeared. (Kumar 2012)

During the Telangana agitation in 2009, dhabas served as the best meeting and networking places for students. Most of the student leaders have their political chats at dhabas. The age-wise friendship can be easily noticed. During agitations, these dhabas serve the strategic meeting points. They talk for hours on different issues and discuss all sorts of matter, from personal to political. As their campus produces dozens of student leaders for Telangana, it provides a historic background for their talk on the movement. New strategies are prepared for agitations. All leaders spend their free time at dhabas; it has become part of the campus culture.

In one of the protests on 15 February 2010, students marched from Arts College to NCC gate. They were attacked repeatedly by police. More than 50 students were injured. The police destroyed *Sudhakar Chai Dabba* and beat the owner. After a few days, students collected some money and contributed to rebuilding the dhaba. This incident shows how authorities destroy public space of meeting point in the time of crisis. Pinsker (2013) uses the concept (in reference to Viennese cafes) of a 'third space' that emerges both from the recent work of sociologists such as Ray Oldenberg and from the work on the 'production of space' and 'lived environment' of cultural geographers such as Henri Lefebvre and Edward Soja. To explain the concept of third space as a geographical metaphor, he writes, 'The literary cafes as a third space is "located" at the border-zone between the "public" and the "private", the "inside" and "outside", a third space that mediates between a site of enunciation of identity, lived experience, and contested meaning.' (2013: 54). Therefore, the third space refers to the space that is neither the home nor the formal work space. In case of students, the workplace is the university's formal spaces such as classroom and library. This third space exists outside these formal spaces which is very much part of public sphere, so the 'dhaba' offers a third space which is equated with an informal space like someone's living room; yet, it is in public and a safe place/space where one can be and discuss things and have an audience. The dhabas, an activist named Sunil, comments, 'are the training ground for those who want to become an activist'.

Campus Police Station

Police action played an important role in intensifying the fervour among activists. Mukesh believes, 'Once you go to jail or your name comes in any case, then you have nothing left except being part of the movement as an activist'. It has been oft-quoted in India that one cannot become a famous leader without going to jail. Students refer to freedom fighters like Nehru, Gandhi, Jaiprakash, and many other popular leaders. 'Our journey from going to jail starts from our campus police station where they maintain our record. Many of us have spent nights in this station under police custody; later we were shifted to Chanchalguda jail and many other jails,' Devender, a JAC leader, stated.

Many state universities in India have a police station inside or adjacent to the campus premises which is generally named after the university. The first building at the main road across the campus is the office of police station called 'Osmania University Police Station'. It gives an image of a police 'camp' before entering into the university campus. The campus is under complete police surveillance.

Hostel B became hugely popular in 2009 due to its location across from the police station. During protests, police often put up barricades in front of the hostel. Some activists would keep an arsenal of stones on the hostel's rooftop. When the situation became tense, police fired tear gas and the activists on the roof would hurl stones onto the police. When they would run out of stones, the police would enter and beat each resident of the hostel.

All of the JAC leaders who led the agitation in 2009–10 have had police cases registered against them. They all faced multiple charges of stone pelting on police, guilty of rioting, disobedience, carrying arms and deadly weapons, attempt to murder, and so on.[21] According to all the activists, 'we agitated for our demand. We rallied, we shouted slogan and we were beaten up by the police. Police used tear gas, rubber bullet and we faced severe torture from police. Therefore, we came to the conclusion this is "Andhra" police and their behaviour is very obvious'. There are around 15 top JAC leaders, and each one of them is facing more than 100 cases. According to activists, 'fake cases were registered to spoil our career and our spirit and also to warn the campus students about their career'. Every week or month they have to be present in the court. 'In the eyes of government, we are hard core criminals', Amar laughs while sharing his grief:

> I go more to court than my college. I am facing 115 different cases registered from 2009 to 2012. Our own advocates [OU alumni] are fighting our cases for which they don't even charge because they are also activists. Every week there is some court case date and on a certain date in a month I also have to appear in OU police station to show my face.

Another leader, Umesh, displayed the police FIR cases and commented sadly:

> I am married man and have a kid. I need to get a job and start settling down my life but now I am bound to be part of the movement until these cases go on. We are running after politicians to resolve these cases but there is no hope so far. We all come from poor families and we are first generation learner, we don't have resources even to pay bribe and get the case resolved.

However, state using repressive measures to control youth protests has been a part of the history of every student movement. Filing police cases against students can spoil their career. Thus, FIR was used as a powerful tool by the police. The boundaries of the campus were put under surveillance. A barricade in front of the police station controls the speed of traffic. This barricade becomes powerful during the movement as it is used to stop the student march during agitation. This is the most controversial space which has not been conceptualized by movement studies scholars. It is a 'total institution' existing in an open space of campus which, through its own mechanisms, controls the liberal and democratic space of the campus.

Anil, a political science doctoral student, says, 'No, things are not as easy to explain. These few characters cannot decide the future of the movement. I know there are some dedicated student leaders who have left everything for their movement and they have mastery over ideology of the movement but the problem is that media does not want to highlight them.'

The media helps the image of a leader in the making. Media 'politics' is well known by activists but not discussed widely, as students also look for their self-interests and to fulfil their political aspirations. The media helps them in enhancing their personality as well as their aspirations. This is the other side of activism. Mahesh claims that he was the one who suggested the concept of JAC. Since the beginning, Mahesh was associated with the movement and participated in all the major events. Like Rajiv, he also has prepared a file containing newspaper cuttings. 'It is because of print and electronic media that we have prepared our strong profile. Media keeps us alive among masses and grass root activist,' Sunil comments. While chatting, he picked up a file and shows newspaper cuttings of his pictures, which he had beautifully pasted in it. He shows his biodata, which he calls an 'activist's CV'. He mentions every possible thing he has done for the movement—how many months and years he spent in the jail and how many cases he is charged with. He is seeking a ticket to any party. Hinting at a national level party, he hands over his CV to the researcher which mentions how many times he has been to jail and the length of his association with the movement.

THE ROLE OF LANGUAGE IN MAKING AN ACTIVIST

After the success of the 2009 mass agitation, student activists planned to launch their own political party.[22] However, each of the 15 student leaders had their own political ambitions. Eventually, with extensive consultation of their teachers and former activists (from 1969), students decided to establish the OU-JAC.[23] Later, there were many fragmentations within the JAC, and gradually, some student leaders left to form their own JACs. They were connected with the Telangana Student-Joint Action Committee (TS-JAC), which represented the confluence of all ideologies. Telangana agitations at Osmania were led by a dozen of these student JACs. During agitations, only TS-JAC and OU-JAC leaders gave press statements to the media. The majority of these leaders gave their statements in Telugu. Some of them were also able to speak both English and Hindi. This played an important role in the formation of leadership. Ajay, a prominent leader of the JAC, explains the phenomenon:

> Telugu is our mother tongue and we speak Telugu; thus the movement is limited to the Telugu audience. When the movement gained momentum, English and international media used to cover our news. We have one person who is a third-generation learner and he is fluent in Telugu, Hindi and English, and as a city guy, he was well networked with the media. Therefore, all the media was going to speak to him. Although, he joined the movement in the latter phase, we made him our media spokesperson. But we later realised that the media started portraying him as a mass leader. We know the reality, but that is media politics. They want such people who can speak their language.

'Media politics' and 'media language' are two themes which concern JAC leaders. Kamal, a JAC leader, explains: 'See, *tamdu* [younger brother], media houses are owned by Andhra capitalists. These rich people want to create dummy leaders who can speak their language. You must be thinking that it widens the movement at a national level. But, for the sake of language, the media misrepresented our leadership.'

Commenting on a fellow activist's popularity, another JAC leader, Raj, expresses similar grievances: 'What he knows is only English. He is a kind of leader who can speak any party's language because parties need a face who can speak their language, not his own.'

Raj is a poor Dalit student from Karimnagar and comments on Kamal's popularity:

> He is an elite Dalit who knows Telugu, Hindi and English, and did not take the movement forward. He is a brilliant speaker and has a lot of potential to become a leader. He talks about Ambedkar but students don't find his actions like an Ambedkar'ite. Ambedkar never fought for his personal interests. But he is advertising himself just to gain political interests. Such people generally sell their soul to political parties.

Raj takes a break, makes a phone call, and then takes a puff of his cigarette. In the meantime, Rahul, who is a close ally to Kamal, joins the discussion. When Raj comes back, he changes his tone and focusses more on media.

> The media played an important role in highlighting our issue and the reason behind this was that we had strong social media to try to reach

the maximum number of people. Whenever media ignored our issues, we were highlighting and boycotting the mainstream media on social media. Our Telugu social media was keeping check on mainstream English as well as Telugu media.

The longer agitational phase of 2009–13 cannot be imagined without electronic and social media and its contribution in the 'making' of activists.

DISCUSSION

Network processes build and sustain the essence of a social movement (Diani and Bison 2004). The chapter attempted to highlight these processes through dynamics of campus networks. However, these dynamics are not limited to the university space alone; rather they are enmeshed in the broader network for the movement. The strength of Osmania students' activism lies in their robust networks, produced by the campus culture of activism. This culture has evolved over the past five decades, both on and off campus. Alumni are a prominent part of the campus community of activists and, in fact, many are teachers at OU. Most of the state's bureaucrats, journalists, lawyers, doctors, officers, social workers, police, and politicians are also students of OU. Whenever they meet, they refer to the OU network as 'our Osmania community'. Among the campus community, a culture of honour is firmly in place. This is evident during public meeting or talks on Telangana—if any movement leader appears unexpectedly at the venue, the organizer is bound to request him to address the meeting or announce his presence. That way, student leaders, old and new, become known to each other, thus weaving a stronger network of those who support the Telangana cause.

Specific sites and spaces within the university are used by activists for networking. The main ones are the ubiquitous dhabas, along with the hostels, where boarders and non-boarders mingle with alumni and outsiders. However, social media has also contributed to connecting Telangana activists across time and space.

Thus, campus networks are also built with personal motives, where activists hope to expand their personal agenda, while fighting for the collective cause.

NOTES

1. From an informal chat with the vendor (translated from Telugu).
2. From the interview of a MSF activist, Murali on 11 September 2013.
3. Yates (2015: 3) uses the term social centres, space where alternative living arrangements, social and educational events, and political campaign are hosted. Networks are deliberately stimulated through the organized events and quotidian socializing that take place in and around centres, as well as in communicative or adversarial protest such as demonstrations and direct action.
4. Data 2009–13, Directorate of Admission, Osmania University.
5. Interview, 16 July 2013, at B hostel dhaba.
6. Granovetter (1973) and Pizzorno (1986) focus on 'trust' in understanding the political behaviour of new recruiters.
7. On the other hand, NSUI could not establish a base on campus because, according to activists 'its parent party Indian National Congress has a long history of denial and betrayal' (through interviews).
8. The officer bearers of BSF claim to be a student wing of BSP but there is no official student body of the party.
9. TDP was the last organization to form their student union *Telugu Nadu Student Front* in 2013.
10. In 1970s, a group called RSU (Radical Student Union) was started by George Reddy but it got dissolve after his death. He was murdered by the Right wing group.
11. MRPS movement gained momentum after their violent protest by burning down Gandhi Bhawan in 2006 during Congress chairperson Sonia Gandhi visit to Hyderabad.
12. Interviewed on 28 September 2013.
13. Available at http://www.thehansindia.com/posts/index/Hans/2013-09-14/Upper-caste-ethics-and--spirit-of-Samaikyandhra/71741.
14. The oath was taken by Dr Sridhar Reddy, a student leader in the 1969 agitation.
15. To control students' participations in rallies and meetings, government closed down students' hostels in six major universities in Telangana region for 10 days. Available at https://timesofindia.indiatimes.com/city/hyderabad/Telangana-hostels-to-be-closed/articleshow/5317197.cms, accessed 12 December 2016.
16. While asking the question, 'Why did you choose sociology or history or political science?', there was only one answer: that these are 'food courses'—they are easy to gain admission, and admission guarantees one food and lodging in the hostel.

17. He served as the principal of Arts College during the agitational phase 2007–11. Excerpt is from his interview on 21 September 2013 at his residence.
18. Describing the European café, Haine writes that a cafe is an 'intellectual laboratory' (cited in Rittner, Haine, and Jackson 2013: 13).
19. However, it is not just to have a connection as 'it is not networks per se that matter but connection to similarly (politically) inclined alters and an absence of ties to alters who oppose activism' (Crossley and Ibrahim 2012: 600).
20. Describing the European cafes, Haine also notes that cafe and the newspaper were born at roughly the same time and in the same place (cited in Rittner, Haine, and Jackson 2013: 13).
21. Remand Case Diary. FIR no. 21/2010. Division: Kachiguda, East Zone, Hyderabad. 20 January 2010 at 1230 hrs. Offence U/s.147, 148, 332, 188, 307 IPC r/w.149 IPC Sec. and (1) of Criminal Amendment Act and sec. 3 of PDPP Act. 1984. Name and Address of the complainant: Smt. G. Anitha, RSI, CAR Head Qrts, HQ Coy. Hyderabad.
22. Available at http://www.thehindu.com/news/cities/Hyderabad/ou-students-decide-to-launch-political-party-and-contest-elections/article4863206.ece.
23. The student wing of TRS party, TRSV was not part of this JAC.

4 Learning from the Past, Imagining the Future

Ross (1975), in his study, 'Students for a Democratic Society', in the United States of America, argues that social movements tend to have a generational character. Scholars (Altbach 1974; Braungart and Braungart 1990; Lipset and Schaflander 1971) have referred to the American student movements of the 1930s and 1960s, and identified how they shared similar dynamics. Braungart and Braungart (1990: 84) argue that 'when a political generation forms, not only is there intergenerational conflict between the young and their elders, but intragenerational conflict occurs'. In their studies on cohort groups, Braungart and Braungart (1990: 183) highlight that 'a cohort is viewed as an age group "in itself", whereas a generation is a dynamic age group "for itself"'. Referencing Ortega (1961) and Esler (1984), they state, 'a generation shares a collective mentality and represents a new integration, with its own "vital style" and sense of destiny' (Braungart and Braungart 1990). This chapter attempts to understand the case of Telangana whereby generations of Osmania alumni, who have been part of the movement since their student days, continue their activism by regularly visiting the campus and meeting the new generation of students. Students, professors, government employees, businessmen, lawyers, journalists, and various associations from every social stratum have contributed to the movement by networking with each other. The chapter draws comparisons between two agitational phases—1969 and 2009–13—and examines how the campus became a site of the confluence of these two generations of activists through the formation of Joint Action Committees (JACs). The chapter presents the circumstances in which university students took the reins from politicians' hands and devised their own ways to agitate and mobilize the masses. By tapping into generations of Telanganaites, students and the growing ranks of alumni were able to enlist the masses for their support.

STUDENT–ALUMNI NEXUS

Contemporary Osmania campus activism is a continuation part of the historical upheaval carried out by the student generation of the 1960s. It is the culmination of dreams, inspirations, and aspirations of its alumni and the present students. Not all the students arrive on campus with same political aspirations. Some become politically involved or inclined because they are recruited by their friends. Political aspiration also motivates people to become part of activists' networks. Everyday informal greeting between old and new activists not only creates a collective identity but also sets the basis of collective decision for rallies and protests. Networks provide opportunities for action through the circulation of information about ongoing activities, existing organizations, and people to contact, and a reduction of the practical costs attached to the participation. They may be the source of social pressure on prospective participants ('if you go, I will go too'), although there is possibility of cross-pressure (Kitts 2000; McAdam and Paulsen 1993) and of the opposite mechanism, whereby people participate precisely because they do not expect others do anything (Oliver 1984). Movement scholars underscore how personal ties with leaders or influential members inspire participation in protests. Snow, Zurcher, and Ekland-Olson (1980, in Crossley 2015: 27) emphasized that 'among 60% to 90% of adherents to religious groups were linked with activists before joining collective action'. Diani and Lodi (1988, in Crossley 2015: 27) show that in Milan, '78% of activists had prior connections with ecologists before participating in the environmental movement'. These studies highlight the fact that personal bonds serve to connect prospective activists with an opportunity for protest (Crossley 2015). The Telangana agitation of 2009 was not possible without the help and guidance of Osmania University (OU) alumni who have continued their activism since 1969.

The tradition of inculcating activism to the next generation is characteristic of Osmania activism and has maintained the movement's fervour. Strategies and 'best practices' have been shared as well, adding value to the movement's trajectory. For example, the 1969 movement conveyed their protest strategies, including how to deal with police firing, how to escape a police raid, and how to negotiate with politicians. The phase of 2009–13 agitations proves that OU alumni reproduced the campus legacy of activism. Comparing it with arms revolt of peasants in 1940s, Thirumali states that the intensity and mobilization of the 2009 student agitations was in 'no way lesser than the people's movement in the 1940s. The difference perhaps is that weapons were used earlier but today they are only the *yatras*, *garjanas*, etc.'[1]

One of the reasons for a strong culture of resistance at OU could lie in the fact that there have been no official student union elections since 1988 when the state government banned student union elections at all state universities in Andhra Pradesh.[2] Without elections, youth energy was not channelized solely within the space of the campus. Those who participated in the year-long agitation in 1969 and later joined university and college as faculty have a sympathetic attitude towards new students. In college functions and seminars, they shared their experiences and stories of horrific memories of the friends they lost during the 1969 agitations. 'Interaction with them inspires youth like me,' says Raj, a senior activist, who spent almost 12 years on campus. He states:

> When I heard Professor Jadhav, Professor Vishveshwar Rao and others' speech, I developed a deep attachment with the building of Arts College and all those hostels where these people stayed. Many times, when I get demotivated in my life, I come here; touch the footsteps of Arts College building and look for hours and hours at this building and remember those people who sacrificed their lives for Separate Telangana identity and culture.[3]

Osmania has three important types of activists: students, teachers, and alumni. Alumni constitute a broad range that covers people from every walk of life. Many of those who participated in 1969 agitation formed a group in 2012 under the banner, '1969 Movement Founders Forum'. Along with OU teachers, this group became the guiding force to the subsequent generations. Many people of this group joined journalism, politics, teaching, and other public facing professions. They motivated new students with their experiences.

JAC: A COLLABORATIVE EFFORT

As discussed in Chapter two, Osmania alumni were instrumental in the formation of Telangana Rashtra Samiti (TRS) in April 2001, which provided a platform to channelize emotions, passion, and energy of the new generation students. It reignited the demand and aspirations for separate Telangana among masses. From 2001 onwards, countless student organizations appeared in the movement network landscape. With a larger presence of scheduled caste (SC), scheduled tribe (ST), and Other Backward Class (OBC) students and activists, new organizations such as Telangana Girijan Vidyarathi Parishad (TGVP), Telangana Democratic Student Federation (TDSF), Bahujan Students' Federation (BSF), Madiga Students' Federation (MSF), Telangana Student Association (TSA), and many more were formed. Many Dalit student organizations (especially MSF and BSF) articulated the ideology of national Dalit leaders such as Kanshi Ram, Mayawati, and Manda Krishna Madiga.[4] Tribal students were more concerned about local politics and caste issues, and later supported the demand for 'Dalit-Bahujan Telangana'. Their activism also charged up the student wings of mainstream political parties such as National Student Union of India (NSUI) and Akhil Bhartiya Vidyarthi Parishad (ABVP). Though these organizations had a small following on campus, they played a vital role in publicizing the movement in the media. In April 2001, with the formation of TRS, Kalvakuntala Chandrashekhar Rao (henceforth KCR) promised intellectuals that Telangana would form through democratic means. After winning his first assembly and parliamentary elections in 2004, KCR served as a minister in the central government from 2004 to 2006. During his ministership, the separate Telangana issue was not pursued. One after the other, TRS won all elections and by-elections and continued performing well in the state and parliamentary elections. However, in 2009 state assembly elections, TRS's poor performance raised critical questions among intellectuals and supporters who had their hopes high from KCR. The party that was formed with one agenda of separate statehood started diverting its attention to other political issues.

In November 2009, the state government of Andhra Pradesh made Hyderabad a 'Free Zone'[5] for jobs. This policy overruled the existing one which ensured some seats for the Telangana region but now anybody from any part of state can fight for jobs in Hyderabad. This rule would create a tough competition for rural students from Telangana. With their educational background they were in no position to compete with city people of Andhra. Sensing this fear, Osmania students, along with students from other universities, led various protests to boycott this rule. The agitation turned intense and violent when police arrested few agitators.

It was first time that a JAC on separate Telangana was formed in November 2009 by Osmania students (though on July 2006, a JAC, Telangana Aikya Karyacharana Samiti, was formed, comprising 56 organizations with the aim to democratize Telangana and unite different sections of Telangana people). A few days after agitation started, Progressive Democratic Student Union (PDSU), All India Student's Federation (AISF), SC, ST *Vidyarthi Sangham*, and *Chaithanya Mahila Sangam* (CMS) had joined the JAC. These organizations together formed JAC on 15 November. Some organizations expressed their support to the proposed indefinite hunger strike, while others organized rallies and agitations. Osmania became the epicentre of this confluence of ideologies that culminated into a JAC. The following organizations supported initially:

1. BSF
2. BC Vidyarthi Sangham
3. MSF
4. Girijana Vidyarthi Sangham (GVS)
5. Telangana Rashtra Samithi Vidhyarthi Vibhagam (TRSV)
6. Telangana Students' Organization (TSO)
7. Telangana Vidyarthi Sangam (TVS)
8. Telangana Vidyarthi Vedika (TVV)

JAC members met KCR and convinced him that it was time to raise the Telangana demand powerfully. Raju,[6] a JAC leader, explains what happened:

> In a meeting at TRS party office, students gave a call that to kick start the agitation, KCR should fast-unto-death. There was a long

> discussion over this issue. Then, all of a sudden, students started shouted and telling him that hundreds of young students have ended their life for Telangana issues, to regard their sacrifice KCR should take this challenge.

After sensing the students' anger, TRS chief KCR[7] agreed to sit on an indefinite hunger fast for a separate Telangana. Osmania students gave assurance of complete support to KCR and hundreds of students started fasting with him. While KCR was fasting, students planned protest marches and rallies across Hyderabad. News reported that during rallies, students attacked public property such as shopping complexes in Panjagutta and surrounding areas. Many of them were arrested and detained by the police. Osmania alumni felt that the 'history of 1969 agitation is repeated once again'. Government did not respond to the agitation for more than a week. From 8 to 9 December, 22 people committed suicide (see Nag 2011: 156). This ignited anger among the youth. The agitation and its wide coverage by the national media made KCR a hero of the movement. With each new day, the number of protests increased but there was no response from the government. On the other hand, KCR's health started deteriorating. Sensing the danger, on 9 December 2009, at 11 pm, the central home minister, P. Chidambaram, on behalf of the Government of India, stated to the press:

> The process of formation of Telangana will be initiated soon. An appropriate resolution will be moved in the state assembly. We requested the Chief Minister of Andhra Pradesh to withdraw cases filed on or after November 29, 2009 against all leaders, students and others associated with the present agitation. We are worried about the health condition of KCR and we are requesting him to stop the hunger-strike, as well as to stop agitation especially the students involved.[8]

The next day, government officials met KCR and broke his fast by offering him a glass of juice. This was telecast live on television. In response to this, Suraj, an Arts College student activist, stated:

> We saw visuals on TV that KCR was drinking juice. He broke the strikes without even consulting us. Many of us were also fasting with him. KCR broke his fast without their consultation; they became distrustful to us and to the common masses of Telangana. We gave the press statement that he drank not the juice, but the blood of Telangana

> youth. We took out his *shava yatra* [symbolic funeral procession] on the Osmania University campus.[9]

In a TV interview, an OU leader expressed his resentment, 'He is a Telangana traitor; his feudal lordship cannot stand before the youth power of Telangana. We will carry his coffin. We will lead the movement. Even if we lose our lives, had to face severe repression and police lathis, bullets and fencing, we won't stop.'[10]

This marked a divide between student activists, who felt cheated by KCR, and TRS politicians. Students had nothing to look forward to, as other political parties such as Congress, BJP, or CPM remained unclear on their stand on separate Telangana. The ambiguous stand of political parties created enough of confusion leaving in the course a large political void (Haragopal 2010b: 157). In this situation, to deal with Telangana issues, a political JAC was also created by all the political parties[11] and they chose OU professor and civil liberty activist, M. Kodandaram, to head this forum. Because of the widespread suspicion of the political parties, there sprung a number of other JACs—first among university students, and then journalists, employees, writers, democrats, women, SCs, backward castes, and local committees including village level JACs (Haragopal 2010b: 159). From this point onwards, students took the movement into their hands and made a powerful attempt to reach out the masses. They became intolerable of any anti-Telangana voice. On 25 December 2009, Mr Nagam Janardhan Reddy, a Telangana politician from TDP, visited OU with a delegation. During his speech, he made a reference to party leader Chandrababu Naidu, which enraged students. They attacked him as he was leaving, kicking and beating him with sandals (chappals). Students also destroyed the guests' vehicles. Mr Reddy suffered bruises and nearly fell unconscious.[12] Later, in the evening, a convoy of TDP politicians arrived at Arts College and requested the students to peacefully discuss their concerns and demands. They were not received well. As they stepped out, students mobbed them, raising 'Go back' slogans. Protesters did not want to hear the name Chandrababu Naidu, as he opposed the idea of separate Telangana.

By far, it was the result of students' unity through JAC that 'wielded considerable power and influence' (Janardhan and Raghavendra 2013: 553). They chalked out their programme from January 2010 onwards, demanding the immediate declaration of separate Telangana. A rally called *Vidyarthi Mahagarjana* was organized on 3 January 2011 in front of Arts College. Over 80,000 students and other activists gathered at the sprawling campus, and it was estimated that 12,000 police and paramilitary personnel were guarding the university, which resembled a fortress, writes Kingshuk Nag (2011: 177) in his journalistic account of the agitation. Addressing *Garjana*, CPI Maoist Central Regional Bureau Secretary Mr Anand remarks:

> The more repression unleashed on students, by arresting in hundreds, lathi charging and firing tear gas and by filing more than 30 fabricated cases will soon transform into resistance. Rulers should recognise that this is not a law and order problem. This is people's problem. Our party believes that people themselves will solve it. Our party from the beginning has been emphasizing on militant mass struggles and in this, students have to play an active role.[13]

After their huge success, Osmania University-Joint Action Committee (OU-JAC) decided to launch another programme called *Pada Yatra*, starting on 19 January 2010 from OU and ending at Kakatiya University. Through this yatra, students spread awareness among the masses living in villages. This 600-kilometre-long march marks a historic journey of student movements. When students arrived in villages, they were welcomed warmly. According to Amar, one of the founding members of JACs,[14] 'We used to walk 30–40 km every day. Rural people gave a very hearty welcome. We used to deliver speeches at every stop from city, small town, village and each village had taken responsibility to host us'.

Expressing the same, Krishan,[15] an OU-JAC representative, also recalls: 'All of our team members were so overwhelmed with the response we received from common people. Our eyes were in tears when village women welcomed us with *pad-abhisheka*.[16] This was a symbol of trust and responsibility on us that we would bring their Telangana a statehood.'

The village women washing students' feet with milk was telecast live. This was a landmark in the movement's history, as society publicly showed tremendous respect at the students' loyalty to the movement. Politicians now felt they were in competition with students. This caused an existential crisis for established politicians like

KCR. In an effort to regain political clout, KCR, along with local politicians, promptly supported the students. He offered financial support and provided them with t-shirts and caps with *Jai Telangana* printed on them. With his generous efforts, he managed to recover many students' trust.

In contrast with politicians, Osmania student activists and intellectuals analysed the Telangana issue from different ideological angles. This led to the formation of countless JACs with a common objective of 'Telangana first'. All JACs culminated into two main JACs: Osmania University (OU-JAC) and Telangana State (TS-JAC). Every section of the society became a part of the movement—from bureaucrats to businessmen, office clerks to politicians, washermen to ironsmiths, *paan-wale* to vendors. People from every walk formed their JAC and participated in the movement to make it a democratic representation. Listed below are some of the popular ones:

1. Telangana Caste Association (Viswakarma, Rajaka, Gouda, Padmashali, Budaga, Jangalu, Yadava)
2. Telangana Rashtra Munuru Kapu Mahasabha
3. Telangana Mudiraj Mahasabha
4. Telangana Dalit Associations JAC, Tribal Association JAC, Women's Associations JAC,
5. Telangana Businessmen's JAC, Telangana *Rythu Bazar* JAC, Toddy Tappers' JAC, City Cable Operators' JAC, Construction Workers and Mason's JAC, Electronic Media Workers' JAC, RTC Employees JAC
6. Employees JAC, Telangana JAC for Private Employees,
7. Telangana *Prajasanghala* Joint Action Committee
8. Telangana Intellectuals Forum
9. Telangana Mass and Social Organisations Forum (TMAS Forum)
10. Telangana Gazetted Officers' JAC
11. Telangana RTC Employees JAC
12. Telangana Electricity Contract JAC
13. *Aanganwadi* Teachers' JAC
14. Agriculture Workers' JAC
15. Telangana Uniformed Services JAC
16. Telangana Model Farmers' (*Adarsha Rythu* JAC)
17. Telangana Senior Citizens Association

18. Telangana *Sarpanches'* JAC
19. Telangana MPTC Members' JAC
20. Telangana Social Activists JAC
21. Telangana *Vikalangula* JAC
22. Muslim Forum for Telangana

There were also upper-caste JACs such as Uma Devi Reddy for Women JAC, Jitta Balakrishna Reddy for Youth JAC, Satyam Reddy for Physically Challenged JAC, and several others at the district level.

The representation of various social groups in the movement indicates the conscious of their Telangana identity vis-à-vis their Andhra counterparts. Students nurtured this consciousness by organizing a series of seminars, meetings, and discussions at the district and village levels. Arts College became the command centre for activists. Heavy attendance of youth and students in everyday meetings in front of the College was evidence of the growing intensity of Telangana issues.[17] This intensity of the movement differed from the 1969 agitation, which was an unplanned upsurge divided into two major student factions raising different demands, characterized by fragmented leadership. On the other hand, the 2009 phase was a result of a protracted struggle of agitations, rallies and discussions, and unyielding commitment. Here students became mainstream political leaders whereby the 'history of political betrayals' was used as a medium to criticize the politics of the TRS party. In 1969, there was a debate on the justification of the demand for separate Telangana. Contrary to this, 2009 onwards agitation was primarily centred on 'how quickly can Telangana be separated from Andhra'? In both time periods, Osmania student activism served as a strong and stable pillar.

The growing influence of JACs can be measured by adding the fact that in 2010, 12 MLAs resigned from their posts as part of the concern for the spate of young students who had committed suicide in the name of Telangana statehood. As a result, there was a by-election, and Osmania students diligently campaigned for these MLAs against to get their seats back. Opposition candidates from TDP and Congress suffered huge losses. According to Haragopal (2010b: 161), 'it suggests that demand for a separate state has percolated deeper in popular consciousness.' Thus, emergence of JACs in the regions was the direct result of misleading and manipulative politics of Telangana leaders. This new (non-party) political culture earned a great reputation in the region which influenced political formations in the state. Each agitation from 2009 onwards achieved mass support and made students the heroes of the Telangana movement. The schedule of their activism indicates their continuous struggle. Below is a calendar of the movement which chronicles activism from the end of 2009 to the end of 2011—a period of intense activism.

2009–2011 Calendar of the Movement

- 2009:
  - 29 November: TRS launched agitation and KCR sat on indefinite hunger strike along with hundreds of students
  - 4 December: Suicide of K. Srikanth Chari that led to violent agitation
  - 9 December: Historic announcement by the Government assuring the formation of separate Telangana. KCR broke his fast without consulting students
  - 10 December: *Chalo Assembly* call by OU-JAC
- 2010:
  - 3 January: OU students' massive rally *Vidyarthi Mahagarjana*
  - 5 January: Union home minister's meeting with all party leaders[18]
  - 18 January–7 February: Students started padayatras to mobilize people to boycott any commission set up by the government. It started from Osmania University, Hyderabad to culminate at Kakatiya University, Warangal after covering all the district of Telangana.
  - 28 January: Political JAC gave deadline to ministers to resign
  - 3 February: Formation of the 'Committee for Consultation on the Situation in Andhra Pradesh'
  - 20 February: Chalo Assembly Call by OU-JAC
  - March: Split in JAC (PDSU, AISF, TVV, Telangana Student Union (TSU) expelled)
  - August: By-elections of the 12th assembly segments in five districts in Telangana
  - 30 December: Srikrishna Committee submitted its report

- 2011:
  - 5 January: Students agitated and boycotted the report; violence erupted with police use of tear gas and lathi charged and arrested dozens of student leaders
  - 20 January: Three student suicides led to violent clash between police and students[19]
  - February: *Sakala Janula Samme*
  - 17 February: Non-Cooperation Agitation (*Sahaya Nirakarana Vudymama*) by Telangana Employee JAC
  - 21 February: Chalo Assembly call by OU-JAC
  - 21 February: Another self-immolation by a student galvanized society[20]
  - 10 March: Million March
  - 3 July: 81 MLAs, 17 MLCs, and 12 MPs (from Telangana region) resigned[21]
  - 5–6 July: Call for 48-hour bandh
  - 13 September: 42-day historic strike
  - 24 October: Strike was called off
  - 15–16 November: Student–police violent clash at Osmania

The passion and fervour for the movement ignited in 2009, and by 2010, a single call for a rally or protests would gather tens of thousands youth and students of Telangana. The OU-JAC started a 'non-cooperation' movement in Telangana with a slogan of 'Pen Down, Chalk Down, Tool Down, Mouse Down',[22] with the aim of closing all official activities. The movement was compared with the Indian National Movement by many newspaper and magazines. 'Telangana state is our Birth Right' and '*Telangana Ichchedi Meme, Telangana Thechchedi Meme*' (We will give Telangana, We will bring Telangana) was another popular slogan that became iconic among the youth due to students' growing influence. A Telangana scholar and activist wrote about Telangana movement and compared its 'Million March' with Cairo's March in Egypt.[23]

Azad, an OU-JAC activist, recalls his participation in an agitation, which ended in his hospitalization:

> Just two days before, I bought my phone and it was early morning, I received a call from my girlfriend and she wished me, 'Happy Valentine, comrade'. She asked about the plan. I told her that I was busy in

organizing a rally this evening. We had a lovely chat for few minutes and then suddenly I got busy with other calls. Then the same evening, I was arrested and my phone got smashed under a police vehicle during clash with police. Valentine ended up with violence on us. I was injured and was hospitalized for a month.

Recalling the same incident, a local police officer,[24] who reported several OU agitations, describes it as one of the more violent agitations of Osmania students, in which he himself was injured. While meeting for tea at dhaba with the researcher, he narrates the incident's details:

> It was 14 February, around 5 pm, about 400 students of Osmania University, majority of them were from Arts College, led by Vangapalli Srinivas, Rajaram Yadav, Praveen Reddy and Pidamarti Ravi took out a rally from Arts College to NCC gate to burn the effigy of Central Government as a part of ongoing agitation for Separate Telangana. Disturbed by the recent student suicides, the students' leaders announced that except TRS Party MLA, no other MLA resigned, for students who sacrificed their lives for separate Telangana. The Political leaders are making mockery of students' suicide. These words spread like wild fire and the mob increased up to 1000 approximately. After a while students tried to push police by raising provocative slogans like Police go back, is it a students' campus not a police campus etc. and jumped over the gates of Osmania University. Police maintained maximum restraint, formed human chain and persuaded protesters to not to take out rallies as prohibitory orders under section 144 CRPC were promulgated in Hyderabad City. After a lot of persuasion, they burnt effigy within the campus and started returning. After burning the effigy, the agitating students reached to ladies hostel by raising slogans in unparliamentary language as 'Telangana Drohulara Kabardar, Telanganaku Adduosthe Addanga Narkestam' (if you stop us, we will cut you in pieces) and 'police go back'. Since, the strength of students increased the students' slogans made girl students to come out of their hostels and join them in College of Management lane.

To see the unruly crowd, ACP announced additional force to occupy campus. This unlawful rally of students reached Arts College and stopped. Meanwhile a few students started talking to media. The inspector, along with ACP Kachiguda and police force, returned to Arts College bus stop. The JAC leaders Pidamarti Ravi, Suman, Rajaram Yadav, Praveen Reddy, along with around 300 other students, came to

Arts College bus stop and suddenly started pushing the police personnel to go out of the Osmania University campus, and insisted that not 'they will show their power at Tarnaka not in the campus'. Among them, some others tried to set fire to the tents, where the police personnel were taking rest. Police tried to convince and persuade them not to resort to such violent activities. However, a group of students ran behind Arts College towards Manikeshwar Nagar with slogans '*Telangana Drohulara Kabardar Kabardar Telanganku Addosthe Addanga Narekestam*', while another group ran towards B hostel, Tarnaka side, and students present there started pelting stones from Arts College on police.

Meanwhile, the police pickets at MK Nagar was also alerted. Then police started announcing that the unlawfully assembly is not permissible as the prohibitory orders are in force and if they do not disperse immediately tear gas will be used. Instead the mob became more violent and started pelting stones under the cover of darkness and trees.

Then, in self-defence and with no option left, the police fired three rounds of tear gas shells because of which the mob ran helter-skelter. However, as the tear gas shells were ineffective, they regrouped immediately and started pelting stones again. The police, once again, warned them that lathi charge will be resorted to, if they do not disperse. The students continued pelting stones because of which police did mild lathi charge dispersing the mob. In the meantime, a group of students came from rear side of tents and set fire to all four tents. Equipments like stone guards, lathis, chairs, dragon lights, ropes, and police vehicles were also damaged in this confrontation.

> DCP East zone arrived at the scene around 7 pm and directed all policemen to withdraw to police station. Around this time, Joint Commissioner of police also came to B-hostel junction to monitor the situation. During this time, the students regrouped again under cover of darkness and resumed pelting of stones from all the directions on police officers and personnel. They started charging towards police, who were returning to police station, with 80–100 girl students providing cover to them. This mob turned more violent and started hurling stones, glass pieces and sticks keeping the girls as shield with an intention to cause injuries to the police. In selfdefence, the police fired tear gas shells and rubber bullets at B hostel junction. However, the unruly students' mob persisted with attacking police with stones, glass pieces etc. The police used 'Vajra' vehicles for firing

of three tear gas shells but soon the vajra operator got hurt as he was hit by a stone on his right hand.

The police officer described that it was his first time seeing so many women activists aggressively taking part in the agitation. 'For a while we were confused how to handle the situation,' he said,

> Around this time, when the police ordered for chasing away the crowd, the students' mob ran into B hostel and some students ran towards Arts College. Subsequently, it was learnt that some girl students who were providing cover for male students probably could not run on par with their counterparts and appear to have fallen on the road and received injuries. They were wearing simple sandals and flipflops. On the other hand, boys were in their proper sports shoes. For girls, it is hard to run in chunnis and suits.
>
> Next day on 15 February, around 9:45 am, one police vehicle was attacked by the students near B Hostel and was damaged due to pelting of stones on the vehicle. The vehicle was suddenly stopped and there was a lot of slogan shouting. The police from rushed to the spot and protected the vehicle. Meanwhile, about 200 to 300 students gathered at Arts College, and simultaneously, they all started pelting stones on the police force as well as on Police Station. In the time of stone pelting, some of the police personnel sustained injuries. Another mob got mobilized around Arts College area and started moving towards B hostel while pelting stones and broken glass pieces etc. on the police.
>
> After some time around 11 am, the mob came on to the main road and reached near the police station and damaged barbered wire fencing meant for blockade and indulged in stone pelting. The police made announcements through asking students to move away but the students continued stone pelting etc. The police in self-defence fired tear gas shells. The students of B hostel standing on terrace and from 1st floor windows were in elevated position and in the stone pelting that followed, some police personnel received injuries along with some journalists.

The officer ended by stating, 'Our previous experiences reveal that whenever there is an attack on students by the police, students formed several groups during agitations; they come on to the main road, rush to Tarnaka, Habsiguda and Manikeshwar Nagar, damage public and private property and also cause injuries to the passers-by.'

This particular incident of violence was condemned by civil society, as the police personnel claimed. According to him, on the same day, about 70 media personnel and lawyers entered the campus to protest against alleged manhandling and assault on media by the police personnel. Some members of State Human Rights Commission visited the university campus again and attempted to convince the students not to resort to violence.

In this agitation, student leaders Sri Bhaskar (TRSV), Mahesh (TRSV), Kumar Swamy (MSF), Yellender and Jagan (PDSU), Ashok (AISF), and D. Srinivas (OU-JAC) were arrested under various charges of rioting, destroying public properties, inciting violence, and so on. Women participated equally, especially the leaders and activists from PDSU. Female PDSU participants like Nagamani, Swapana, Srivani, Sumati, Hymavathi, Anju, Kavitha, Koteshwari, Mani, and Sujitha were also arrested and sent to jail.[25]

Thus, student agitations from 2009 to 2013 followed a unique strategy in framing slogans. Many of their protests ended up with violence because they provoked police. But as with anything, there are two versions of the same story. One is about police blaming students' behaviour as being rowdy and using vulgar language. On the other hand, students claim that they had to be aggressive only because government purposely appointed Andhra officers who were ready to throw all of them in jails. According to Rajiv, a popular JAC leader:

> We made this a successful protest because we mobilised our girls and boys both and from NCC gate to Ladies Hostels to Arts College and then to Tarnaka … our network was so strong that even police could not understood the intensity of the protest. When police reapplied that we were fearless, they started registering hundreds of fake cases on us to put us in jails.

Rajesh,[26] one of the OU-JAC leaders, describing the supremacy of student power, states, 'It was February 2010 there was a lathi charge by the police on some women activists. Regarding this matter, I called directly to minister Savita Indira Reddy. She not only responded nicely but within half an hour she came to Osmania University and apologized to the lady warden for police action.'

By this time, the government began to acknowledge growing student authority. Rajesh continues to explain:

> I still remember the time when we were so powerful due to our activism. Media used to wait outside Arts College for our press statement. We had

> a super busy schedule. We had sleepless nights during that time. We had no time even to attend our family calls. I remember, the then state minister Karim Srihari and many others contacted us through some other friends and had to wait to get our appointments.

To make a protest successful, the key is to mobilize students, and for that, activists' networks are crucial. Organizing a successful protest requires many things. The leader should be a good orator. Cultural programmes have been used as crowd pullers as well as to make the masses conscious and sensitive about the Telangana issue. Explaining the 2009 strategies, Krishank Manne (2013: 91) describes in his account of the 2009 movement that OU-JAC was the perfect combination of dynamic leaders with their qualities:

> If Pidamarthi Ravi and Rajaram Yadav were think tank's, Mandala Bhaskar and Balka Suman were crowd pullers, If Durgam Bhaskar, Gadari Kishore, Kailash Neta and Balraj were good speakers then Dharuvu Ellanna, Vijay were singing warriors, if Vangapally Srinivas was daring then TGVP boys were dashing, if Stalin, Rajesh were committed then Kota Srinivas, Ashappa, Azad, and Karate Raju were confident. Balalakshmi, Satyavati and Suguna were the face for women.

Success of any movement depends on the strategies used by its members. These strategies exist in the form of decision-making, schedule-planning, making use of the resources, motivating masses by highlighting various issues, using mass communication tools, and so on. Organizing a 'protest' is part of a strategy in a movement. Generally, student unions such as TRSV and NSUI (who belong to ruling party like TRS and the Indian National Congress) are expert in organizing a quick protest as they get full resources from their parent parties. Secondly, they have good networking in the media and know how to handle the situation. Main student leaders of these parties even have a television in their hostel rooms to keep themselves up to date with the news and political activities. If there is a protest going on in Delhi, Osmania activists plan an agitation in no time and alert media personnel. Some activists even have an effigy that they prepare in advance, ready to use at a moment's notice. That way, they only need to tag it with a name when they plan to burn it at a protest. Similarly, they keep banners and posters ready to protests any time when they need. They call some close friends in media and some activists and within no time, they organize a full protest.

The role of media, including social media, played a crucial role in 2009 agitations. It helped them in conveying their message to every corner of the state. During 1969, there were only three popular newspapers: *The Hindu*, *Deccan Chronicle*, and *Andhra Bhoomi*. On the contrary, in 2009, media became the centre of the movement, and people's sentiments were guided by the media. Telangana people owned two newspapers and a news channel. According to an industry analyst, by the end of 2010, Andhra Pradesh had 19.9 million television households, of which 11.3 million were cable and satellite households (Reddy 2010). Thus, television served as a connector between the movement and masses. The live telecast of the students' self-immolation caused intense public anger against the government and strengthen the public support for the separate Telangana movement. These visuals had such a deep effect on masses that on one call by student JAC, youth could reach and rally in Hyderabad within no time.

Along with the use of media and technology, activists strategically selected cultural symbols from Telangana folklore, assimilated them in the movement, and manoeuvred them as historical symbols and tools of assertion. *Dappu* is one of those traditional symbols used by the Osmania students to assert their rights. Dappu is a traditional medium of communicating the official announcements in the villages. It highlights the 'life-world' of lower castes. In 2009, it was used as a cultural symbol to reach out to masses and served as the beat of the movement. As an indigenous instrument of the region, it could reach to that section of society which has been on the margins for ages. In every movement, agitation, or strike, dappu caught the centre stage. There are doctoral students at Arts College who research the sociology and history of dappu. Some journalism students are exploring the role of dappu in traditional communication. There are Facebook group called *Madiga Dappu Yuvasena*, which organize various shows and claims that they have the 'best dappulu team in the state'. There are hundreds of activists who add dappu with their name on their Facebook accounts.

Similarly, activists worship Telangana Talli (mother goddess) to oppose Telugu Talli which is a cultural symbol worshipped by Andhra Telugus.[27] In many places, statues of Telugu Talli were vandalized. This created an outrage among Andhra people as well. Similarly, new Facebook groups were formed such as *Telangana Blackvoice*. Madan,[28] one of the active members of Blackvoice explains, 'Blackvoice represents the voice of oppressed and discriminated people. Black is the symbol of the oppressed. Black symbolizes dried blood and is therefore closely related to the bloodshed of oppressive rule and the suffering, hunger, misery and death of the ruled masses'.

Their logo is a phoenix with a red star on the Telangana map. According to its activists, 'Telangana map denotes self-respect, self-rule and a separate state, Map in Blue means symbol of social justice and phoenix represents ashes to glory, and immortality. Red star is the symbol of revolt, liberty and revolution and Raised fist expresses Unity, Strength, Resistance, Solidarity and support.'

Every symbol and colour finds a new meaning when it is linked to a movement. While designing a logo, an activist considers those who sacrificed their lives. A simple insignia of a party can appeal masses. It is a part of attracting people or a symbol of protesting against others.

JACs organized programmes in Hyderabad and mobilizing people from rural area. From September to December 2011, Telangana JAC organized series of agitation such as *rail-roko*, *rasta-roko* (road-blockade), and so on. Auto-rickshaw drivers JAC was instrumental in making these blockades successful. During rail-roko programme in Hyderabad violence erupted due to intervention of police which also led to arrest of several student union leaders. There were series of agitations to oppose arrest of student leaders and army on campus.[29] For many days, Osmania campus turned into an army camp, as Mukesh,[30] leaned against the wall, then sank into the chair and sighed, while describing that period:

> Agitations were going on in Hyderabad. We were literally living in an army camp. Nearby area like *Basti* and *Taranaka* were under surveillance. Many army people were staying in these areas to watch over student's activities. For weeks there was no food supply. That was the festive season but many of us couldn't go home. There were fire-crackers in our homes and we were hiding in our rooms listening to the sounds of bullets.

During 2009 agitations, the 'non-boarders' became a serious issue for the university administrator as they were a large participation of them in protests. To tackle this, police kept the campus under surveillance. While holding a tea cup and a cigarette, Naresh,[31] an activist who prepared the design of the posters for one organization, lowers his tone and tells two of his friends:

> Once I had some work in the police station. The city police in-charge was my known people. He asked us who else is living in your room and what is his name and other details. Then, he showed the full detail of how many people legally and illegally residing in every room of the hostel. What is happening in our rooms and how many out-borders are staying in hostels. They have their own informants. Police also knows that how many student leaders are extorting money in the name of movement. But they don't arrest them because otherwise student would think they are against the movement.

Mukesh's face shows a sign of surprise. However, the movement had much complex dynamics not just for the activists but also for the administration and police. For student activists, it was not easy to organize end number of talks and protests on campus.

> There is a job crisis world over. Our state is no different from other. But separation is not going to solve any problem. What this agitation, rallies and movements are doing basically creating bunch of goons, bunch of middle-man who bargain for students' interests and their own benefits. Bunch of student leaders will get their political benefit. It is not going to benefit common student. These leaders have no vision for anything.

Suresh, another resident of NRS hostel who is the next door neighbour of a JAC leader, reveals:

> In our hostel, many students are aware what our student leaders are doing. Except two-three leaders, everyone has sold their soul to cheap politicians. They enjoy a lavish life. But by living in the hostels with us they show that they are like us. It is a known fact that they extort money from business in the name of movement. They are rowdies; they can beat anybody in the name of Telangana movement. Andhra businessmen are afraid of doing businessmen in Hyderabad. A bunch of these students are creating terror in the city.

CHANGING MOVEMENT STRATEGIES AND DYNAMICS

Ways of protesting and mobilizing students differed for this generation than for the first generation of activists. If we compare it with the 1969 phase, we can draw following comparisons:

1. Student composition was different in 1969, in that there was a large percentage of Andhra students at OU. At that time, Osmania was the only university in the area. Later, Kakatiya was founded, and by 1990, many educational institutions appeared on the map of Andhra Pradesh, but the Telangana area was not given much attention. On the other hand, student composition in 2009 at OU was dominated by students from the Telangana region, while students from the Andhra region had several institutions to choose from.
2. In the 1969 movement, student movement leadership reflected the upper-caste majority on campus. By 2009, SC, ST, and OBC students constituted almost 90 per cent of the population in Osmania. Also, in contrast with the earlier generation that was mostly in the natural sciences and medical fields, by 2009, most students on campus belonged to the social sciences. This is in part due to the declining academic reputation of the university and diminishing intellectual and financial resources. Economically well-off students were no longer drawn to OU as they were in its heyday.
3. In 1969, there were three main leading organizations (Telangana Praja Samithi, Osmania University Student Union, Telangana NGO's Union). By 2009, countless organizations and sub groups emerged. Apart from that, the movement received its support from abroad and networked closely with Osmania students. 'Without this networking, it was hard to organise a single protest,' says Jai, an activist who was invited by an NRI association in Singapore.

The strategy differed in 1969 because 'there was no time for analysis', according to 1969 activist, Advocate Ramdas. 'We did untiring agitations continuously for 10 months. By that time, we exhausted our energies and resources. That was a bad strategy; actually, there was no strategy. We focus on our goal of getting separate Telangana and in a way, we did but our political class betrayed us'. Activist leader K. Srinivasulu,[32] an engineering student at the time, remembers those days:

> In the 1969 movement, farmers used to get involved. From all section used to participate. Caste was not there. Class was not there. Those days Left, Right or Centre was not clearly known. All these communalisms and all were not well known that time. We have not read Marx, Lenin or anyone else. Poet Sri Sri was our inspiration. Our concern was to react to the societal problem. Everyone fought for one cause.

On the other hand, the 2009–13 movement occurred in a planned manner. Students learnt from the mistakes of 1969 agitation. They systematically used the university space and its intellectual and academic resources. The kinds of ideologies formed and implemented were never planned earlier. According to Professor G. Krishnareddy, 'the important contribution of 2009 agitations is the formation of the Joint Action Committees (JACs) by the students'. Through JAC, students get the participation of every section of the society which helped the movement in creating a strong ideological base.

ROLE OF FOLK, THEATRE, AND ART

During 2009 agitations, campus produced many cultural activists. Many activists on campus are part of these groups and make music albums on Telangana movement. Enjoying as much popularity and respect as politicians, they have performed with famous singers such as Rasmai Balkrishna (Dhoom-Dhaam group), Gaddar, Belli Lalitha, and Varavara Rao. During the 2009 movement, these activists became the voice of the movement. Their music revived the spirit of movement among masses. Therefore, the 2009 movement was turned into a cultural revolution by the university students. Student activists of Osmania have written plethora of literature in Telugu to reach out to masses. They recorded their music cassettes, albums, and YouTube videos to highlight their sufferings and feelings about their Telangana identity. Some popular movies were also made after the 2009 student movement. Print and electronic media also helped them to highlight their programmes. There were no popular cultural activists in Telangana. It was an Andhra poet, Sri Sri, who captivated the youth. Sridhar Reddy,[33] who led his own group supporting separate Telangana in 1969, explains: 'Sri Sri was a progressive poet who suffered with poverty in his young age. In his twenties, he wrote great poetry that energized and inspired youth of our generation, especially me as I used to write poetry at that time'.

Sri Sri's poems became the voice of the generation of radical activists as well as student activists of the separate Telangana movement. On the contrary, post-2000 Telangana phase of the movement produced a range of young poets who became the face of 2009 agitations. Manoj arrives at the dhaba in front of B Hostel with three other friends, Raju,

Mohan, and Yunus. He is holding a piece of paper in his hand. Raju calls out at the *chaiwala* to make them tea. Mohan lights his cigarette and makes himself comfortable, then says, 'Yes Anna, please recite now'. Manoj,[34] a history student and a popular poet, shares his story:

> One of my activist friends encouraged me to write my poetry and sing it to every programme organised by the university. I have a great passion for poetry but it was all sad love poetry. After coming here one day we saw that one of the students of Nizam College committed suicide in front of Arts College, I have seen his close friend crying. It was such a pathetic scene which shook my consciousness. We organised many condolence meetings on campus. In these meetings, I have seen activists from different parts of Telangana came to participate. Some of them recited poetry for Telangana. I was so impressed with the reality of the problems. I felt bad that I was somehow writing more about utopian things which does not have any meaning for my state people. Since then, I decided to join hard core activism. I started writing poetry about Telangana in Telugu and started sharing it with my activists' friends. Now, I have four books on Telangana issue. Now, I go to villages and people love my poetry as they can relate themselves with it. The latest one contains the picture of Arts College in its cover page. Whatever I am today is because of this campus.

The movement has produced countless poets, writers, novelists, artists, musicians, and local global leaders. Students feel proud to associate themselves with the movement. These artists have a strong following in rural areas as well. Among Osmania student singers, Daruvu Yellanna became a popular voice of Telangana. His song, '*Veerullara vandanam Vidyarthi, Amarlara Vandanam Paadalaku*' (A Salute to Students) became the voice of Telangana youth. Common students and activists sang this song in their groups. This song was dedicated to the martyrs of Telangana and evoked patriotic feelings for Telangana. Yellanna was among those who sacrificed their career for the movement. To him, it was the love for common people which made him what he is today. The rented house of one of the student activists, Daruvu Ellana,[35] is full of awards and medals which he received as 'Telangana movement singer' from every part of Telangana. He was invited by the Mumbai JAC to sing revolutionary songs at the meetings and also helped the OU-JAC by providing financial support. He described the event as follows: 'The happiest moment of life was when I was invited to Mumbai by Telangana activists. I am proud that I represented my Telangana in the economic capital of India where thousands of Telangana people came to listen and appreciate my revolutionary song for separate Telangana.'[36]

Since 2009, he has been invited as a guest artist to most of the programmes organized by Osmania students.[37]

Like Mumbai, there were many other cities, where Telangana people are settled and protested for Telangana. Similarly, there was a strong network between Telangana diaspora settled in China, UK, Europe, the United States of America, Canada, and other countries. All the global networks have financially contributed to the groups working in Hyderabad. These networks, through social media, made the movement more vibrant at the national level.

During 2009–10 agitations, the government shut down the university and hostels to curb movement activities. Notice was given to all the students to leave the hostel. Water, food, and electricity supply was cut. The entire campus was put under surveillance. Police had control over all the activities. Students gathered and set up a huge stage in front of Arts College. Their motivational speeches continued around the clock. They invited popular Telangana activists to address their gathering. The government did not allow anybody to enter that area except students. However, balladeer Gaddar and musicians Rasmai Balkishan, Vidyasagar Rao, and Deshpati Srinivas used to come regularly. But activists as well as common students had records of all of Gaddar's songs on Telangana. In NRS hostel, it is common to see many students playing Gaddar Anna's song. Rasmai Balkishan played a vital role in sensitizing students through his staged dramas during agitation. An activist, Mukesh, describes the impact of these dramas:

> The students had set up their stage in front of Arts College. We stayed, eat and sleep there. The cultural program, revolutionary speeches and stage dramas were keeping our spirit high. In one of the play by Rasmai Balkishna depicted 'Andhra' police who was brutally beating Telangana students with their boots and lathis and firing bullet on their head. These scenes projected in such a real manner what we all had experienced during our agitations. These scenes were so touching at every dialogue we had goose bumps and our eyes were full of tears.

CHANGING STRATEGIES

The period from 2009 to 2014 witnessed many agitations, rallies, marches, and strikes for the separate statehood for Telangana. On the other hand, the Andhra region was protesting for 'United Andhra' (*Samaikhayandra*). However, there was no major agitation led by the Andhra region as they did not have proper leadership.[38] Andhra activists resorted to following the strategy of Telangana activists' initiatives such as *Vanta Varapu*, *Rail Roko*, and so on. In 2013, they formed many JACs to oppose the demand of Telangana but their protests remained largely limited to the Hyderabad city. A history professor from OU, commenting on the Samaikhyandhra movement, found no comparison between the two:

> We have been writing books and publishing it for past 50 years but media never highlighted us. These Andhra leaders will publish a pamphlet about united Andhra and they will gain lots of popularity in media. But leaflets, pamphlets are just information; it is not an intellectual material. And without intellectuals you cannot launch any serious movement. Tell any name of the book written by their activists. Our activists have written hundreds of books and thousands of songs were composed only for Telangana.

Telangana Samburalu[39] (food festivals) were organized in the college premises and used to express resentment against commercialization of culture, art and conventions, and food. The demonstrators distributed boiled *channa*. To gain public support, TRS involves in funding these festivals. The people were mobilized for different types of protests—strikes, dharnas, mass processions and rallies, gheraos, civil disobedience, *Vanta Varapu* (cooking on the streets), cultural programmes, and political meetings. In the name of reasserting the cultural identity of Telangana, the traditional *Bathukamma* (goddess of life) festival, where women offer flowers to a goddess and seek her blessings to become good housewives, was organized and celebrated in public with the blessings and support of Telangana ideologues and activists. Along with long-established Bathukamma songs, which have patriarchal overtones, new ones on the plight of Telangana and in praise of those who died for the cause of the state were composed and sung in public celebrations.

Students planned new programmes and used various protest strategies. 'Fasting' was opted as the last form of protest. On the other hand, some civil society groups have organized fasting. Taking a critical stand on hunger strike as a protest strategy, Dr Surepally,[40] an Osmania alumni from Telangana, questions its efficacy: 'Poor people think they can change India by fasting or by hunger strike. Fasting is just one form of protests, isn't it? But can it bring any change? Can't we do opposite of it—cook well and eat well—be more effective?'

To oppose the traditional way of fasting as protest, Telangana students organized *Vanta Varapu*—cooking and eating in public places such as roads or railways tracks. Through this strategy, they united their fellow students. As one activist pointed out, 'Who will come to have fast with you and suffer hungry? But everyone will always ready to come to feast. *Vanta Varapu* strategy also helped building student-mass relations stronger and connecting all our activists'.

The form of protest decides the future of movement. In the case of Telangana movement, students adopted new network strategies to connect with the masses. Food was used as a medium to protest. Students, teachers, politicians, businessmen, doctor, lawyers, engineers, civil right activists, and daily wage labourers joined these protests with their families to participate in the protests. Male and female activists helped each other cut vegetables and cook three times a day for everyone in temporary community kitchens. More than 20,000 stoves were lit in different locations to feed the protesters. Every caste and community came up with a unique way of protesting. Potters depicted the Telangana flag on pots, drew the map of Telangana, and inscribed the word 'Telangana' with colours; embroiders weaved 'Telangana' on cloth, and so on. Women JAC[41] was spreading a 200-metre-long fabric on the road with the word 'Telangana' hand-printed on it. Paan seller made a map of Telangana on the paan leaf. The agriculture class took up their ploughs and etched the word 'Telangana' in the soil. An activist cannot imagine himself without networking. The service castes of Telangana expressed their solidarity with the Telangana movement through remonstrative forms of shaving, washing clothes in public space. 'These protests forms are rooted in their desire to turn the political system to listen to their voices'[42] (Thirumali 2010).

In 2013, when movement was at its peak, a doctoral student (also a former Indian army personnel and closely associated with 69 activists), returned his degree during convocation at Osmania and shouted the slogan '*Jai Telangana*' on the stage. In his press statement, he said, 'What is the use of accepting a doctorate when the issue of Telangana is still pending?' He further stated, 'My only wish is that when I die I should be cremated in Telangana. And if I die early, I ask my son to put me in the mortuary and only bury me when Telangana is declared as my own soil.'[43] Such statement evoked sympathy and motivated youth who used this as a strategy saying that 'degree is not as important as Telangana'. Such strategy became part of protest and resistance.

ACTIVIST, CLICKTIVIST, AND 'TICKETIVIST'

Many activists, who joined a political party, maintained their loyalty to it. Apart from campus activism, their political motive was to get the party ticket for elections. Close to the state assembly elections, these activists demonstrated their strength to influence the party. They organized various meetings on Telangana at the campus and invited their political party leaders. Most of the leaders who formed their own JACs claim to have been with the movement 'since the beginning'. They maintain a physical folder of newspaper clippings and flyers of their activism, as well as regularly updating their profile on Facebook. For Krishank and other student leaders, the movement is no longer one that is just about identity or access to resources, but also about opportunities:[44] 'If you look back, you will realise that in 2009, the issue raked up once again during the allocation of SI posts.[45] For us, the formation of Telangana is a way of ensuring that everyone is given equal opportunity—whether it is in education or jobs. As students that's what we have been fighting for—better opportunities'.

Social media has elevated some activists' stature and created a global awareness of the movement. Many 'Facebook leaders' got more popularity than those who really had a mass base. From 2009 onwards, there were more than 50 groups on Facebook in the name of Osmania and Telangana at the national and global level (by 24 December 2014). Some common pictures such as Telangana map and Telangana agitation were widely shared by the activists. On every picture, students generally comment 'Jai Telangana' and 'Osmania Students' struggle long live', the popular slogans of the movement. Social media movements produced thousands of activists who, as per social movement literature, can be called 'clicktivists' or 'slacktivist'. The Facebook group *Blackvoice Telangana* is run by Osmania alumni and some current students of Osmania. A history student, Krishna, posts messages like 'Boycott Andhra Movies in Telangana: Be a Fan of Your Mother and Motherland Telangana—*Jai Jai Telangana*' and 'I cannot openly publish this message otherwise the police will kill me because they are from Andhra. I am spreading messages through Facebook to express my feelings for Telangana. Our group has a huge fan following.'[46]

Citing the role of mainstream media in making a movement, Ajit, a professor of journalism, opines:

> It is not the movement but the political parties which decide who will be the activist. All media houses are run by the political parties. Media focuses on certain people who are visible but the grassroots activists are not highlighted because media follows an elitist approach. If you talk to a real activist, he will use a very crude language and his real experience. Such language is not liked by the mainstream media as it does not make a news.

The researcher met many activists who were reluctant to interact with media, in spite of their strong ideological beliefs. They have their own resentment with the movement and its leadership but they have no resources to launch their own group. But they have spent much time in the movement; they cannot leave it at this stage. Therefore, they continued their activism without compromising with their principles. JAC leaders were accused of 'turning puppets in the hands of political parties'.[47] Sharing such experience, Shyam,[48] a 41-year-old resident in NRS hostel, shares his thoughts on the movement:

> I don't want to talk about Telangana activists. In the name of activism, they are extorting money. They call themselves Ambedkar'ites. There is no ideology of those who extort money. When I questioned their practices, they gave logic that finances are important for a movement. They also get funding from political parties. What do they do with the money? Students are committing suicide here in Telangana. There are deeper roots of feudalism.

Shyam takes out a piece of paper and draws a diagram to show the caste atrocities by Reddys and Velammas. His voice gets louder as his frustration begins to show, and he tears apart the diagram. 'Do these student leaders have any answer to the caste question in Telangana?' he asks angrily. He pauses and continues:

> I don't want to waste my time talking about this non-sense movement. It has produced just a bunch of goons and middlemen. That is not what Ambedkar or Kanshi Ram has imagined for Dalit society. They are all PhD students but you ask them any book of Ambedkar, you will get no answer. They have no vision. They are surviving only because they are associated with glorified Osmania University. They themselves did nothing to glorify it.

Ignoring the question posed, Shyam, in his prophetic style, reveals:

> You will see various characters of the Left, *Dalit-Bahujan* and Telangana movement. Leftist leaders would convince you how they are attached to the masses. A Dalit leader would say he is attached with Dalits. But Telangana student leaders would say, 'I am closely attached with TRS'. This is the irony of Telangana politics. To them, it is just about how to get a ticket from TRS.

A defining characteristic of an activist is his or her adherence to a particular ideology. Ambedkar, Periyar, and Phule appear to play an important role in the lives of many campus activists. Images of such social thinkers hang in the rooms of all the activists the researcher encountered. For the radical Left, the icons are Marx, Lenin, Mao, and Bhagat Singh. Some activists have posters that nearly cover the entire wall. Yet, out of the 47 present-day Osmania student activists interviewed, only one had a complete collection of Dr Ambedkar's writings translated in Telugu and some of Phule's writings. Thus, it is difficult to define these activists on the basis of their ideological leanings. For example, the majority of activists are office bearers in several organizations which are often ideologically antagonistic. The understanding of their ideology is limited to iconic representations of above mentioned social thinkers. This can help us understand the proliferation of student unions in the NRS hostel alone. Popular politics and the desire to be in the limelight propel many students into activism such that combined with the lack of ideological mentors there is not one single ideology that has defined the movement.

Thus, campus activism does not represent any particular ideological understanding among student activists; rather, it is a combination of their regional identity, political aspirations and the 'ultra local' vision of the movement. Close to the elections, ideology is compromised, and student leaders of from left-wing and right-wing parties run after every political party to get election tickets. Like mainstream politics, campus politics turns to be very opportunistic. All their activism and politics ends up into a struggle of getting election ticket. Those who do not get the ticket continue with their ideological activism. They prove themselves as popular leaders in the eyes of mainstream party leaders. There are two ways to show their strength. One is by showing the real strength in numbers by taking their supporters with them when they attend any party function or any public ceremony where their party leaders are also invited. For example, in the marriage function of the university student, all the student leaders enter the hall with dozens of their supporters behind them; they meet with all the popular leaders. Second is the virtual way—through social media. All student leaders have Facebook accounts. They upload the pictures and videos of their programmes, agitations, confrontations with the police, addresses to large gatherings, meetings with ministers and bureaucrats, organizing protests, and so on. This account is generally maintained by the closest friend who is considered the 'right hand' of the student leader. He manages all his appointment and schedules. Common students from other universities and colleges approach this right hand to get their work done.

Krishank Manne writes in his agitational account, 'Movement and agitation are done by people who are hungry and angry' (Manne 2013: 24). Manne, with other senior activists, was jailed twice. Many JAC leaders have a history of being jailed in two of the well-known jails of the area: Chanchalguda Central Jail and Cherlpally Jail. Sharing his experiences, Rajiv[49] explains, 'See, in India, without going to jail, one cannot become leader. From Gandhi, Nehru, and Patel to Lalu Yadav, everyone survived jail which made them the mass leader. I can go to jail again and again for my people of Telangana. I exist because of Telangana'.

His statement shows the power of region in a federal system of democracy. Most of the regional movements in democracy have gained momentum because the regional identity was presented in such a manner that evoked the cultural feeling of its people. For example, the basis for the demand of separate Jharkhand state from Bihar was the tribal identity that spurred a mass movement. Similarly, Chhattisgarh was formed on the basis of the Chhattisgarhi language spoken in the region. Therefore, there is a correlation between culture, language, and region. Firoz, a sociology student at Arts College, states:

> I come from Warangal district which is known for its struggle and sacrifices. When I joined here, I met many senior activists from my area who carry forward the legacy of the radical left. I started attending their program and rallies, agitation. Now, you see I am speaking to the media on the behalf of Osmania students. My family does not own a TV in my village but when they heard that I was on TV and they called me I was the happiest person on earth. This campus is the most pious place for students like me who come from extremely poor families.

During the 1969 agitation, OU led the movement and hundreds of students lost their lives. The majority of these students were from Khammam and Warangal districts. Therefore, these two districts are generally represented in student leadership.

Caste has been used as a mobilizing factor in Telangana movement since the 2009 agitations. There are only a few Osmania student leaders who gained fame and emotional support mass across the party. As argued earlier, emotions are rooted in cultural practices, and it takes cultural activism to stimulate them. The dedication, use of slogans, and fearless actions of the activist turns him into a mass leader. Such action catches media attention, which brings them closer to the mainstream leaders. That was the strategy followed by Pidamarthi Ravi, Rajaram Yadav, and Balka Suman, who were ready to fight and take action. Their actions, in police language, are illegal and rowdy. During the 2010–11 agitations, there were cases of government property destruction. Some TVV student leaders were accused of setting New Necklace Road and Jamai Somalia railway station on fire on 21 February 2011 (Editorial 2011: 3).[50]

On the other hand, Left ideologue such as Kota Rajesh and Nagam Kumaraswamy, Jagan remained ideologically committed, and gained mass support but never got involved in any violence. Another Left activist like Kota Srinivas, Stalin and others refrained from violent activities. Regardless, each of these group leaders was charged with more than 100 cases by the local police. Their history of activism shows a particular trend from being an ordinary student to becoming a popular student leader. For example, Pidamarthi Ravi grew up in extremely poor economic conditions, studied in government schools, and reached OU and opted for Telugu literature for his doctoral. His friends revealed that he was always found in library reading for competitive exams and they were confident that he would easily crack state civil services. But they believe that it is his generous nature that made him a leader. He never said no to any of his friends who sought any kind of help. While he was with the SC/ST Students' Association, Ravi publicly shattered an idol of the Hindu god Lord Ganesha to oppose Brahminism on campus, which cast him into limelight. To counter the slogan of *Bharat-Mata* [Mother India], he coined the slogan *Ambedkar Pitah* [Father Ambedkar][51] and offered his support to BSP.

During interviews with the old generation of activists (1969–72) and then the present generation of activists (2000–14), the researcher found an interesting connection between these generations—that both are first generation learners. Except one or two activists, all of them belonged to economically poor backgrounds. Students from elite backgrounds used to attend Arts College, but now it is only first-generation learners who do so. Between November 2009 and February 2010, 60 young students aged 18–25 committed suicide. Many of them were self-immolations (Government of India 2010: 387). This was a distinct phenomenon in 2009 agitations. On the contrary, there was not even a single suicide during 1969 agitations. Dr Chiranjeevi became visibly emotional while talking about this phenomenon: 'We used to face the police bullets directly and many of our friends sacrificed their lives but we never quit even in the extreme hopeless situations. This generation is losing hope'.

During 1969, there was a low number of faculty members from Telangana region, but it was predominantly students who devised their own strategies. But during 2009, the ratio was different. Arts College had the largest faculty from Telangana, and it became a joint struggle for both students and teachers.

DISCUSSION

The university campus is a site where 'identities are actively made, remade' (Vennela 2014) and strengthened. Most of the students who were part of the movement were first generation students. Their families had high expectations of them to secure a government job in Hyderabad. Thus, they do not necessarily come with the aim of engaging in politics or activism on campus. Yet, it is the image of the university as an 'activists' campus' that contributes to and strengthens their Telangana identity. As more and more students from small towns and villages came to Hyderabad to join OU, they learned more about the difficulties of settling in Hyderabad. Living in the city forced them to think more of their career. Seeing first-hand the difficulties and struggle to gain employment coupled with the lack of representation of people like themselves in government jobs and positions of power, students from Telangana felt the only solution to these social inequities was forming a separate state. Thus, the university provided the consciousness and understanding of the problems and offered a solution. Daily life experiences in Hyderabad magnified reasons to become an activist and the university campus provided a safe haven.

Activists define collective identities in opposition to other groups in society, including targeted groups such as the state or countermovement groups. Collective identity is an interpretation of a group's collective experience: who these members of the group are, what their attribute are, what they have in common, how they are different from other groups, and what is the political significance of all this (Whittier 2002: 302). It emerges from interaction within movement contexts as participants transform their sense of themselves. It is grounded in the group's social location, that is, its structural position, its common experiences, and dominant definition of the group. It, thus, is shaped by forces external to the movement, but it is never a straightforward result of a shared social location. The collective identity of JACs fragmented into various segments. On the one hand, it was narrowing the collective identity but at the same time, it was democratizing the movement. Three ideological concepts—'Geographic Telangana', 'Democratic Telangana', and 'Dalit-Bahujan Telangana'—represented a vision, a strangery and planning for their dream state. This ideological grouping not only rekindled activists' aspirations and mobilization process for separate statehood, but also highlights intellectuals' contributions to the movement. One can argue that it fragmented the movement and put it on the righr path. Looking at it from another point of view, the movement can be understood as an identity-resistance movement, in which caste and sub-caste identity mobilization affected its internal structure. It helped the marginalized section to gain pride in their identity.

Telangana movements brought together individuals from different social locations at one platform. The comparison of 1969 and 2009 generations of activists provides important similarities and differences. For example, the state repression was much severe in 1969–72 agitations but there was no suicide during 1969 agitation. On the other hand, during 2009–13, several students committed suicide for statehood. This explains how external dynamics (state and power structure) influence the movement actors' decisions and strategies. By 2009, students had lost all hope. The strength of the 2009 movement, compared to the 1969 one, lies in the activists' awareness and pride in collective identity of Telangana, their cultural understanding of the movement, which created a feeling of self-empowerment through identities that were inward-looking. Due to caste and sub-caste JACs, identity of Telangana was constantly negotiated as the specific question of 'whose Telangana is this?' became the central question of the movement. Dalit-Bahujan Telangana, Madiga Student Union focussed more on identity empowerment.

In other words, caste-based groups have a strong presence on campus, but all these groups culminated into a common platform of JACs. Under the broader umbrella of OU-JAC and TS-JAC, several internal substructures like caste, minorities, gender, and region played a crucial role. The strategies and goals of these JACs were largely shaped by the media, local politics, and state and national politics. Moreover, political culture of Osmania campus and youth leadership as well as an individual's aspirations contributed to more dynamic and powerful protests and agitations, posing threats to the existing structures of state power and politics. Thus, individual, culture, and structural transformation are inseparable (Whittier 2002: 306). In caste-based JACs, activists explored caste connections within and outside the country (among diasporas) to widen their political space. It challenged the existing leadership of the movement and their bargaining power with the state. However, internal dynamics of movements was not simply determined by external contexts. The JAC as a concept became popular among every section of Telangana society, from elite to the common masses. Each social class had formed their own groups, first on the basis of collective identity of Telangana, then on the basis of primordial identities, and then on the basis of ideology ('Geographic', 'Democratic', and 'Dalit-Bahujan' Telangana). In the longer run, such groupings strengthened the movement at grassroot level. Interestingly, this basis strengthened the movement and made it more democratic by introducing concepts such as 'Democratic', 'Geographic', and 'Dalit-Bahujan' Telangana.

A movement only takes an agitational route when it generates a collective identity. The success of Telangana movement was the combination of various internal and external factors. For example, dappu, as a traditional symbol of caste-based occupation, was presented as a symbol of assertion by the activists. Telangana dappu was popularized as a new identity to solidify Telangana identity. Similarly, the individual talent of singing got a public expression through movement (which otherwise was not possible). There are studies (Braz 1973; Danda 1983; Dasgupta 1983; Mahapatra 1983; Rao 1981; Saikia 1982; Singh 1983) on social movements and collective actions of individuals that demonstrate the emergence of charismatic leadership and how it becomes a symbol of the emotive aspects of the cultural consciousness of a community, articulates the strategies of solidarity, and revitalizes the indigenous traditions (Singh 2001: 169). Castells introduces another concept of identity: project identities. A project identity is formed 'when social actors, on the basis of whichever materials are available to them, build a new identity that redefines their position in society and, by so doing, seek the transformation of the overall social structure' (Castells 1999: 8).

In short, the second phase of the Telangana movement agitation started from 2009 and was qualitatively different from the 1969 phase. Both generations came together and led frequent and successful agitations between 2009 and 2014. They created a tough situation for the political class, who had lost trust of the common masses. Again, OU intellectuals (professors, doctors, engineers, journalist, and so on), and alumni were instrumental in launching successful agitations and they remained the guiding force for other university students as well. Thus, without the institutional contribution of Osmania, it is hard to imagine the movement for the separate statehood of Telangana.

A common factor that binds the two generations of activists is their trust in the democratic (electoral) means for Telangana to achieve statehood. That is why a mass movement could sustain for almost for more than five decades (though some activists from 1969 generations learnt this lesson the hard way, as many of them took the extreme revolutionary path for a while). Both phases of the movement experienced the leadership of seasoned politicians: MCR (Marri Chenna Reddy) in 1969; and KCR (K. Chandrashekhar Rao) in 2000. Such phenomena raise a critical question for us—what is the relation between social movements and politics? Scholars of social movements, especially resource mobilization theorists, consider politics as a resource for the movement, and issues of resource mobilization as important to examine and understand movements. Touraine (1981) argued that a movement must be more than just oppositional and that it must propose alternatives. In the 1969 movement, after forming a separate political party, TPS, and winning the elections, the possibility of creating a political alternative was lost the minute MCR merged TPS with the Congress party. Between 2001 and 2009, the KCR phase paints a similar picture. With the help of Telangana intellectuals, KCR formed TRS party in 2001 and won several elections, served as a cabinet minister in the central government, but the issues of separate statehood had not made a headline during his tenure. Another phase of agitation was started by the university students. The phase of 2009–13 marks an extraordinary commitment of student activists who not only led a mass movement but also provided an alternative to the existing politics by forming JACs. With the advent of JACs, the movement entered an institutional phase which was critical to the movement's success. More illuminating is the assertion among Dalits and OBC students that has changed the basis of caste as a social institution. They produced counter-historical narratives to challenge the existing ones. Castells (1997/2001: 9) notes that the identity building on the basis of history, geography, or biology often results from 'unbearable oppression … making it easier to essentialise the boundaries of resistance'. Resistance identities are defensive socio-cultural formations, and they are products of alienation and resentment in relation to the dominant institutions and ideology of society, which make their reasons for being no less comprehensible. Resistance identities do not generate the institution of civil society because they do not tend to aim primarily at institutional transformation vis-à-vis the state (Castells 1997/2001). Castells provides us framework of NSMs to understand the Telangana movement. Earlier chapters highlighted that within the larger spectrum of the movement, a parallel movement for caste identity assertion was taking place. The tradition and trajectories of their (ongoing) struggle can help us in understanding the contemporary activism. Gore (1989), Oommen (1990), and Singh (2001) agree on the idea that 'movement are not idiosyncratic phenomena that they have some degree of autonomy in relation to the autonomy of society itself' (Singh 2001: 167). Singh (2001: 136–91) raises a question: 'how to comprehend and analyze the growing conflicts, contestation, protests, demands and assertions of people relating to ethnic identity, regional autonomy to nation and sub-nation, monopoly over symbolic heritage, language, culture and religious faith ...' In other words, the formation of collective identity (of Telangana or any regional movement) is primarily cultural which finds its explanation economically, and generally manifests itself politically.

The second theme which we can derive from Telangana movement is the lived experience of its activist and its relationship with movements. Telangana movement has produced several student intellectuals who later emerged as 'organic intellectual' (using Gramscian term who sees a greater challenge among students as they are not tied to the system in the same way like other social groups). The university education is not limited to bookish knowledge but it also provides a space where social learning takes place among students. It is the place where students' everyday interactions (de)construct new narratives, which provides alternatives to the existing forms of knowledge. Understanding these systems of learning and knowledge production helps us in understanding the genesis of social movements.

Democratizing the production of histories by writing subaltern and Dalit literature has challenged the existing liberal and critical school of thought. Pathania (2012), in his ethnography of one of the premier institutions of India, highlights how educational practices were exclusionary in a liberal campus like JNU where 'Ambedkar was not accepted as a scholar until 1990'. But gradually with student activism and engagement with academic discourse of caste, Ambedkar's ideology has developed into a school of thought. The graffiti on campus walls includes Ambedkar who appears larger than Marx, Mao, and Lenin. Thus, the project of building a new kind of historical culture and democratizing the production of history is vital. Movement generates new knowledge, theory, and questions. Space, organizing, learning, and knowledge production are deeply interconnected in the course of activism for social change (Choudry 2015: 86).

NOTES

1. Available at https://www.mainstreamweekly.net/article1970.html, accessed 19 September 2015.
2. The ban was implemented following the death of a Nizam College student leader. See https://timesofindia.indiatimes.com/city/hyderabad/Lift-ban-on-student-polls/articleshow/42067746.cms, accessed 15 January 2015.
3. Interview on 29 June 2013, Hyderabad.
4. Manda Krishna Madiga formed MRPS to fight for subcategorization to oppose dominance of *Mala* caste among SCs. He tried to unite all 59 sub-castes of Dalits. He became popular among students since he formed a group called MSF. In January 2014, he also formed a party called Mahajana Socialist Party (MSP).
5. Available at http://www.thehindu.com/todays-paper/tp-national/tp-andhrapradesh/lsquoHyderabad-cannot-be-viewed-as-a-free-zonersquo/article16477754.ece.
6. Raju was one of the JAC leaders who attended several meetings at TRS office during 2009. From his interview on 2 June 2013.
7. KCR was the cabinet minister in the Congress government from 2004 to 2009. After four years of his tenure, Osmania students realized that he was not raising the separate Telangana demand.
8. *Deccan Chronicle*, 24 December 2009.
9. To express their anger, the student activists told the media that 'this coloured thing he drank was our urine'.

10. In an interview with TV9 and NDTV on 31 November 2009. Gaddar, a famous balladeer and the radical face of the movement, echoed the sentiment by saying *KCR is the traitor of Telangana movement*. For details see, *Andhra Jyothi*, 31 November 2009.
11. Congress party was the first one to get out of this JAC and then TDP.
12. TDP leaders attacked on Osmania Campus, *The Hindu*, 25 December 2009.
13. CPI (Maoist) CRB secretary Interview. *Andhra Jyothi*, 1 January 2010.
14. Interviewed on 27 September 2013 at B hostel.
15. From his interview on 30 August and 23 September 2013 at the Department of Journalism, Arts College.
16. *Pad-abhisheka* is the act of dousing milk over one's feet. It is a form of honour and reverence, usually performed on Hindu gods.
17. During 2012–13, around one hundred talks were organized in the Arts College premises by activists regarding themes of development, economy, Dalits, Madiga, reservation, agriculture, peasants, labour, and women of Telangana. The most common word was 'Jai Telangana' and 'struggle' in the title of these talks.
18. INC, BJP, CPI-M, CPI, TDP, AIMIM, TRS, PRP attended this meeting.
19. Available at https://economictimes.indiatimes.com/news/politics-and-nation/telangana-erupts-again-3-students-commit-suicide/ articleshow/5482695.cms.
20. Available at https://timesofindia.indiatimes.com/city/hyderabad/Student-who-set-himself-ablaze-for-Telangana-cause-dies/articleshow/5598698.cms.
21. Available at http://www.thehindu.com/news/national/crisis-looms-as-81-telangana-mlas-some-mps-submit-resignations/article2158170.ece, accessed 18 February 2014.
22. From *Nadustunna Telangana* (2011: 1).
23. *Nadustunna Telangana*. 2011. 'Editorial'. (3): 5 (The editor also writes all across the world people are revolting against imperialism, hegemony, dictatorship, capitalism, feudalism, p. 4).
24. The officer's name has been withheld as he would only speak on the condition of anonymity. The narrative is from several informal conversations with him held in August 2013.
25. A copy of police FIR is attached in the Appendix. Mentioned narratives is from ethnographic notes of authors' everyday discussion with police officials.
26. From his interview on 28 August and 11 September 2013.
27. Available at http://www.thehindu.com/todays-paper/tp-national/tp-andhrapradesh/telugu-talli-statue-unveiled/article5307531.ece.
28. Interviewed on 17 June 2013 at the Arts College, Osmania University.

29. Available at http://www.thehindu.com/news/national/andhra-pradesh/Telangana-bandh-Students-police-clash-at-Osmania-Univer-sity/article15454760.ece.
30. He is a resident of Dr B.R. Ambedkar (PG) hostel known as NRS.
31. Resident of hostel B, who generally hangs out at tea shops every evenings with his close friends. Excerpt is taken from my ethnographic notes on 2 November 2013.
32. Interviewed on 19 June 2013 at the department of political science, Arts College, Osmania University.
33. From interview at his home on 22 June 2013.
34. The researcher met with Manoj several times. He was invited to sing his revolutionary songs. The narrative is from his interview conducted on 22 December 2013 at his rented accommodate at Taranaka.
35. In 1999, Daruvu formed a team called *Daruv Kala Brundam*. His idea was that Telangana should be sung and led by Dalits not by the upper castes. He also formed *Telangna Rashtra Vidhyarthi Samiti* in 2001. He himself belongs to Madiga caste but married to an OBC girl. He got a job as teacher but he left it for the movement.
36. Interviewed on 10 October 2013 at his residence.
37. 'Telangan Etlostadi' (How to get Telangana?): a programme organized by TSJAC and OU-JAC on 12 June 2013.
38. See *The Hindu*, 2 November 2013.
39. Available at http://www.thehindu.com/news/national/telangana/students-celebrate-bathukamma-samburalu/article6429983.ece.
40. Interviewed on 19 September 2013 at Satvahana University, Karimnagar.
41. Professor Revathi, Professor Vimala, and Dr Sujatha were actively involved in the women's JAC. They celebrated Chakali Illama's birth anniversary as Telangana Women's Day.
42. Available at www.mainstreamweekly.net/article1970.html.
43. Captain L. Pandu Ranga Reddy in his interview to Deccan Chronicle on 2 October 2013. Available at http://archives.deccanchronicle.com/130208/news-current-affairs/article/osmania-university-student-rejects-degree-telangana-statehood.
44. Available at http://www.firstpost.com/politics/how-student-leaders-were-the-driving-force-behind-telangana-996213.html.
45. Police sub-inspector, a government post that is respectable and highly sought-after.
46. Posted on Blackvoice Telangana wall on 10 January 2013.
47. 'Students Attack OU JAC Leaders'. Available at http://www.thehindu.com/news/cities/Hyderabad/Students-attack-OU-JAC-leaders/article15456975.ece, accessed 14 October 2017.

48. From several informal conversation at the hostel during ethnographic observation between 2013 and 2014.
49. Interviewed on 5 September 2013.
50. The editorial of Nadustuna Telangana magazine compared this incident with the historical *chora-chori* incident during non-cooperation movement of 1920.
51. See *Nadustua Telangana* (2011: 10).

5 New State, Old Narratives

The political map of India has been drawn and redrawn several times since independence, according to recommendations made by the States Reorganisation Commission Act of 1953. Demands for new states have reshaped regional power dynamics. Starting with Andhra Pradesh, many new states were created, including Himachal Pradesh, Kerala, Madhya Pradesh, and Manipur. In the decades since, states and boundaries have been created and shifted for linguistic or political reasons. With the exception of Chhattisgarh, all such demands began with protests and resistance. The territorial reorganization had different socio-political undercurrents. Tillin (2013: 5–6) identifies three processes behind the state formation: (*a*) compromise between historic social movements and new political parties in the 1970s; (*b*) challenges to the upper-caste dominance in the Hindi heartland by Dalits and Other Backward Classes (OBCs); and (*c*) Bharatiya Janata Party's (BJP) changed approach to federalism and their emergence as national party (also see Heath 2002). On the other hand, Weiner (1978) highlighted the 'sons of the soil' theory to understand the demand for the separate statehood. All the analyses of state formation are centred on political (representational or electoral benefits) and economic gains.

After more than six decades of struggle, on 2 June 2014, Telangana appeared on the map as the 29th state of India. Contrary to above mentioned approaches, this book unfolds cultural contours to explain the emergence of Telangana movement for separate statehood. There are historical factors that guide these cultural resistances. William Sax (2011: 173), in his study on Uttarakhand statehood, argues that 'cultural and ethnic factors have been prominent in the creation of new Indian states (with the exception of Uttrakhand)'. Mitra (1995: 59) observes that 'culture is the ubiquitous, common element of all separatist movements'. No other state has witnessed as violent or intense a struggle as that preceding the formation of Telangana. Nowhere in modern Indian history have as many youths lost their lives as they did for Telangana. One cannot imagine history of Telangana without the sacrifice and struggle of university resistance. For a separate statehood from Andhra Pradesh, thousands of students sacrificed their lives. On 20 February 2010, 19-year-old Siripur Yadaiah set himself ablaze in public view at Osmania University (OU).[1] His suicide note read: 'I am an orphan, I was hopeful of getting a job in Telangana. But it appears that a separate state will not happen'. Like Yedaiah, hundreds of young students committed suicide between 2005 and 2014, citing lack of a Telangana state as the kernel of their despair. These suicide notes present a counter-narrative to the state's 'promised' narrative of 'inclusive' development and growth. Each death doused the anger of Telangana activists until 2 June 2014.

The present movements based on identities is an effort to create a culture of resistance. Culture is not a sphere, but a dimension of all institutions—economic, social, and political (Jordan and Weeden 1995: 8). The assertion of culture is *sui generis*, independent of political nationalism, but it may manifest politically or economic motivations may operate in parallel with cultural factors, which makes culture a complex phenomenon. On the other hand, 'ethnically based nationalism arises out of a sense of alienation, on the one hand, and resentment against unfair exclusion, whether political, economic or social' (Scheff 1994: 281). Della Porta et al. (2006) claim that territorial identities do not fade but are increasingly impacted by other places and cultures. This leads to resistance movements to defend traditional cultures, which in turn, leads to a resurgence of nationalism, ethnic movements, and religious mobilization (2006:15).

The ruling class of any state serves as the 'means and the end of the political oppression and cultural suppression that are imposed on the indigenous communities,' as Chomsky observes (cited in Meyer and Alvarado 2010: 16). The Telangana movement has been symptomatic of the existing cultural hegemony of 'settlers' (which they term as 'Andhra dominance') that was reflected in every walk of life of the state and which led to exclusion and underdevelopment of Telangana region. This inevitably resulted in the concept of '*Samajik*' or 'socially inclusive' Telangana, an ideology projected by Osmania intellectuals and alumni (C.H.H. Rao 2009). Many felt that Telangana had 'not received its due share in investment allocations, and that the "surpluses" from Telangana, were diverted to the other regions' (Rao 1969, cited in Rao 2009). The 'feeling of injustice' due to these disparities is greater among the educated classes because of their awareness of injustices faced in terms of job promotions or career mobility (Rao 2009). 'Representation and inclusiveness is not easy to be achieved in a bigger state as the voice of the marginalized sections remained fragmented,'[2] argues C.H.H. Rao (2009) in his article on regional disparities pertaining to Telangana.

POLITICS OF NARRATIVES

Generally, a social movement provides counter-narratives to existing narratives. These new narratives gradually become part of our socio-cultural understanding. The history of Telangana regional politics has been a history of countless narratives by the government of 'constituting', 'establishing', 'forming', and 'setting up' dozens of 'safeguards' 'committees', 'commissions', 'agreements', 'pacts', 'government orders', 'official statements', 'negotiation', 'promises', 'assurance', and so on. These words appear thousands of times in the modern history of Telangana politics. The Telangana movement engaged with the state by opposing government policies known as 'safeguards' says Dr A. Gopala Kishan, who was one of the founding fathers of Telangana Praja Samiti (TPS). According to him, 'none of our interests—relating to health, education, self-governance, and sale of agricultural lands—was safeguarded'.[3] These 'safeguards' were planned to ensure equal development in the region, but many of them were never implemented. Yet, they remained part of the state's narrative.

The first chapter highlights the discrimination, humiliation, and neglect of Telangana people and culture, specifically in government employment and financial allocation by the 'dominant' culture of Andhra. Employees hailing from Telangana faced constant humiliation as their culture and accent were considered 'inferior'. As OU is located in the capital city of Hyderabad, its students recognized the cultural politics at hand. When agitations to uphold the policy of safeguards were repeatedly ignored by the government, OU students raised the demand for separate statehood in 1969 and formed the TPS, rallying widely for support. Their collective anger burst onto the streets of Hyderabad in the form of the first violent student agitation, accelerating the movement, and creating turmoil in the city for nearly a year. Hundreds of students lost their lives in these protests, which fuelled more protests and resulted in a mass satyagraha across Telangana. For the entire academic year, students were on the road confronting the police. Jails quickly became overpopulated with students, and even schools in Telangana were used as detention centres. At the movement's peak, students invited Dr Marri Chenna Reddy (MCR), a Congress party leader, to head the TPS. After a year-long failed agitation in 1970, student activists set their eyes to the parliamentary election of 1971. 'This election was the only hope left for us. We coined the slogan—*Employment, Status and Pride.* We had no experience of any election except campus election of 1968 which was fought on Separate Telangana issues and we won that with this hope we were so ready to take the challenge and responsibility of parliamentary election.'[4]

In the 1971 election, TPS won 11 of 14 parliamentary seats, the most remarkable victory in the history of students' struggle. With high hopes, pamphlets were published announcing 'Telangana State'. However, Reddy's politicking and the eventual merger of TPS with the ruling Congress party led to widespread frustration among students, as they lost trust in the state. This new narrative was accepted by those who opted for a peaceful approach to remain close to power. But many activists rejected the Reddy–Congress narrative and imagined a new narrative. Sympathies began to sway towards the extreme Left with many student leaders joining the Naxal movement and People's War Group. Activism on campus waned and the emotions and forces generated by the 1969 movement did not find a political platform. More than a decade later, students became disillusioned with the Left's inaction. Nevertheless, the vision of a separate Telangana never wavered in the minds of the leading intellectuals who had experienced the 1969 agitation and lost friends in police firings. In 1986, they formed the 'Telangana Information Trust', where they penned their experiences of the movement. Later, many of them became popular writers and poets. In addition, OU alumni formed many socio-cultural organizations such as *Telangana Jana Parishad, Telangana Mahasabha* and *Telangana Sanskruti Samakhya*, to evoke consciousness among the masses.

In an effort to forge unity among people of the Telangana and Andhra regions, N.T. Rama Rao (NTR) offered a new narrative called 'Telugu Unity': *Telugu Jathi Manadi, Ninduga Velugu Jathi Manadi* (Ours is a Telugu nation, ours is a flourishing nation). Yet, many saw this as a ploy to distract attention from the Telangana cause. Telugu unity was just another narrative, which, according to Srinivasulu (2012), was 'a myth invented by Andhra people to justify their exploitation and oppression of the Telangana region'. 'In reality, it was "Andhra Unity,"' Ramesh,[5] a 1969 activist claims. 'In governments' eyes, Telangana does not even exist but this identity is well documented in our minds'. Most of the actors involved in agitations and protests were the university educated class.

Similarly, Telugu Talli[6] is another narrative created by the state to keep Telugus united by promoting common linguistic and cultural heritage. New departments were established in universities to enhance research on Telugu language and literature. The song, *Man Telugu Talli ki Malle Poodanda* (A jasmine garland for our mother of Telugu), was sung at every government office function. During the Telangana movement, activists rejected Telugu Talli and coined Telangana Talli. Later, at the peak of the movement, Dalit activists questioned whether Telangana Talli representing the 'real mother of Telangana'. Instead, they chose to celebrate Chakali Ilamma as Telangana Talli. After Telangana became a state, Joint Action Committee (JAC) leaders and government planned to erect statues of her across various districts of Telangana.[7]

When the Indian government created new states of Jharkhand, Chhattisgarh, and Uttarakhand, aspirations rekindled among Telangana supporters. They pushed their agenda to the national-level authorities. In 2001, with the help of intellectuals, activists, and politicians, the TRS formed under the leadership of K. Chandrashekhar Rao (henceforth KCR) and Telangana activism experienced a robust revival. Many activists had reservations with KCR and feared history would repeat itself, as they compared him to MCR. From this point onwards, through various programmes, pamphlets, and songs, students spread awareness in cities and villages about social backwardness of Telangana, an absolute deficit of governance and nepotism in employment practices, as well as the unjust exploitation of Telangana's natural resources. During this phase, the movement expanded and diffused into different ideological camps, no longer clinging to the Left.

The movement entered the second phase on 29 November 2009, when KCR's announcement of a fast-unto-death caught national attention. At this time, Osmania students played a crucial role: before KCR began his fast, he ensured he had the support of students. Yet, nine days later, when his health started deteriorating, the government became concerned about the consequences of his death. A new narrative crafted by the Congress government 'assured' the creation of a separate state by forming another commission called the Sri Krishna Commission. It was seen as another 'political betrayal' in the eyes of activists, who sensed a repetition of 1969 with KCR in place of MCR. This time, they declared, they 'would not let history repeat itself'. When KCR abruptly broke his fast, students cut all ties with him. They took the movement into their own hands and made a powerful attempt to reach the masses by forming a JAC—a non-political organization. Students were successful in their grassroot outreach, as the masses not only understood students' narratives, but also warmly accepted them. However, KCR managed to rebound and regained public sympathy by helping student padayatras. The period from 2009 to 2013 was characterized by rallies, meetings, marches, protests, agitations, and strikes.

At the height of the movement, KCR vowed that his party would appoint a Dalit as chief minister if Telangana became a state.[8] This was to counter the growing popularity of the Madiga (Dalit) leader, Manda Krishna Madiga[9] who formed his own party to fight elections. However, after TRS won the state election with a clear majority, KCR and his family members were given key positions. Before he took oath as the first chief minister of the new Telangana state, he pledged to rescind the police cases lodged against Telangana activists during the movement, as well as create one lakh jobs for the new state's youth.

Many former student activists have received retroactive government orders from the police for their involvement during the Telangana movement—activists call it a 'betrayal'. The handful of activists given election tickets by the TRS party and who are currently in power remain silent about their fellows' plight. As organic intellectuals, they strongly believe that they must continue their struggle to achieve a truly democratic Telangana. 'Those who are enjoying power now, should remember that it was our fellow students who sacrificed their lives to create this state which they claim as their now,' expresses an angry agitator in a rally organized by the Telangana Unemployed JAC.

Thus, they find little difference in their struggle pre and post-state formation.

Post-State Formation Narratives

Within a few months after the new government formation, students were back on the streets protesting against the state which they fought so hard to bring into existence. Angry and dissatisfied with the present government's neglect of its own promises, they formed the 'Student Unemployed Joint Action Committee' and protested against the government for not doing enough to provide employment opportunities to educated youth. They are raising the same issues of unemployment, poverty, and farmers' suicides, and so forth—issues which concerned them prior to the state's formation. According to students, 'all that was achieved was a geographic Telangana and a power transfer from Andhra's feudal Reddys to Telangana's wealth landowner Velammas'.

A prevalent feeling of 'being cheated' is felt among generations of Osmania students, who made countless sacrifices for the state, yet did not reap any benefits from the formation of the state. Osmania students see these actions as yet another 'chapter of betrayal' in the long history of the struggle for a separate Telangana. *Neellu-Nidhulu-Niyamakaalu* (water, resources, and employment) are still discussed in activist meetings. These are the common issues that still need to be addressed.

In the aftermath of the state's formation, mainstream media and new school textbooks have portrayed KCR as the architect of Telangana. His close ally from OU, Professor M. Kodandaram, one of the founders of T-JAC, has denied this claim, citing the collective effort of civil society in achieving statehood. He alleged that KCR 'indulged in horse trading of MLAs and MPs' and implemented unilateral decisions without consulting ministers or senior officials.[10] In 2016, Professor Kodandaram, with the help of students and other civil society groups, mobilized people from every part of Telangana and raised burning issues in the region. In addition, several non-governmental organizations (NGOs) such as the Telangana Development Forum, Telangana Intellectuals Forum, Telangana Resource Centre, *Telangana Jagruthi*, and Telangana Information Task Force are actively involved in disseminating the idea of a separate Telangana. Their websites provide free access to academic books and articles, literary works, biographies of

Telangana heroes, and video clips of speeches by Telangana leaders and political events. Once again, we see how intellectuals chose their own path towards social justice, rather than curry favour with power. The coalition of intellectuals and student community served as the basis of radical opposition and deepening democratic practice (Haragopal 2010b; Kannabiran et al. 2010: 69–88). This is reflected in the largely violence-free and disciplined response to protracted political negotiation since 2009 (Shaw 2014).

Politics of Ideological Narratives

In general, ideology needs to be problematized in the context of movements. This would help us in exploring why movements' organization or leadership splits up and divides. In this regard, educational institution such as school and university are an important site where social hierarchies, rituals, and traditions are reproduced through a dominant ideology. The recent critical debates on ideology highlight that class and ideology are neither empirical nor epistemological realities. They are materially and relationally continued through the infinite semiosis of linguistic meaning and the historical contingency of discursive practices (Bhabha 2015: 6). Ideology is not necessarily the expression of a class interest. It never stands on its own but involves in relations with other ideology. It is never complete, but continues to evolve and modify itself (Sigel 1990). It is the way certain class interests and other social forces attempt to intervene in the sphere of signification, to articulate or harness it to a particular project to hegemonize (Hall 1997: 30–1). Thus, ideology is not a monolithic entity that drives all facets of our thinking (for example, class ideology). It is also a realm of contestation and negotiation (Eagleton 2007: 101). Therefore, in contemporary times, whether political parties and movements have any concrete ideology or not is the key question to be raised. The leadership in the Telangana movement used different strategies, tactics, and mechanisms for their cause. Yet, if we analyse them from the traditional Marxist or functionalist ideological paradigm, it does not explain the ambiguities of caste and regional aspirations. Over 60 years, the movement has experienced varied leadership, demands, and countless ideological spectrums. These demands ultimately seek the representation of every social group, seeking a truly socially democratic state.

Therefore, in any identity based movements or mobilization, the word 'ideology' does not convey a serious message.

For the past two decades, identity has been an important theme capturing the attention of new social movement scholars. Snow and McAdam (2010: 46) look at identity as 'constructive perspective' which focusses on the construction and maintenance of collective identity in social movements (also see Hunt, Benford, and Snow 1994; Lichterman 1999). Identity work in social movements is not necessarily confined to discussion about creating 'we'. Bernstein (2008: 288) uses the term 'deconstructive movements', which may target the state, institutions, and more general cultural practices. These movements are motivated by activists' understandings of how categories are constituted and how those categories, codes, and ways of thinking serve as axes of regulation and domination (Crossley 2002; Eyerman and Jamison 1991; Melucci 1996; Rochan 1998). Taking the concept of identity movement critically, Bernstein (2008: 291) argues that 'collective action' is highly researched that centres around issues of domination and so on. Therefore, it not only defines who 'us' is, but also acknowledges some injustice done to 'us' and attributed it to structural causes (Gamson 1992; Morris and Braine 2001; Taylor and Whittier 1992).

To oppose the historical injustice, Osmania students formed a musical band called *Bheem Drum* to represent the traditional symbol of a community. Similarly, the dappu emerged as a powerful symbol for the movement. Identity assertion occurred through food consumption and festivals as well. In celebration of Ambedkar's birthday, a group of Dalit students composed a *Beef Anthem* at OU in 2012. Through these cultural resources they invoke a 'collective memory' (Eyerman and Jamison 1998: 70). Icons, symbols, and food practices, which were considered derogatory, have become part of the activists' toolkit in resisting cultural hegemony. The emerging middle class in India that has largely received higher education are 'harbingers of newness' due to their active participation in agitations and protests (Pathania 2015: 290). Yet, this 'newness' needs to be looked at critically when it comes to the issue of marginalized communities based on caste, region, religion, or gender. Marginalized students use the logic of historic discrimination and injustice done to 'us' *vs.* 'them' as their vantage point for any issue they raise. They claim that 'class' analysis not only misguides but also weakens the fight against casteist forces. Therefore, these binaries of 'us *vs.* them', 'bourgeois *vs.* proletariat', or 'Hindu *vs.* non-Hindu' and so forth, are fixed. This leaves little scope for any change in ideology.

The narratives of Telangana ideologues justify the movement as a struggle for identity and autonomy, and rationalize it as a struggle against domination, exploitation, discrimination, deception, and humiliation (Srikanth 2013: 42). Political parties not only ignored the socio-cultural history of the state but also bypassed the people's aspirations. Hundreds of student suicides were labelled as 'political strategy'. Radical left parties used students' energy for their party interests while Telangana issue was given only a token inclusion in their agendas. Amidst all this, OU intellectuals' efforts over half a century to research and understand the Telangana problem of writing and publishing literature, forming organization, and mobilizing masses finally achieved success. What is important to understand is that a movement occurs when the inequality becomes intolerable and there is no space left for negotiation. It occurs when there is no other option left, when representation becomes redundant, and existence becomes meaningless.

The Telangana movement is the combination of various identities assertion and above mentioned challenges. The grouping, organization, mobilization, and the strategies of the movements are loose and unstructured in these new movements. The changing student (social) composition has also changed the context of higher education, which led to the identity assertion. It takes us back to the question that Bernstein (2008: 289) asks: 'How do movements negotiate identity for empowerment when the identity around which the movement is organised is also the basis for grievance?' It also provides us insight to understand the weakness of the Telangana movement. Before the movement is unified, it splintered into various caste and sub-caste groups. The process of formation of Telangana identity and caste assertion did not work in tandem. In fact, unlike the assertion of caste and sub-caste identity occurred before identity formation for separate Telangana. In other words, lower castes were doubly deprived of their identity as Dalit and being Telanganaite. On the other hand, upper castes appeared to have a single agenda—of attaining statehood. Caste appeared as a dividing factor among Leftist parties but at the same time, it was making a collective identity for Dalits. Ideology of Dalit-Bahujan Telangana ignited aspirations of all the lower castes, including OBCs. Therefore, caste issues may not be the primary agenda item in their ideology, yet, caste is used as a political tool. Therefore, there is a need to problematize the notion of ideology. Any caste movement has the possibility to transform itself into an anti-caste movement if it can develop a democratic culture of its own and challenge the cultural institution. Movement that emerges from identity has some uniqueness that reflects in its cultural practices. The contemporary student activism makes university a potential site for a cultural resistance.

The formation of a new state does not necessarily guarantee the welfare and representation of historically marginalized identities—it demands continuous resistance and agitation for democratic representation. Universities, in this regard, provide fertile ground where students and teachers can question the establishment and devise critical and creative ways to establish organic linkages with the ontological realities of the public. The mass movement led by Osmania activists sets an example for any resistance movement around the world. The university as a democratic institution stands taller than other public institutions.

NOTES

1. Available at http://www.thehindu.com/news/national/Telangana-student-succumbs-to-burns/article16816028.ece, accessed 16 October 2014.
2. Available at http://www.mainstreamweekly.net/article1213.html, accessed 14 March 2016.
3. Available at https://www.telegraphindia.com/1130804/jsp/7days/17193418.jsp, accessed 14 March 2016.
4. Srinivasulu (OU activist in 1969), interviewed on 18 June 2013 at his residence in Gandhi Nagar, Secundrabad.
5. From his speech at Telangana Vidyarthi Vedika prorgram at Arts College on 2 October 2013.
6. Like Bharat Mata in the British era, Telangana Talli is presented as a victim of colonial domination, the victim here is Seemandhra capitalists (Srikanth 2013: 42).
7. Available at https://www.ap7am.com/lv-198321-chakali-ilamma-statue-unveiled-in-warangal-district.html, accessed 6 November 2016. A Telugu movie was also made on the life of Chakali Ilamma.
8. Available at http://indiatoday.intoday.in/story/dalit-telangana-first-chief-minister-k-chandrasekhara-rao/1/298009.html.
9. As Dalit politics, government jobs and position were largely held by Mala community, there was space for the emergence of non-Mala. Madiga

constitute 12 per cent of the population in Telangana region, but had no stake in power. Manda Krishna Madiga tried to bring 59 sub-castes of Dalit together. He led the MRPS agitation for subcategorization in reservation. His growing popularity made Osmania student leaders his close ally. With his help, students formed Madiga Student Federation (MSF) at OU and organized massive gatherings at the Arts College.

10. Available at http://www.thehansindia.com/posts/index/Telangana/2017-10-07/Kodandaram-vows-to-fight-against-KCR-Govt/331643, accessed 10 October 2017.

References

Abraham, M. 2016. 'India's Student Protests: Struggle for a Better World'. *ISA Forum Blog*. https://isafo-rum2016.wordpress.com/2016/03/21/indias-student-protests-struggle-for-a-better-world/.

Adiraju, V.R. 1969. *The People's Struggle*. Hyderabad: The Telangana Publications.

———. 2009. *Telangana: Saga of a Tragic Struggle*. Hyderabad: Anupama Printers.

Agarwal, P. 2009. *Indian Higher Education: Envisioning the Future*. New Delhi: SAGE Publications.

Alam, S.M. and Khan, W. 1972. *Metropolitan Hyderabad and Its Region*. Hyderabad: Asia Publishing House.

Alatas, S.H. 1977. *The Myth of Lazy Native*. London: Frank Cass Company Limited.

Altbach, P. 1966. 'The Transformation of the Indian Student Movement'. *Asian Survey* 6 (8): 448–60.

———. 1967. 'Student Politics'. *Transition* 28: 25–7.

———. 1968. 'Student Politics and Higher Education in India'. *Daedalus: Journal of the American Academy of Arts and Science* (Winter Issue): 254–73.

———. 1972. *The University in Transition: An Indian Case*. Mumbai: Sindhu Publications.

Altbach, P.G. 1966. 'A Wide-Angle View: The Student Movement and the American University'. *The Phi Delta Kappan* 47 (8): 424–7.

———. 1968a. *Student Politics in Bombay*. Mumbai: Asia Publishing House.

———. 1968b. *Turmoil and Transition: Higher Education and Students Politics in India*. Mumbai: Lalvani Publishing House.

———. 1969. 'Student Politics and Higher Education in India', in *Students in Revolt*, ed. S.M. Lipset and P.G. Altbach, pp. 241–62. Boston: Houghton Mifflin.

———. 1970a. *Student Revolution: A Global Analysis*. Mumbai: Lalvani Publishing House.

———. 1970b. 'Student Movement in Historical Perspective: The Asian Case'. *Journal of Southeast Asian Studies* 1 (1): 74–84.

———, ed. 1974. *University Reforms: Comparative Perspectives for the Seventies*. Cambridge, Mass.: Schenkman.

———. 1982. *Student Politics: Perspective from the Eighties*. New Jersey: The Scarecrow Press.

———. 1984. 'Student Politics in the Third World'. *Higher Education* 3 (16): 635–55.

———. 1987. 'A New Student Militancy'. *Economic and Political Weekly* 22 (13): 543–4.

———, ed. 1996. 'The International Academic Profession: Portraits of Fourteen Countries'. *Higher Education* 35 (3): 364–6.

Alavi, H. 1973. 'Peasants and Revolutions', in *Imperialism and Revolution in South Asia*, ed. K. Gough and H.P. Sharma. New York: Monthly Review Press.

Apple, M.W. 1996. *Cultural Politics and Education*. New York: Teachers College Press.

———. 2001. 'Comparing Neo-Liberal Projects and Inequality in Education'. *Comparative Education* 37 (4): 409–23.

———, ed. 2010. *Global Crisis, Social Justice and Education*. New York: Routledge.

———. 2011. *Education and Power* (Third Edition). New York: Routledge.

Armstrong, E. and Bernstein, M. 2008. 'Culture, Power, and Institutions: A Multi-Institutional Politics Approach to Social Movements'. *Sociological Theory* 26 (1): 74–99.

Aspinall, E. 2005. *Opposing Suharto: Compromise, Resistance, and Regime Change in Indonesia*, pp. 140–3. California: Stanford University Press.

Attewell, P. and Thorat, S. 2007. 'The Legacy of Social Exclusion: A Correspondence Study of Job Discrimination in India'. *Economic and Political Weekly* 42 (41): 4141–5.

Ball, S. 2004. *Class Strategies and the Education Market: The Middle Classes and Social Advantage*. London: Routledge Falmer.

Beckford, J. 1989. *Religion and Advanced Industrial Society*. London; Boston: Unwin Hyman. Beissinger, M., Jamal, A., and Mazur, K. 2012. 'Who Participate in Democratic Revolutions? A Comparison of Egyptian and Tunisian Revolutions'. Paper presented at 'American Political Science Association Meetings', New Orleans. http://www.princeton.edu/~mbeissin/beissinger.tunisiaegyptcoalitions.pdf.

Benichou, L.D. 2000. *From Autonomy to Integration: Political Development in Hyderabad State 1938–48*. New Delhi: Orient Blackswan.

Bernstein, B. 2000. *Pedagogy, Symbolic Control and Identity: Theory, Research, Critique*. London: Taylor and Francis.

Bernstein, M. 1997. 'Celebration and Suppression: Strategic Uses of Identity by the Lesbian and Gay Movement'. *American Journal of Sociology* 103: 531–65.

———. 2005. 'Identity Politics'. *Annual Review of Sociology* 31: 47–74.

———. 2008. 'The Analytic Dimensions of Identity: A Political Identity Framework', in *Identity Work in Social Movements*, pp. 277–301. Minneapolis: University of Minnesota Press.

Beteille, A. 2007. 'University at the Crossraod'. *Current Science* 82 (4): 25.

Bhabha, H.K. 2015. *Critical Inquiry* 42 (1): 1–30.

Bheenaveni, R. 2013. 'Division of Andhra Pradesh: Upper Caste Ethics and Spirit of Samaikyandhra'. *Hans Indi*. http://www.thehansindia.com/posts/index/Hans/2013-09-14/Upper-caste-ethics-and-spirit-of-Samaikyandhra/71741.

Bhushan, B.N.V. 2009. *Telangana: The State of Affairs*. Hyderabad: AdEd Value Ventures.

Bhushan M.B. and Venugopal, N. 2009. *Telangana: The State of Affairs*. Hyderabad: AdEd Value Ventures.

Bhushan, S. 2013. 'Higher Education in 12th Plan'. *Economic and Political Weekly* 48 (4): 17–19.

———. 2016. 'Public University in a Democracy'. *Economic and Political Weekly* 51 (17): 35–40.

Biao, X. 2007. *Global Bodyshopping: An Indian Labour System in the Information Technology Industry*. Princeton; Oxford: Princeton University Press.

Bischof, G., Karner, S. and Ruggenthaler, P., ed. 2010. *The Prague Spring and the Warsaw Pact Invasion of Czechoslovakia in 1968*. Lanham, MD: Lexington Books.

Blehl, V.F. 1963. *The Essential Newman*. New York: Omega Books.

Bombongan, D.J. 2008. 'Revisiting Newman's Idea of a University for Our Times'. *Philippiniana Scara* XLVIII (129): 469–83.

Bourdieu, P. 1983. 'The Field of Cultural Production or the Economic World Reversed'. *Poetics* 12 (4–5): 311–56.

———. 1985. 'Social Space and the Genesis of Groups'. *Theory and Society* 14 (6): 723–44.

———. 2003. *Firing Back against the Tyranny of the Market 2*. New York: New Press.

Brand, K.W., ed. 1983. *Aufbruch in eine Andere Geselleschafi*. Frankfurt Campus.

———, ed. 1985. *Neue Soziale Bewegungen in Westeuropa und den USA. Ein Internationaler Vergleich*. Frankfurt: Campus.

Braungart, R.G. 1984. 'Historical Generations and Generation Units: A Global Perspective'. *Journal of Political and Military Sociology* 12: 113–35.

Braungart, R.G. and Braungart, M.M. 1990. 'Youth Movements in the 1980s: A Global Perspective'. *International Sociology* 5: 157–81.

Braz, R. 1973. Student Movement, Political Development and Modernisation in India. Master's thesis, Graduate School of the University of Massachusetts, Amherst. https://scholarworks.umass.edu/theses/2460.

Brooks, R., ed. 2016. *Student Politics and Protest: International Perspective*. New York: Routledge.

Buechler, S.M. 1995. 'New Social Movement Theories'. *The Sociological Quarterly* 36 (3): 441–64.

———. 2011. *Understanding Social Movements: Theories from the Classical Era to the Present*. Boulder, CO: Paradigm Publishers.

Butalia, U. 2012. 'Let's Ask How We Contribute to Rape'. *The Hindu*, 26 December. http://www.thehindu.com/opinion/op-ed/lets-ask-how-we-contribute-to-rape/article4235902.ece.

Calhoun, C. 1993. 'New Social Movements of the Early 19th Century'. *Social Science Journal* 17: 385–427.

Carnoy, M. 2000. *Globalisation and Educational Restructuring*. Paris: International Institute of Educational Planning.

Carter, D.J. 2007. 'Why the Black Kids Sit Together at the Stairs: The Role of Identity-Affirming Counter-Space in Predominantly White High School'. *The Journal of Negro Education* 76 (4): 542–54.

Castells, M. 1978. *City, Class and Power*. London: Macmillan.

———. 1983. *The City and the Grassroots: A Cross-Cultural Theory of Urban Social Movements*. Berkeley: University of California Press.

———. 1997/2001. *The Power of Identity*, as a part of *The Information Age: Economy, Society and Culture, Volume 2*. Oxford, UK: Blackwell.

———. 1999. *The Rise of Network Society*, as a part of *The Information Age: Economy, Society and Culture, Volume 2*. Oxford, UK: Blackwell.

Chaitanya, K. 1994. 'JNU Rebuff to Communal Fascism'. *Economic and Political Weekly* 29 (4): 160–1.

Chandran, R. 2012. 'Exactly Whose Sentiments are Hurt by Beef and Pork?' *Round Table India: For an Informed Ambedkar Age*. Accessed 3 February 2015. https://roundtableindia.co.in/~roundta3/index.php?option=com_content&view=article&id=5764:exactly-whose-sentiments-are-hurt-by-beef-and-pork&catid=119:feature&Itemid=132.

Chandra, P. 1938. *Student Movement in India*. Lahore: All India's Student Federation.

Charon, C.E.T. 2004. 'Re-Encountering Cuban Tastes in Australia'. *Journal of Anthropology* 15 (1): 40–53.

Chatterjee, P. 1997. *The Present History of West Bengal: Essays in Political Criticism*. New Delhi: Oxford University Press.

Chattopadhyay, S. 2009. 'The Market in Higher Education: Concern for Equity and Quality'. *Economic and Political Weekly* 46 (29): 53–61.

———. 2012. *Education and Economics: Disciplinary Evolution and Policy Discourse*. New Delhi: Oxford University Press.

Chaturvedi, B.N. 1956. *A Descriptive Atlas of Hyderabad State*. Allahabad: Indian Press Private.

Chomsky, N. 2013. *On Anarchism*. New Delhi: Penguin.

Choudry, A. 2015. *Learning Activism: The Intellectual Life of Contemporary Social Movements*. New York: University of Toronto Press.

Ciotti, M. 2006. 'At the Margins of Feminist Politics? Everyday Lives of Women Activists in North India'. *Contemporary South Asia* 15 (4): 437–52.

Clark, T.N. and Hoffmann-Martinot, V. 1998. *The New Political Culture*. Boulder, CO: Westview Press.

Cohen, J.L. 1985. 'Strategy of Identity: New Theoretical Paradigm and Contemporary Social Movements'. *Social Research* 52 (4): 663–716.

Crossley, N. 2002. *Making Sense of Social Movements*. Philadelphia: Open University Press.

———. 2012. 'Student Perspective: A Perspective from the UK'. *Mobilising Ideas*. Accessed 10 June 2016. https://mobilizingideas.wordpress.com/2012/05/02/student-protest-a-perspective-from-the-uk/.

———. 2015. 'Relational Sociology and Culture: A Preliminary Framework'. *International Review of Sociology* 25 (1): 65–85.

Crossley, N. and Ibrahim, J. 2012. 'Critical Mass, Social Networks and Collective Action: Exploring Student Political Worlds'. *Sociology* 46 (4): 596–612.

Culler, A.D. 1965. *The Imperial Intellect: A Study of Cardinal Newman's Educational Ideal*. London: Yale University.

Curran, J.A. 1951. *Militant Hinduism in Indian Politics: A Study of the R.S.S.* New York: Institute of Pacific.

Daenekindt, S. and Roose, H. 2015. 'De-Institutionalisation of High Culture? Realised Curricula in Secondary Education in Flanders, 1930–2000'. *Cultural Sociology* 9 (4): 515–33.

Damle, Y.B. 1966. College *Youth in Poona*. Pune: Deccan College.

Damodaran, H. 2008. *India's New Capitalists: Caste, Business, and Industry in a Modern Nation*. New York: Palgrave Macmillan.

Danda, A.K. 1983. 'Gahira Guru and His Sant Samaj Movements', in *Tribal Movements in India: Volume 2*, ed. K.S. Singh, pp. 197–208. New Delhi: Manohar.

Dasgupta, P.K. 1983. 'The Adi Samaj Movement among the HO', in *Tribal Movements in India: Volume 2*, ed. K.S. Singh, pp. 93–107. New Delhi: Manohar.

Dasgupta, R. 2006. 'Towards the "New Man": Revolutionary Youth and Rural Agency in the Naxalite Movement'. *Economic and Political Weekly* 41 (19): 1920–7.

Dasgupta, S., Bhattacharjee, R., and Singh, S. 1974. *The Great Gherao of 1969: A Case Study of Campus Violence and Protest Methods*. Mumbai: Orient Longman.

Deccan Chronicle. 2013. 'Statehood Refused Due to T-Case in UNSC'. https://www.pressreader.com/india/deccan-chronicle/20130210/281801396353407.

Della Porta, D., Andretta, M., Mosca, L., and Reiter, H. 2006. *Globalization from Below: Transnational Activists and Protest Networks*. Minneapolis, MN: University of Minnesota Press.

Desai, M. 2008. 'Where Did We Go Wrong', in *Beyond Degree*, ed. I. Panda, pp. 178–83. New Delhi: India International Centre.

Deshmukh, C.D. 1968. 'Student Violence Part of a Vicious Circle'. *The Tribune*, 24 April.

Deshpande, S. 2013. 'Towards a Biography of the "General Category" Caste and Castelesssness'. *Economic and Political Weekly* 48 (15): 32–9.

DeSouza, P.R. 2015. 'Living Between Thought and Action', in *The Public Intellectuals in India*, ed. R. Thapar, S. Sarukkai, D. Raina, P.R. DeSouza, N. Bhattacharya and J. Naqvi, pp. 79–100. New Delhi: Aleph Book Company.

Dewey, J. 1961. *Democracy and Education*. New York: Macmillan Publishers.

Dhangare, D.N. 1983. *Peasant Movements in India*. Delhi: Oxford University Press.

Diani, M. and Bison, I. 2004. 'Organizations, Coalitions, and Movements'. *Theory and Society* 33: 281–309.

Diani, M. and McAdam, D. 2003. *Social Movements and Networks: Relational Approach to Collective Action*. New York: Oxford University Press.

DiBona, J. 1966. 'Indiscipline and Student Leadership in an Indian University'. *Comparative Education Review* 10 (2): 306–19.

DiMaggio, P. 1991. 'Social Structure, Institutions and Cultural Goods: The Case of United States', in *Social Theory for a Changing Society*, pp. 133–67. Boulder: Westview.

D'Souza, E. 2004. 'IIMs-I: Market and Equity in Education'. *Economic and Political Weekly* 13: 1107–9.

Duncombe, S. 2002. *Cultural Resistance Reader*. London; New York: Verso.

———. 2012. *Cultural Resistance Reader*. New Delhi: Adarsh Books.

Eagleton, T. 2007. *Ideology: An Introduction*. New Delhi: ABS Publishers and Distributors.

Nadustunna Telangana. 2011. 'Editorial' (4): 17.

Edward, J. 2009. *Language and Identity: An Introduction*. NY: Cambridge University Press.

Elavarthi, S.P. and Vamireddy, V. 2015. 'Telangana and Language Politics of Telugu Cinema'. *Anveshi-Broadsheet* 2 (4 and 5). http://www.anveshi.org.in/wp-content/uploads/2015/01/Language-Region-and-Community-English.pdf.

Eliot, T.S. [1934] 1968. 'Choruses from "Rock"', in *Selected Poems*, pp. 161–85. London: Faber.

Elliot, C.M. 1972. 'The Problem of Autonomy: The Osmania University Cas', in *Education and Politics in India: Studies in Organization, Society and Policy*, ed. S.H. Rudolph and L.I. Rudolph, pp. 273–312. Cambridge, Mass.: Harvard University Press.

Emmerson, D., ed. 1968. *Students and Politics in Developing Nations*. New York: Praeger.

Eyerman, R. and Jamison, A. 1991. *Social Movements: A Cognitive Approach*. University Park, PA: Pennsylvania State University Press.

———. 1998. *Music and Social Movements: Mobilizing Tradition in the Twentieth Century*. Cambridge, UK: Cambridge University Press.

Fantasia, R. 1988. *Cultures of Solidarities: Consciousness, Action, and Contemporary American Workers*. Oakland: University of California Press.

Ferree, M.M. 1992. 'The Political Context of Rationality: Rational Choice Theory and Resource Mobilization', in *Frontiers in Social Movement Theory*, ed. A. Morris and C. McClurg Mueller, pp. 29–52. New Haven: Yale University Press.

Ferree, M.M., Gamson, W.A., Gerhards, J., and Rucht, R. 2002. 'Four Models of the Public Sphere in Modern Democracies'. *Theory and Society* 31 (3): 289–324.

Frank, A.G. and Fuentes, M. 1987. 'Nine Theses on Social Movements'. *Economic and Political Weekly* 22 (35): 1503–10.

Fraser, N. 1997. *Injustice Interrupts: Critical Reflections on the 'Postsocialist' Condition*. New York: Routledge.

Freire, P. 1970. *Pedagogy of the Oppressed*. New York: Continuum.

Friberg, M. and Galtung, J., ed. 1984. *Rorelserna*. Stockholm: Akademilitteratur.

Furedi, F. 2004. *Where Have All The Intellectuals Gone?* London, UK: Continuum.

Gamson, J. 1995. 'Must Identity Movements Self-Destruct? A Queer Dilemma'. *Social Problems* 42 (3): 390–407.

———. 1996. 'The Organisational Shaping of Collective Identity: The Case of Lesbian and Gay Film Festivals in New York'. *Sociological Forum* 11: 231–61.

Gamson, W. 1992. *Talking Politics*. New York: Cambridge University Press.

Gamson, W.A. and Meyer, S.D. 1996. 'Framing Political Opportunity', in *Comparative Perspectives on Social Movements: Political Opportunities, Mobilizing Structures and Cultural Framing*, ed. D. McAdam, J.D. McCarthy, and M. Zald, pp. 275–90. Cambridge, UK: Cambridge University Press.

Garalyte, K. 2015. 'Subaltern Autonomy: Dalit Students' Identity Politics in India'. *Groups and Environment* 4: 49–76.

Geiger, R.L. 2009. *Curriculum, Accreditation and Coming of Age of Higher Education* (First Edition). New York: Routledge.

Giroux, H. 1981. *Ideology, Culture and Process of Schooling*. Philadelphia: Temple University Press.

———. 1983. *Theory and Resistance in Education: A Pedagogy for the Opposition*. South Hadley, Mass.: Bergin and Garvey.

———. 1989a. *Teachers as Intellectuals: Towards a Critical Pedagogy of Learning*. Massachusetts: Bergin and Gravey.

———. 1989b. *Schooling for Democracy: Critical Pedagogy in Modern Age*. London: Routledge.

Giroux, H.A. 1977. *Pedagogy and the Politics of Hope—Theory, Culture and Schooling: A Critical Reader*. Boulder. CO: Westview Press.

———. 1991. 'Democracy and the Discourse of Cultural Difference: Towards a Politics of Border Pedagogy'. *British Journal of Sociology* 12 (4): 5.

———. 1999. 'Rethinking Cultural Politics and Radical Pedagogy in the Work of Antonio Gramsci'. *Educational Theory* 49 (1): 1–19.

Giroux, H., Freire, P., and MacLaren, P. 1988. *Teachers as Intellectuals*. New York: Bergin and Garvey.

Gitlin, T. 1993. *The Sixties: Years of Hope, Days of Rage*. USA: Bantam Books.

———. 1995. *The Twilight of Common Dreams: Why America Is Wracked by Culture Wars*. New York: Metropolitan Books.

Goodwin, J. and Jasper, J.M. 1999. 'Caught in a Winding, Snarling Vine: The Structural Bias of Political Process Theory'. *Sociological Forum* 14 (1): 27–54.

———. 2003. 'Caught in a Winding Snarling Vine: The Structural Bias of Political Process Theory', in *Rethinking Social Movements*. Boulder: Rowman & Littlefield Publishers.

Gore, M.S. 1989. *The Non-Brahmin Movement in Maharashtra*. New Delhi: Segment Book Distributors.

Gorringe, H. 2005. *Untouchable Citizens: Dalit Movements and Democratization in Tamil Nadu*. New Delhi: SAGE Publications.

———. 2016. 'Drumming Out Expression, or Drumming It In? Identity, Culture and Contention in Dalit Politics'. *Contribution to Indian Sociology* 50 (1): 1–26.

Government of India. 1955. *Report of the State Reorganisation Committee*. Delhi: Government Printer.

———. 2010. *Report of the Committee for Consultations on the Situation of Andhra Pradesh*. New Delhi: Ministry of Home Affairs.

———. 2016. *National Policy on Education 2016: Report on the Committee for Evaluation of the New Education Policy*. New Delhi: Ministry of Human Resource Development.

Gramsci, A. 1971. *Selections from the Prison Notebooks of Antonio Gramsci*, ed. and trans. Q. Hoare and G.N. Smith. New York: International Publishers.

Granovetter, M.S. 1973. 'The Strength of Weak Ties'. *American Journal of Sociology* 78 (6): 1360–80.

Gray, H. 1974. 'The Failure of the Demand for a Separate Andhra State'. *Asian Survey* 14 (4): 338–49.

Guha, R. 2008. 'Crucibles of Modernity', in *Beyond Degree*, ed. I. Pande, pp. 2–17. New Delhi: India International Centre.

Gundimeda, S. 2009. 'Democratisation of the Public Sphere: The Beef Stall Case in Hyderabad's Sukoon Festival'. *South Asia Research* 29 (2): 322–42.

Gupta, R.C., ed. 1968. *Youth in Ferment*. Delhi: Sterling.

Guru, G. 1995. 'Dalit Women Talk Differently'. *Economic and Political Weekly* 30 (41/42): 2548–50.

———. 2012. 'Egalitarianism and the Social Sciences in India', in *The Cracked Mirror: An Indian Debate on Experience and Theory*, ed. G. Guru and S. Sarukkai, pp. 9–28. New Delhi: Oxford University Press.

———. 2017. 'Taking Indian Nationalism Seriously', in *What the Nation Really Needs to Know: The JNU Nationalism Lectures*, ed. JNU Teachers' Association, pp. 2–13. New Delhi: Harper Collins.

Habashi, J. 2014. 'Langauge of Political Socialisation', in *Social Movements: Transformative Shifts and Turning Points*, pp. 326–46. New Delhi: Routledge.

Habermas, J. 1967. *On the Logic of the Social Sciences*. Cambridge, MA: MIT Press.

———. 1981. New Social Movements. *Telos* 49: 33–7.

———. 1984. *The Theory of Communicative Action: Reason and Rationalisation of Society*. Boston: Beacon Press.

———. 1987. *The Theory of Communicative Action*, trans. T. McCarthy. Cambridge, UK: Polity Press.

Habermas, J. and Blazek, J.R. 1987. 'The Idea of the University'. *New German Critique* 41: 3–22.

Haine, W.S. 2013. 'Introduction', in *The Thinking Space: The Cafe as Cultural Institution in Paris, Italy and Vienna*, ed. L. Rittner, W.S. Haine, and J.H. Jackson, pp. 1–22. UK: Ashgate Publishing.

Hall, S. 1997. 'Culture and Power'. *Radical Philosophy* 86 (Nov/Dec): 24–42.

Hall, S., Evans, J., and Nixon, S., ed. *Representation* (Second Edition). London: Sage.

Haragopal, G. 2010a. 'The Telangana People's Movement: The Unfolding Political Culture'. *Economic and Political Weekly* 45 (42): 51–60.

———. 2010b. 'Emergence of a New Political Culture in Andhra Pradesh', in *The Telangana Struggle for Identity*, ed. K.R. Velchala, J.V. Raghavendra Rao, and B. Narsing Rao, pp. 155–66. Hyderabad: Telangana Cultural Forum Publication.

Hardtmann, E.M. 2009. *The Dalit Movement in India: Local Practices, Global Connections*. New Delhi: Oxford University Press.

Harinath, S. 2013. *Dalit Women and Dropout Rates in Collegiate Education: A Study of the Warangal District of Andhra Pradesh*. Newcastle Upon Tyne, UK: Cambridge Scholars Publishing.

Heath, O. 2002. 'Anatomy of BJP's Rise to Power: Social, Regional and Political Expansion in 1990s', in *Parties and Party Politics in India*, ed. Z. Hasan, pp. 232–57. New Delhi: Oxford University Press.

Heredia, R. 1996. 'Tribal Education for Development: The Need for a Liberal Education'. *Journal of Education and Social Change* X (1–2).

Hobson, B. 2003. *Recognition Struggles and Social Movements: Contested Identities, Agencies and Power*. Cambridge, UK; New York: Cambridge University Press.

Huffinton Post. 2016. 'Shoot Anti-National JNU Students & Profs, Says BJP Official'. Accessed 1 April 2016. https://www.huffingtonpost.in/2016/03/09/jnu-row_n_9415292.html.

Hugar, G.B. 2015. 'Vande Mataram Movement in Hyderabad Karnataka 1938–39, India'. *International Research Journal of Social Sciences* 4 (9): 30–3.

Humboldt, W.V. 1970. 'On the Spirit and the Organisational Framework of Intellectual Institutions in Berlin'. *Minerva* 8: 242–50.

Hunt, S.A., Benford, R.D., and Snow, D.A. 1994. 'Identity Fields: Framing Processes and Movement Identities', in *New Social Movements*, ed. E. Larana, H. Johnston, and J.R. Gusfield, pp. 185–208. Philadelphia: Temple University Press.

Hyderabad Forum for Telangana. 2009. *Whose Hyderabad Is It? Myths, Facts and Realities*. Secunderabad: Hyderabad Forum for Telangana.

———. 2010. *Appeal to Political Parties on People's Demand for Separate State of Telangana*. Hyderabad: Hyderabad Forum for Telangana.

Ilaiah, K. 2001. *God as a Political Philosopher: Buddha's Challenge to Brahminism*. Kolkata: Samya.

The Indian Express. 1953. 'High-Power Commission (on the Re-Organisation of States) by Year-End'.

Indiresan, J. 1999. 'Campus-Community Linkages: A Dialogue on Diversity', in *Diversity and Unity: The Role of Higher Education in Building Democracy*, ed. M. Cross, N. Cloete, E. Beckham, A. Harper, J. Indiresan and C. Musil, pp. 128–54. Cape Town: Maskew Miller Longman.

Jadhav, K.R. 1997. 'Towards a History of the Telangana Movement', in *Telangana: Dimensions of Under-Development*, ed. S. Simhadri and P.V. Rao, pp. 5–14. Hyderabad: Centre for Telangana Studies.

Jafar, S.M. 1977. *Student Unrest in India: A Selected Bibliography*. Gurgaon: Indian Documentation Services.

Janardhan, V. and Raghavendra, P. 2013. 'Telangana: History and Political Sociology of a Movement'. *Social Change* 43 (4): 551–64.

Jaoul, N. 2006. 'Learning the Use of Symbolic Means: Dalits, Ambedkar Statues and the State in Uttar Pradesh'. *Contributions to Indian Sociology* 40 (2): 175–207.

Jasper, J. 1997. *The Art of Moral Protest: Culture, Biography and Creativity in Social Movements*. Chicago, IL: University of Chicago Press.

Jayaram, N. 1979. 'Sadhu No Longer: Recent Trends in Indian Student Activism'. *Higher Education* 8 (6): 683–99.

———. 2006. 'India, in Forest', in *International Handbook of Higher Education, Part Two: Regions and Countries*, ed. J.F. James and P.G. Altbach, pp. 747–67. Dordrecht: Springer.

Jeffrey, C. 2001. 'A Fist Is Stronger than Five Fingers: Caste and Dominance in Rural North India'. *Transaction of the Institution of British Geographers, New Series* 25: 1–30.

———. 2003. *India's Silent Revolution: The Rise of the Lower Castes in North India*. London: Hurst and Company.

———. 2007. 'Kicking Away the Ladder: Student Politics and the Making of an Indian Middle Class'. *Environment and Planning, D: Society and Space* 26: 517–36.

———. 2008. 'Generation Nowhere: Rethinking Youth through the Lens of Unemployed Young Men'. *Progress in Human Geography* 32 (6): 739–58.

———. 2010. 'Timepass: Youth, Class, and Time among Unemployed Young Men in India'. *American Ethnologist* 37 (3): 465–81.

Jeffrey, C. and Young, S. 2012. 'Waiting for Change: Youth, Caste and Politics in India'. *Economy and Society* 41(4): 638–61.

Jeffrey, C., Jeffrey, R., and Jeffrey, P. 2004. 'Degree without Freedom: The Impact of Formal Education on Dalit Young Men in North India'. *Development and Change* 35 (5): 963–86.

Jessop, B. 2002. *The Future of the Capitalist State*. Cambridge, UK: Polity Press.

Johnston, H. and Klandermans, B., ed. 1995. *Social Movement and Culture*. Minneapolis: University of Minnesota Press.

Jordan, G. and Weeden, C. 1995. *Cultural Politics: Class, Gender, Race and the Postmodern World*. Oxford, UK: Blackwell.

Joshi, P.M. 1972. *Student Revolts in India: Story of Pre-Independence Youth Movement*. Mumbai: Popular Prakashan.

Kakkar, S. and Chowdhury, K. 1969. *Conflict and Choice: Indian Youth in Changing Society*. Mumbai: Somaiya Publication Pvt. Ltd.

Kamat, S. 2011. 'Neo-Liberalism, Urbanism and the Education Economy, Producing Hyderabad as a Global City'. *Discourse: Studies in the Cultural Politics of Education* 32 (2): 18–202.

Kannabiran, K., Ramdas, S.R., Madhushan, N., Ashalatha, S., and Kumar, P.M. 2010. 'On the Telangana Trail'. *Economic and Political Weekly* 24 (13): 69–88.

Kavitha, K. 2014. 'Telangana: A Brush with History'. *Deccan Chronicle*, 2 June.

Khagram, S. 2004. *Dams and Development: Transnational Struggles for Water and Power*. New Delhi: Oxford University Press.

Khora, S. 2015. 'Questioning Excellence: Expelling 73 Students in IIT Rookee'. *Economic and Political Weekly* 50 (33). http://www.epw.in.ezproxy.jnu.ac.in/node/145675/pdf.

———. 2016. 'Removing Discrimination in Universities: Situating Rohith Vemula's Suicide'. *Economic and Political Weekly* 51 (6). http://www.epw.in.ezproxy.jnu.ac.in/node/146468/pdf.

Kincheloe, J.L. 2008. 'Critical Pedagogy and the Knowledge Wars of the Twenty-First Century'. *International Journal of Critical Pedagogy* 1 (1): 1–22.

Kirylo, J. 2013. *A Critical Pedagogy and Resistance*. Rotterland: Sense Publishers.

Kitts, J. 2000. 'Mobilising in Black Boxes: Social Networks and Participation in Social Movement Organisations'. *Mobilisation: An International Quarterly* 5 (2): 241–57.

Klandermans, B., Kriesi, H., and Tarrow, S., ed. 1988. *From Structure to Action: Comparing Social Movement Research across Culture*. Greenwich, CT: Jai Press.

Kothari, R. 'The Centre and Indian Reality'. By H. Ahmed, P. Vijaisri, and A.K. Dubey. *Seminar* 639. pp. 3–5. http://www.india-seminar.com/2012/639/639_interview_kothari.htm.

Kriesi, H. and Giugni, M.G. 1995. 'Introduction', in *New Social Movements in Western Europe: A Comparative Analysis*, ed. H. Kriesi, R. Koopmans, J.W. Duyvendak, and M.G. Giugni, pp. ix–xxvi. Minneapolis: University of Minnesota Press.

Kumar, A. 2002. *The Black Economy in India* (Revised Edition). New Delhi: Penguin.

———. 2012. '"Banda-Canteen" Broadcasts: Reminiscences of George Reddy – Budding Physicist and Revolutionary'. *george.reddy.amar.rahe*. Accessed 13 February 2014. http://georgereddyamarrahe.blogspot.com/2012/02/banda-canteen-broadcasts.html.

Kumar, P.K. 2010. 'Popular Culture and Ideology: The Phenomenon of Gadar'. *Economic and Political Weekly* 45 (7): 61–7.

Kumar, V. 2005. 'Understanding the Politics of Reservation'. *Economic and Political Weekly* 40 (9): 803–6.

———. 2007. *Social Exclusion and Different Shades of Dalit Movement*. Pune: Department of Sociology, Pune University.

———. 2016. 'Discrimination on Campuses of Higher Learning: A Perspective from Below'. *Economic and Political Weekly* 51 (6): 12–15.

Kumar, V.M.R. 2016. 'History of Indian Environmental Movement: A Study of Dr B.R. Ambedkar from the Perspective of Access to Water'. *Contemporary Voice of Dalit* 8 (2): 239–45.

Lall, M. and Rao, S.S. 2011. 'Revisiting the Equality Debate in India and the UK', in *Education and Social Justice in the Era of Globalisation: Caste, Race and Class Intersection in Education*, ed. M. Lall and G.B. Nambissan, pp. 25–55. Delhi: Routledge.

Laraña, E., Johnston, H., and Gusfield, J.R. 1994. *New Social Movements: From Ideology to Identity*. Philadelphia: Temple University Press.

Laxamaiah, M. 2007. *Nurella Telugu Dalitodyamam*. Hyderabad: Samantaara Publications.

Lee, N. 2005. 'Representing the Worker: The Worker–Intellectual Alliance of the 1980s in South Korea'. *Journal of Asian Studies* 64 (4): 912.

Lee, S.H. 2007. *Debating the New Social Movements: Culture, Identity and Fragmentation*. Lanham, MD: United Press of America.

Lichterman, P. 1999. 'Talking Identity in the Public Sphere: Broad Visions and Small Spaces in Sexual Identity Politics'. *Theory and Society* 28 (1): 101–41.

Lipset, S.M. 1960. *Political Man*. London: Mercury Books.

———. 1968. *Revolution and Counter-Revolution*. New York: Basic Books.

———. 1971. 'Youth and Politics', in *Contemporary Social Problems*, ed. R.K. Merton and R. Nisbet (Third Edition), pp. 752–4. London: Harcourt Brae Jovanovich.

Lipset, S.M. and Schaflander, G.M. 1971. *Passion and Politics: Student Activism in America*. Boston, Mass.: Little Brown.

Lukács, G. 1968. *History and Class Consciousness*. Cambridge, MA: MIT Press.

Lukose, R. 2006. 'Re(casting) the Secular: Religion and Education in Kerala, India'. *Social Analysis: The International Journal of Social and Cultural Practices* 50 (3): 38–60.

———. 2010. *Liberation's Children: Gender, Youth and Consumer Citizenship in Globalising India*. Durham, NC: Duke University Press.

Lynch, K., Crean, M., and Moran, M. 2010. 'Equality and Social Justice: The University as a Site of Struggle', in *The Routledge International Handbook of Sociology of Education*, ed. M.W. Apple, S.J. Ball, and L.A. Gandin, pp. 296–305. New York: Routledge.

Mahapatra, S. 1983. 'Raghunath Murmu's Movement for Santal Solidarity', in *Tribal Movements in India: Volume 2*, ed. K.S. Singh, pp. 129–59. New Delhi: Manohar.

Manne, K. 2013. *No One Dies: The Scrambling of Student Movement*. Hyderabad: Good Tree Publications.

Mantena, R.S. 2014. 'The Andhra Movement, Hyderabad State and the Historical Origins of the Telangana Demand: Public Life and Political Aspiration'. *India Review* 13 (4): 337–57.

Maringanti, A. 2010. 'Telangana: Righting Historical Wrongs or Getting the Future Right?' *Economic and Political Weekly* 45 (4): 33–8.

Marisha, Banshal, S.K., and Singh, V.K. 2017. 'Research Performance of Central Universities in India'. *Current Science* 112 (11): 2198–207.

McAdam, D. 1986. 'Recruitment to High-Risk Activism: The Case of Freedom Summer'. *American Journal of Sociology* 48: 735–54.

———. 1988. 'Micromobilisation Contexts and Recruitment to Activism'. *International Social Movement Research* 1: 125–54.

McAdam, D. and Paulsen, R. 1993. 'Specifying the Relationship between Social Ties and Activism'. *American Journal of Sociology* 99 (3): 640–67.

McAdam, D., Tarrow, S., and Tilly, C. 2001. *Dynamics of Contention*. Cambridge, UK: Cambridge University Press.

McCully, B.T. 1940. *English Education and the Origin of Indian Nationalism*. New York: Columbia University Press.

McLaren, P. 2000. *Che Guevara, Paulo Freire, and the Pedagogy of Revolution*. Lanham, MD: Rowman & Littlefield Publishers.

———. 2005. *Capitalists and Conquerors: A Critical Pedagogy against Empire*. Lanham, MD: Rowman & Littlefield Publishers.

Mehta, P.B. 2017. 'Closing of the University'. *The Indian Express*, 3 March. http://indianexpress.-com/article/opinion/columns/closing-of-the-university-4551570/.

Melucci, A. 1980. 'The New Social Movements: A Theoretical Approach'. *Social Science Informations* 19 (2): 199–226.

———. 1985. 'The Symbolic Challenge of Contemporary Movements'. *Social Research* 52 (4): 789–816.

———. 1986. *Nomads of the Present*. London: Radius.

———. 1989. *Nomads of the Present: Social Movements and Individual Needs in Contemporary Society*. Philadelphia: Temple University Press.

———. 1996. *Challenging Codes: Collective Action in the Information Age*. New York; Cambridge: Cambridge University Press.

Menon, N. 2016. 'Why Our Universities Are in Ferment'. *The Hindu*, 15 February.

Metta, S. 1967. 'Professional, Scientific and Intellectual Students in India', in *Student Politics*, ed. S.M, pp. 357–71. Lipset. New York: Basic Books.

———. 1970. 'The Partisan Student in India', in *The Student Revolution: A Global Analysis*, ed. P. Altbach. Mumbai: Lalvani Publishing House.

Meyer, D. and Corrigall-Brown, C. 2005. 'Coalitions and Political Context: U.S. Movements Against Wars in Iraq'. *Mobilization: An International Quarterly* 10 (3): 327–44.

Meyer, D. and Whittier, N. 1994. 'Social Movement Spillover'. *Social Problems* 41 (2): 277–98.

Meyer, D.S. 1999. 'A Civil Disobedience and Protest Cycles', in *Waves of Protest: Social Movements since the 1960s*, ed. J. Freeman and V. Johnson, pp. 267–76. Lanham, MD: Rowman & Littlefield Publishers.

Meyer, D., Whittier, N., and Robnett, B. 2002. *Social Movements: Identity, Culture and the State*. New York: Oxford University Press.

Meyer, L. and Alvarado, B.M., ed. 2010. *New World of Indigenous Resistance: Noam Chomsky and Voices from North, South and Central America*. San Francisco: City Lights Books.

Mills, C.W. 1960. 'Letter to the New Left'. *Marxists Internet Archive*. https://www.marxists.org/subject/humanism/mills-c-wright/letter-new-left.htm.

Mishra, A. 1993. 'A Left Resurgence? JNU Students' Union Election'. *Economic and Political Weekly* 28 (48): 2579–80.

Mitchell, D. 2003. *The Right to the City: Social Justice and Fight for the Public Space*. New York: The Guilford Press.

Mitchell, L. 2010. *Language, Emotion, Politics in South India: The Making of a Mother Tongue*. Ranikhet: Permanent Black.

Mitra, S.K. 1995. 'The Rational Politics of Cultural Nationalism: Sub-National Movements of South Asia in Comparative Perspective'. *British Journal of Political Science* 25 (1): 57–77.

Morris, A. and Braine, N. 2001. 'Social Movements and Oppositional Consciousness', in *Oppositional Consciousness: The Subjective Roots of Social Protest*, ed. J. Morris and A. Mansbridge, pp. 20–37. Chicago: University of Chicago Press.

Morris, A. and Mueller, C.M. 1992. *Frontiers in Social Movement Theory*. New Haven; London: Yale University Press.

Mosse, D. 2012. *The Saint in the Banyan Tree: Christianity and Caste Society in India*. Berkeley: University of California Press.

Nag, K. 2011. *Battleground Telangana: Chronicle of an Agitation*. New Delhi: Harper Collins.

Nair, J. 2017. 'Introduction: A Teach-in for a JNU Spring', in *What the Nation Really Needs to Know: Extracts from JNU's Nationalism Lectures*, ed. JNU Teachers' Association, pp. ix–xxv. Delhi: HarperCollins Publishers India.

Nandy, A. 1997. *Creating a Nationality: The Ramajanam Bhoomi and Fear of Self*. New Delhi: Oxford University Press.

Narain, I. 1976. 'Cultural Pluralism, National Integration and Democracy in India'. *Asian Survey* 16 (10): 903–17.

Neelakandan, S.M. and Patil, S.M. 2012. 'Complexities of Inclusion and Exclusion: Dalit Students and Higher Education in India'. *Journal of Social Inclusion* 3 (1): 86–100.

Newman, J. 1982. *The Idea of a University*. Notre Dame: University of Notre Dame Press.

Noorani, A. 2001. 'Of a Massacre Untold'. *Frontline* 18 (5). http://www.frontline.in/static/html/fl1805/18051130.htm.

Nurullah, S. and Naik, J.P. 1962. *A Students' History of Education in India* (Revised Edition). Kolkata: The Inland Printing Works.

Offe, C. 1985. 'New Social Movements: Challenging the Boundaries of Institutional Politics'. *Social Research* 52 (4): 817–68.

Oliver, P.E. 1984. 'If You Don't Do It, Nobody Will: Active and Token Contributions to Local Collective Action'. *American Sociological Review* 49: 601–10.

Omvedt, G. 1993. *Reinventing Revolution: India's New Social Movements*. New York: M.E. Sharpe.

———. 1994. *Dalits and the Democratic Revolution: Dr Ambedkar and the Dalit Movement in Colonial India*. New Delhi: SAGE Publications.

Oommen, T. 1985. *From Mobilisation to Institutionalisation: The Dynamics of Agrarian Movement in 20th Century Kerala*. Mumbai: Popular Prakashan.

———. 1990. *Protest and Change: Studies in Social Movements*. New Delhi: SAGE Publications.

———. 2010. *Social Movements I: Issues of Identity*. New Delhi: Oxford University Press.

Oommen, T.K. 1974. 'Student Politics in India: The Case of Delhi University'. *Asian Survey* 14 (9): 777–94.

———. 2005. *Crisis and Contention in Indian Society*. New Delhi: SAGE Publications.

Ortega, Y.G.J. 1961. *What Is Philosophy?* New York: W.W. Norton.

Paik, S. 2016. 'Education and Exclusion of Dalits: A History of Hurt and Humiliation'. *The Wire*. Accessed 15 August 2016. https://thewire.in/education/education-and-exclusion-of-dalits-a-history-of-hurt-and-humiliation.

Pandian, M.S.S. 2002. 'One Step outside Modernity: Caste, Identity Politics and Public Sphere'. South-South Exchange Programme for Research on the History of Development (SEPHIS), Amsterdam; the Council for the Development of Social Science Research in Africa (CODESRIA), Dakar, http://www.sephis.org/pdf/pandian.pdf.

Panikkar, K. 2007. *Colonialism, Culture and Resistance*. New Delhi: Oxford University Press.

Pant, H. 2008. 'In Defense of Liberal Education', in *Beyond Degree*, ed. I. Pande, pp. 168–77. New Delhi: India International Centre.

Paris, R. 1981. 'Soziale Bewegung und Offtentlichkeit'. *Prokla* 43 (2): 103–28.

Passi, A. 2003. 'Region and Place: Regional Identity in Question'. *Progress in Human Geography* 27 (4): 475–85.

Passy, F. 2001. 'Socialisation, Connection, and the Structure/Agency Gap: A Specification of the Impact of Networks on Participation in Social Movements'. *Mobilisation: An International Quarterly* 6 (2): 173–92.

Pathak, A. 2017a. 'From JNU to Ramjas, Where Has the Spirit of Studentship Disappeared?' *The Wire*. Accessed 4 March 2017. https://thewire.in/113948/jnu-ramjas-college-spirit-studentship-disappeared/.

———. 2017b. 'The Spirit of Being a University Teacher in These Turbulent Time'. *The Wire*. Accessed 5 October 2017. https://thewire.in/173802/university-teacher-teachers-day/.

Pathania, G.J. 2011. 'Marx Sipping Tea at Nehru's Dhaba'. *Mainstream Weekly* XLIX (47). https://www.mainstreamweekly.net/article3123.html.

———. 2012. University as a Site of New Social Movements: Identity Based Student Activism in Jawaharlal Nehru University. MPhil thesis, Jawaharlal Nehru University, Delhi.

———. 2015. 'Middle Class Resistance in Contemporary Urban India: How "New" Are These New Social Movements', in *The Trajectory of India's Middle Class: Economy, Ethics and Etiquette*, ed. L. Lobo and J. Shah, pp. 274–95. Newcastle Upon Tyme, UK: Cambridge Scholars Publishing.

———. 2016. 'Food Politics and Counter-Hegemonic Assertion in Indian University Campuses'. *South Asia Research* 36 (2): 261–77.

———. 2017. 'University and the Politics of Narrative'. *Cafe Dissensus Everyday*. https://cafedissensusblog.com/2017/09/15/jnusu-elections-the-university-and-the-politics-of-narratives/.

Pathania, G.J. and Tierney, W.G. 2018. 'An Ethnography of Caste and Class at an Indian University: Creating Capital'. *Tertiary Education and Management – The Journal of European Higher Education Society*. https://www.tandfonline.com/doi/full/10.1080/13583883.2018.1439998.

Patil, S. 1992. 'Ambedkarism-Marxism'. *Nalupu*, ed. B. Tharakam 4 (6): 28–32.

Patnaik, P. 2007. *Alternative Perspective on Education*. New Delhi: National University of Educational Planning and Administration.

Peterson, R.A. and Anand, N. 2004. `The Production of Culture Perspective'. *Annu. Rev. Sociol.* 30: 311–34.

Pingle, G. 2014. *The Fall and Rise of Telangana*. Delhi: Orient Blackswan.

Pinner, F.A. 1972. 'Students—A Marginal Elites in Politics', in *The New Pilgrims: Youth Protest in Transition*, ed. P.G. Altbach and R.S. Laufer, pp. 28–84 New York: David McKay.

Pinsker, S. 2013. 'Jewish Modernism and Viennese Cafes 1900–1930', in *The Thinking Space: The Cafe as Cultural Institution in Paris, Italy and Vienna*, ed. L. Rittner, W.S. Haine, and J.H. Jackson, pp. 51–64. Farnham, England: Ashgate Publishing Ltd.

Pizzorno A. 1986. 'Some Other Kinds of Otherness: A Critique of "Rational Choice" Theories', in *Development, Democracy and the Art of Trespassing: Essays in Honor of Albert O. Hirschman*, ed. A. Foxley, M.S. McPherson, and G. O'Donnell, pp. 355–72. Notre Dame, IN: University of Notre Dame Press.

Polletta, F. 1999. 'Free Space'. *Collective Action, Theory and Society* 28: 1–38.

———. 2004. 'Culture Is Not Just in Your Head', in *Rethinking Social Movements: Structure, Meaning and Emotions*, ed. J. Goodwin and J.J. Jasper, pp. 97–110. Lanham: Rowman & Littlefield Publishers.

Polletta, F. and Jasper, J.M. 2001. 'Collective Identity and Social Movements'. *Annual Review of Sociology* 27: 283–305.

Prakash, S. and Vemmireddy, V. 2015. 'Telangana and Language Politics of Telugu Cinema'. *Anveshi-Broadsheet on Contemporary Politics* 2 (4 and 5): 7–8. http://www.anveshi.org.in/telangana-and-language-politics-of-telugu-cinema/.

Prakash, V. 2007. 'Trends in Growth and Financing in Higher Education in India'. *Economic and Political Weekly* 42 (31): 3249–58.

———. 2011. 'Concern about Autonomy and Academic Freedom'. *Economic and Political Weekly* 46 (16): 36–40.

Raagmaa, G. 2002. 'Regional Identity in Regional Development and Planning'. *European Planning and Studies* 10 (1): 55–76.

Rajeev, M. 2009. 'Plank of Self-Respect'. *Frontline* 26 (26). http://www.frontline.in/static/html/fl2626/stories/20100101262600900.htm.

Ramulu, B.S. 2007. 'Bisilaki Jajkiya Adhikaram: Avagaahana'. Party Nirmanamu, Karykramamu, Ennikala Pranalika, Smajika Tatvika Vishwavidhyalayamu, Hyderabad.

Rao, A.V. 1969. *The People's Struggle*. Hyderabad: The Telangana Publication.

Rao, C.H.H. 2009. *Regional Disparities, Smaller States, and Statehood for Telangana*. New Delhi: Academic Foundation.

Rao, E.S. 2010. 'I Am from Telangana—I Am Not a Naxalite', in *The Telangana Struggle for Identity*, ed. K.R. Velchala, J.V. Raghavendra Rao, and B. Narsing Rao, pp. 118–22. Hyderabad: Telangana Cultural Forum Publication.

Rao, J.V.N. 1969. *Separate Telangana: A Suicidal Slogan*. Hyderabad: Department of Information and Publicity, Government of Andhra Pradesh.

Rao, K.S. 2010. 'Emotional Needs for Separate Telangana State', in *The Telangana Struggle for Identity*, ed. V.K. Rao, J.V. Raghavendra Rao, and B. Narsing Rao, pp. 89–92. Hyderabad: Telangana Cultural Forum Publication.

Rao, K.V.N. 1972. *Telangana: A Study in the Regional Committees in India*. Kolkata: The Minerva Associates.

Rao, M.S.A 1981. 'Prophecy and Heritage in Social and Cultural Movements'. *Social Action* 31 (2): 174–81.

Rao, R.R.M., Reddy, V.S., and Rao, N.R.K. 2014. 'Hyderabad: Then and Now'. *Telangana State Info*. https://www.telanganastateinfo.com/hyderabad-then-and-now/.

Rao, V.K. 2010. 'Cultural Incompatibilities Are at the Root of All Other Incompatibilities', in *The Telangana Struggle for Identity*, ed. K.R. Velchala, J.V. Raghavendra Rao, and B. Narsing Rao, pp. 178–81. Hyderabad: Telangana Cultural Forum Publication.

Ray, R. and Katzenstein, M.F., ed. 2005. *Social Movements in India: Poverty, Power and Politics*. Lanham, MD: Rowman & Littlefield Publishers.

Reddy, C.A. 2009. 'The Grammar ofTelugu Culture'. *Wichaar: A Comprehensive Pubjabi Journal*. Accessed 25 May 2018. http://www.wichaar.com/news/295/ARTICLE/17663/2009-12-14.html.

Reddy, G.R. 1967. 'Social Composition of Panchayati Raj: Background of Political Executives in Andhra'. *Economic and Political Weekly* (23 December): 2211–14.

Reddy, G.R. and Sharma, B.A.V. 1979. *Regionalism in India: A Study of Telangana*. New Delhi: Concept Publishing Company.

Reddy, M. 1949. *Whither Students? Nidubrolu*. Hyderabad: Kisan Publishers.

Reddy, N.M. 2014. 'Review of S.V. Srinivas's Cinema as Politics, Politics as Cinema'. *Himal South Asian*. Accessed 12 January 2016. http://himalmag.com/cinema-politics-politics-cinema/.

Reddy, P.H. 1969. 'Indian Student Rebellion: Some Neglected Factors'. *Economic and Political Weekly* 4 (7): 357–60.

Reddy, S. 2010. 'Telugu Television Rewrites Script in 2010'. www.indiatelevision.com, www.indi-antelevision.com/special/y2k11/sanjay_reddy_Yearender.php.

Reddy, S.K. 1978. Telangana: A Study in Reginoalism. PhD diss., Osmania University, Hyderabad.

Reddy, S.S. 2017. 'When OU Was a Red Bastion'. *The Hans India*, 22 April.

Reed, I.A. and Alexander, J.C., ed. 2007. *Culture, Society and Democracy: The Interpretative Approach*. The Yale Cultural Sociology Series. London: Paradigm Publisher.

Rege, S. 2006. *Writing Caste/Writing Gender: Reading Dalit Women's Testimonies*. New Delhi: Zubaan Books.

Rege, S. 2010. 'Education as Trutiya Ratna: Towards Phule–Ambedkarite Feminist Pedagogical Practice'. *Economic and Political Weekly* 45 (44–45): 88–98.

Rikowski, G. 2002. '*Globalisation and Education*'. Paper Prepared for the House of Lords Select Committee on Economic Affairs, Inquiry into the Global Economy. London. http://www.leeds.ac.uk/educol/documents/00001941.htm.

Rochan, T.R. 1998. *Culture Moves: Ideas, Activism, and Changing Values*. New Jersey: Princeton University Press.

Ross, A.D. 1969. *Student Unrest in India: A Comparative Approach*. Montreal: McGill-Queen's University Press.

Ross, R. 1975. 'Generational Change and Primary Groups in a Social Movement'. Unpublished Paper. Clark University, Worcester.

Roth, R. 1984. 'Analysen af Nye Sociale Bevægelser—Teorier og Begreber'. *Kurasje* 34: 49–68.

Rucht, D. 1982. 'Neue Soziale Bewegungen oder: Die Grenzen Bürokratischer Modernisierung', in *Politische Viertelsjahresschrift*. Sonderheft 13: 272–91.

Saikia, M.C. 1982. 'The Brahma Movement among the Bodo-Kacharis of Gopalpura Districts', in *Tribal Movements in India: Volume 1*, ed. K.S. Singh, pp. 241–51. New Delhi: Manohar.

Sakrikar, D.A. 'History of the Student Movement in India'. Unpublished Manuscript. Mumbai.

Sarkar, C. 1960. *The Unquiet Campus*. New Delhi: The Statesman Press.

Satyanarayan, R. 1969. 'Foreword', in *The Telangana Movement: An Investigative Focus*, ed. A.R. Thota. A Research Volume. Hyderabad: A.R. Thota.

Satyanarayana, K. and Tharu, S. 2011. *No Alphabet in Sight: New Dalit Writings from South India*. New Delhi: Penguin Books.

Sax, W. 2011. 'Religion, Rituals and Symbols of Belonging: The Case of Uttrakhand', in *The Politics of Belonging in Himalayas: Local Attachments and Boundaries Dynamics*, ed. J. Peaff-Czarnecka and G. Toffin, pp. 167–81. New Delhi: SAGE Publications.

Savage, M. and Butler, T. 1992. 'Assets and the Middle-Classes in the Contemporary Britain', in *Property, Bureaucracy and Culture: Middle Class Formation in Contemporary Britain*, ed. M. Savage, J. Barlow, P. Dickens, and T. Fielding, pp. 245–59. London: Routledge.

Scheff, T. 1994. 'Emotions and Identity: A Theory of Ethnic Nationalism', in *Social Theory and the Politics of Identity*, ed. C. Calhoun, pp. 277–303. Oxford: Blackwell.

Schwartz, T. 1992. 'Anthropology and Psychology: An Unrequited Relationship', in *New Directions in Psychological Anthropology*, ed. T. Schwartz, G.M. White, and C.A. Lutz, pp. 324–49. Cambridge, UK: Cambridge University Press.

Scott, A. 1990. *Ideology and New Social Movements*. London: Unwin Hyman.

Sen, A. 2009. 'On Interpreting India's Past', in *Modern Indian Culture and Society: Critical Concepts in Asian Studies*, ed. K.A. Jacobsen, pp. 10–35. London; New York: Routledge.

Shah, G. 2004. *Caste and Democratic Politics in India*. London: Anthem Press.

Shah, G., Mander, H., Thorat, S., Deshpande, S., and Baviskar, A. 2006. *Untouchability in Rural India*. New Delhi: Action Aid, SAGE Publications.

Shaw, P. 2014. 'The Public Sphere and the Telangana Movement'. *Media International Australia* 152: 143–57.

Shils, E. 1959. 'The Culture of the Indian Intellectuals'. *The Sewanee Review* 67 (3): 401–21.

———. 1961. *Intellectuals between Tradition and Modernity: The Indian Situation*. The Hague: Mouton & Co.

Shyamala, G. 2013. 'Beef, Our Life, Our Culture'. *Anveshi Broadsheet on Contemporary Politics* 1 (4). Accessed 14 August 2014. http://www.anveshi.org.in/beef-our-life-by-gogu-shyamala/.

Sigel, H. 1990. *Educating Reason*. New York: Routledge.

Simhadri, S. and Rao, P.L.V. 1997. *Telangana: Dimensions of Underdevelopment*. Hyderabad: Centre for Telangana Studies.

Singhal, S. 1977. 'Academic Leadership and Student Unrest'. Report Submitted to ICSSR. New Delhi: Newman.

Singharoy, D.K. 2010. 'Changing Trajectories of Social Movements', in *Dissenting Voices and Transformative Actions: Social Movement in a Globalising World*, ed. D.K. Singharoy, pp. 145–88. Delhi: Manohar Publications.

Singh, D. 1942. *The Indian Struggle*. Lahore: Hero Publications.

Singh, K.S. 1982. 'The Gond Movement', in *Tribal Movements in India: Volume 2*, ed. K.S. Singh, pp. 177–85. New Delhi: Manohar.

Singh, R. 2001. *Social Movements, Old and New: A Post-Modern Critique*. New Delhi: SAGE Publications.

Sitapati, V. 2011. 'What Anna Hazare's Movement and India's New Middle Classes Say about Each Other'. *Economic and Political Weekly* 36: 39–44.

Smith, P.J. 2008. 'Going Global: The Transnational Politics of the Dalit Movement'. *Globalization* 5 (1): 13–33.

Snow, D. and McAdam, D. 2010. *Readings on Social Movements: Origins, Dynamics and Outcomes*. New York: Oxford University Press.

Snow, D., Rochford, E.B., Worden, S.K., and Benford, R.D. 1986. 'Frame Alignment Processes, Micromobilisation and Movement Participation'. *American Sociological Review* 51: 464–81.

Snow, D., Zurcher, L. and Ekland-Olson, S. 1980. 'Social Networks and Social Movements: A Microstructural Approach to Differential Recruitment'. *American Sociological Review* 45 (5): 787–801.

Somers, M.R. 1994. 'The Narrative Constitution of Identity: A Relational and Network Approach'. *Theory and Society* 23: 605–94.

Sooryamoorthy, R. 2008. 'Untouchability in Modern India: A Review Article'. *International Sociology* 23 (2): 283–93.

Spencer, M. 1967. 'Professional, Scientific and Intellectual Students in India', in *Student Politics*, ed. S.M. Lipset. New York: Basic Books Inc. Publishers.

Spiro, M.E. 1955. 'The Acculturation of American Ethnic Groups'. *American Anthropologist* 57 (6): 1240–52.

Srikanth, H. 2013. 'Construction and Consolidation of Telangana Identity'. *Economic and Political Weekly* 48 (45–46): 39–45.

Srikrishna Commission. 2010. Committee for Consultations on the Situation in Andhra Pradesh Report. New Delhi: Ministry of Home Affairs, Government of India.

Srinivas, M.N. 1966. 'Students in Turmoil'. *Seminar* 88 (December): 7–48.

Srinivasulu, K. 2002. 'Caste, Class and Social Articulation in Andhra Pradesh: Mapping Differential Regional Trajectories'. ODI Working Paper 179. Overseas Development Institute, London.

———. 2012. 'Tank Bund Idolism: Crisis of Cultural Politics of a Provincial Regime'. *SocialSciences.in*. Accessed 2 March 2014. http://socialsciences.in/article/tank-bund-idol-ism-crisis-cultural-politics-provincial-regime.

———. 2017. 'Celebration and Introspection: Reflections on the Century-Old Osmania University'. *Economic and Political Weekly* 52 (51): 19–21.

Stark, M., Browser, B., and Horne, L. 2008. *Cultural Transmission and Material Culture: Breaking Down Boundaries*. Tuscon: University of Arizona Press.

Steinberg, M.W. 1999. *Fighting Words: Working-Class Formation, Collective Action Framing and Discourse in Early Nineteenth-Century England*. Ithaca, NY: Cornell University Press.

Sukumar, N. 2008. 'Living a Concept: Semiotics of Everyday Exclusion'. *Economic and Political Weekly* 43 (46): 14–17.

———. 2016. 'Gatecrashing the Gurukuls'. *Himal Southasian*. Accessed 27 February 2017. http://himalmag.com/gatecrashing-the-gurukuls/.

Sundarayya, P. 1972. *Telangana People's Struggle and Its Lesson*. Kolkata: Ghanshakti Printers.

Suri, K.C. 2002. *Democratic Process and Electoral Politics in Andhra Pradesh*. London: Overseas Development Institute.

———. 2016. 'Andhra Pradesh: Political Dynamics of Regionalism, Formation of New States in India'. ISAS Working Papers. National University of Singapore.

Swain, A. 2017. 'Compulsory Classroom Attendance for JNU Students Is a Regressive Idea'. *Outlook*. https://www.outlookindia.com/website/story/compulsory-classroom-attendance-for-jnu-students-is-a-regressive-idea/306219.

Swartz, D.L. 2013. *Symbolic Power, Politics and Intellectuals: The Political Sociology of Pierre Bourdieu*. Chicago: University of Chicago Press.

Tadakamallaa, V. et al. 2009. *Telangana Udyama Charitrapatralu*. Hyderabad: Telangana History Society.

Tamir, Y. 1993. *Liberal Nationalism*. Princeton: Princeton University Press.

Tarrow, S. 1989/1991. 'Struggle, Politics, and Reform: Collective Action, Social Movements, and Cycles of Protest'. *Western Societies Program*, Occasional Paper No. 21, 2nd. Ithaca, NY: Centre for International Studies, Cornell University.

———. 1992. 'Mentalities, Political Cultures and Collective Action Frames: Constructing Meaning through Action', in *Frontiers in Social Movement Theory*, ed. A. Morris and C.M. Mueller, pp. 174–202. New Haven, CT: Yale University Press.

———. 1998. *Power in Movement: Social Movements and Contentious Politics* (Second Edition). New York: Cambridge University Press

———. 2013. *The Language of Contention: Revolutions in Words, 1688–2012*. NY: Cambridge University Press.

Tarrow, S. and Della Porta, D. 2005. 'Conclusion: "Globalization", Complex Internationalism, and Transnational Contention', in *Transnational Protest and Global Activism*, ed. S. Tarrow and D. Della Porta, pp. 227–46. New York: Rowman & Littlefield Publishers.

Taylor, C. 1978. *From Mobilisation to Revolution*. Massachusetts: Addison-Wesley.

Taylor, V. and Whittier, N.E. 1992. 'Collective Identity in Social Movement Communities; Lesbian Feminist Mobilisation', in *Frontiers in Social Movement Theory*, pp. 104–29. New Haven, Conn.: Yale University Press.

Tejani, S. 2007. *Indian Secularism: A Social and Intellectual History 1890–1950*. New Delhi: Permanent Black.

Thakur, M. and Rai, D., ed. 2013. *Democracy on the Move: Reflections on Moments, Promises and Contradictions*. Delhi: Aakar.

Thapar, R. 2015. 'To Question or Not to Question? This Is the Question', in *The Public Intellectuals in India*, ed. R. Thapar, S. Sarukkai, D. Raina, P.R. DeSouza, N. Bhattacharya and J. Naqvi, pp. 1–40. New Delhi: Aleph Book Company.

———. 2016. 'Targeting Institutions of Higher Education: Fear of the Intellectual'. *Economic and Political Weekly* 51 (10): 19–21.

Thapar, R., Sarukkai, S., Raina, D., DeSouza, P.R., Bhattacharya, N., and Naqvi, J. 2015. *The Public Intellectuals in India*. New Delhi: Aleph Book Company.

Thatha, S. 2015. 'Constructing Telangana Identity in the Context of Bifurcation of Andhra Pradesh and Telangana States in India'. *The International Journal of Humanities and Social Studies* 3 (8).

The Hindu. 2013. 'Telugu Talli Statue Unveiled'. http://www.thehindu.com/todays-paper/tp-national/tp-andhrapradesh/telugu-talli-statue-unveiled/article5307531.ece.

The Telegraph. 2016. 'Lawyers Clash with JNU Students as Kanahaiya Case Hearing Comes Up'. https://www.huffingtonpost.in/2016/03/09/jnu-row_n_9415292.html.

Thirumali, I. 2010. 'Lessons from the Telangana Movement'. *Mainstream Weekly* XLVIII (14). https://www.mainstreamweekly.net/article1970.html.

Thirumali, I. 2013. *Telangana-Andhra: Castes, Regions and Politics in Andhra Pradesh*. Delhi: Aakar.

Thomson, M. 2013. 'Hyderabad 1948: India's Hidden Massacre'. Accessed 1 November 2017. http://www.bbc.com/news/magazine-24159594.

Thorat, S. 2004. 'On Reservation Policy for Private Sector'. *Economic and Political Weekly* 39 (25): 2560–3.

Thorat, S. and Newman, K.S. 2007. 'Caste and Economic Discrimination: Causes, Consequences and Remedies'. *Economic and Political Discourse* 42 (41): 4121–4.

———. 2008. 'Emerging Issues in Higher Education: Approach and Strategy of 11th Plan', in *Higher Education in India: Issues Related to Expansion, Inclusiveness, Quality and Finance*, ed. S. Thorat, pp. 1–26. New Delhi: University Grants Commission.

Thota, A.R., ed. 1969. 'The Telangana Movement: An Investigative Focus'. A Research Volume. Hyderabad: A.R. Thota.

Tierney, W.G. and Sabharwal, N. 2016. 'Debating Academic Freedom in India'. *Journal of Academic Freedom* 7: 1–11.

Tilak, J.B.G. 2013a. 'Higher Education in Trishanku: Hanging between State and Market', in *Higher Education in India: In Search of Equality, Quality and Quantity*, ed. J.B.G. Tilak, pp. 391–407. New Delhi: Orient BlackSwan.

———. 2013b. 'Higher Education in the BRIC Member-Countries'. *Economic and Political Weekly* 48 (14): 41–7.

Tillin, L. 2013. *Remapping India: New States and Their Political Origins*. London: Hurst and Company.

Tilly, C. 1978. *From Mobilisation to Revolution*. Reading, MA.: Addison-Wesley.

Touraine, A. 1971. *The May Movement: Revolt and Reform*. New York: Random House.

———. 1981. *The Voice and the Eye: An Analysis of Social Movements*. Cambridge: Cambridge University Press.

———. 1985. 'An Introduction to the Study of Social Movements'. *Social Research* 52 (4): 749–87.

———. 1997. *What Is Democracy*. Boulder: Colorado.

Tuomainen, H.M. 2009. 'Ethnic Identity (Post) Colonialism and Foodways: Ghanaians in London'. *University of Warwick Journal* 12 (4): 525–54.

Turner, S.P. 1994. *The Social Theory of Practices*. Chicago: University of Chicago Press.

United Nations Development Programme. 1999. 'Globalisation with a Human Face'. Human Development Report. New York; Oxford: Oxford University Press.

Varshney, A. 1998. 'Why Democracy Survives'. *Journal of Democracy* 9 (3): 36–50. Accessed 13 April 2014. https://scholar.harvard.edu/files/levitsky/files/varshney.pdf.

Vennela. 2014. 'What Makes a Man or Woman on Campus? Reviewing the Stakes of Desirability, Agency, and Power in the Movies Sye (2004) and Happy Days (2007)'. *Anveshi Broadsheet*. http://www.anveshi.org.

in/what-makes-a-man-or-woman-on-campus-reviewing-the-stakes-of-desirability-agency-and-power-in-the-movies-sye-2004-and-happy-days-2007/.

Venugopal, N. 2009. 'Demand for Separate Telangana towards Understanding the Core Issues', in *Telangana: The State of Affairs*, ed. M. Bharath Bhushan and N. Venugopal, pp. 33–54. Hyderabad: AdEd Value Ventures.

Vidyarthi, L.P. 1976. *Students Unrest in Chhotanagpur, 1960–70.* Kolkata: Punthi Pustak.

Vinayak, J.P. 1972. 'Student Violence'. *Hindustan Times*, 15 October, 6.

Visvanathan, S. 2016a. 'Dividing Lines: The Death of the University'. *Deccan Chronicle*, 30 April. http://www.deccanchronicle.com/opinion/columnists/290416/dividing-lines-the-death-of-the-university.html.

———. 2016b. 'The "Everydayness" of Our Violence'. *The Hindu*, 10 May. http://www.thehindu.com/opinion/lead/the-everydayness-of-our-violence/article8576738.ece.

———. 1999. 'Democracy, Plurality and the Indian University', in *Diversity and Unity: The Role of Higher Education in Building Democracy*, ed. M. Cross, E.N.C. Beckham, A.H. Musil, J. Indiresan, and C. Musil, pp. 49–79. Cape Town: Maskew Miller Longman.

Wasserstrom, J. and Xinyong, L. 1989. 'Student Protest and Student Life: Shanghai, 1919–49'. *Social History* 14 (1): 1–29.

Weinberg, I. and Walker, K.N. 1969. 'Student Politics and Political System: Towards a Typology'. *American Journal of Sociology* 75: 82.

Weiner, M. 1978. *Sons of the Soil: Migration and Ethnic Conflict in India.* New Jersey: Princeton University Press.

Weiss, M.L. 2011. *Student Activism in Malaysia: Crucible, Mirror, Sideshow.* Ithaca: Cornell Southeast Asia Program Publications.

Welch Jr., C.E. 1980. *Anatomy of Rebellion.* Albany: State University Press of New York.

Whittier, N. 2002. 'Meaning and Structure in Social Movements', in *Social Movements: Identity, Culture, and the State*, ed. D.S. Meyer, N. Whittier, and B. Robnett, pp. 289–307. New York: Oxford University Press.

Williams, J.P. 2011. *Subcultural Theory: Traditions and Concepts.* Cambridge, UK: Polity Press.

Yashpal Committee. 2009. 'Report of the "Committee to Advise on Renovation and Rejuvenation of Higher Education"'. New Delhi: Ministry of Human Resource Development, Government of India.

Yates, L. 2015. 'Everyday Politics, Social Practices and Movement Networks: Daily Life in Bercelona's Social Centres'. *The British Journal of Sociology* 66 (2): 236–57.

Zahir, A. 2008. 'Dakhni Language', in *Hyderabad Hazir Hai: Writings from the City of Nizam.* New Delhi: Rupa Publishers.

Zaretsky, E. 1994. 'Identity Theory, Identity Politics: Psychoanalysis, Marxism, Post-Structuralism', in *Social Theory and the Politics of Identity* ed. C. Calhoun, pp. 198–215. Oxford: Blackwell.

Zavos, J. 2000. *The Emergence of Hindu Nationalism in India*. Oxford: Oxford University Press.

Zimmerman, J. 2017. *Campus Politics*. New York: Oxford University Press.

Index

About the Author

Gaurav J. Pathania is visiting scholar at University of Massachusetts, Amherst, USA, and also associated as post-doctoral researcher with Pullias Centre for Higher Education at the University of Southern California. He completed his PhD in sociology of education from Jawaharlal Nehru University, New Delhi, and served on an international project with University College London that explored the distress and discrimination in Indian higher education. His articles and reviews have appeared in journals such as *South Asia Research, Economic and Political Weekly*, and *Cafe Dissensus.* His latest research paper, published by the European Higher Education Society, explores the caste and class discrimination among university students. Relying primarily on ethnographic method, Pathania's research applies insights from cultural sociology to understand social movements in education, and critically examines contemporary student activism and its global networks and solidarities.

Pathania has also contributed to various literary journals. He is the winner of the All India Poetry Competition 2016, organized by The Poetry Society (India).